LEGENDARY LOCALS

OF

GREENVILLE

SOUTH CAROLINA

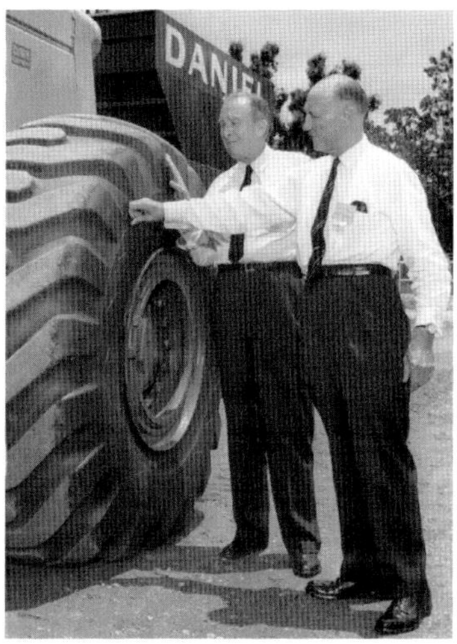

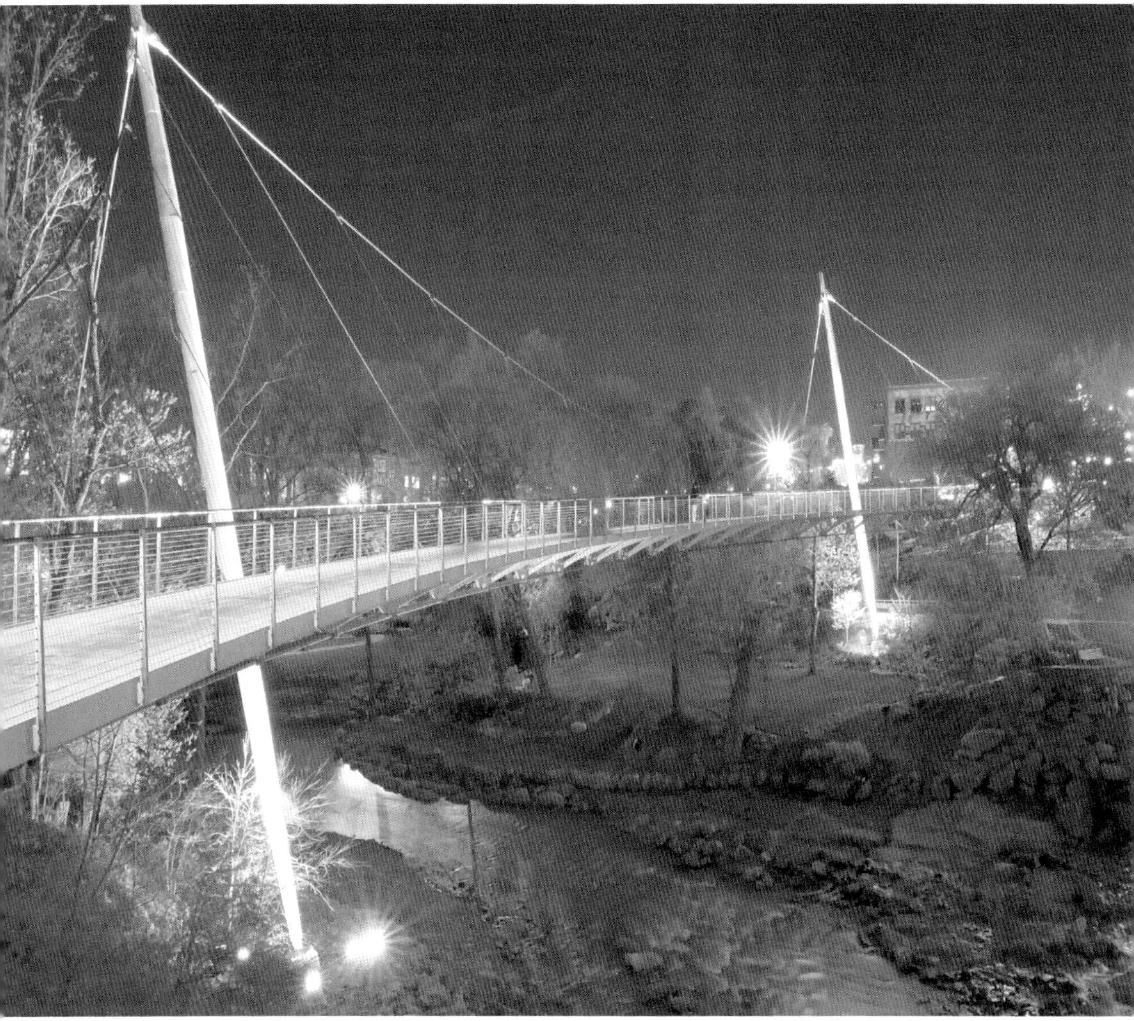

Liberty Bridge at Night

Harriet Wyche spearheaded an effort to get rid of a vehicular bridge and build Falls Park in downtown Greenville. The Liberty Bridge, a pedestrian bridge that curves around Reedy Falls in the park, has become Greenville's iconic landmark. For more information, see page 31. (Photograph by Cindy Landrum.)

Page 1: Charles E. Daniel

Daniel Construction Co. founder Charles E. Daniel (left) and Sen. Strom Thurmond are pictured examining a tire on a construction site. For more information, see page 113. (Courtesy of Fluor Corp.)

LEGENDARY LOCALS

OF

GREENVILLE

SOUTH CAROLINA

CINDY LANDRUM

LEGENDARY LOCALS

ISBN 978-1-4671-0203-2

Legendary Locals is an imprint of Arcadia Publishing
Charleston, South Carolina

Printed in the United States of America

Library of Congress Control Number: 2014956646

For all general information, please contact Arcadia Publishing:
Telephone 843-853-2070
Fax 843-853-0044
E-mail sales@arcadiapublishing.com
For customer service and orders:
Toll-Free 1-888-313-2665

Visit us on the Internet at www.arcadiapublishing.com

Dedication

This book is dedicated to my dad, Gary Heck, who has supported me in each and every one of my endeavors. It is also dedicated to all those who have made Greenville what it is today.

On the Front Cover: Clockwise from top left:
Shoeless Joe Jackson, professional baseball player (Courtesy of Upcountry History Museum–Furman University; see page 81), Jesse Jackson, civil rights activist (Courtesy of the Library of Congress; see page 61); Edvard Tchivzhel, conductor (Courtesy of the Greenville Symphony Orchestra; see page 72); Knox White, mayor and attorney (Courtesy of the *Greenville Journal*; see page 46), Llyn Strong, jeweler (Courtesy of the *Greenville Journal*; see page 76), James C. Furman, founder of Furman University (Courtesy of Special Collections and Archives, Furman University; see page 86), Frank Halter, real-estate company chairman and community activist (Courtesy of Caine Co.; see page 110), Sarah Reese, opera singer (Courtesy of Special Collections and Archives, Furman University; see page 69), Frank Selvy, basketball player (Courtesy of Special Collections and Archives, Furman University; see page 82)

On the Back Cover: From left to right:
Roger Peace, Bony Hampton Peace, B.H. Peace Jr., and Charlie Peace, newspaper family and community leaders (Courtesy of Betty Stall; see page 24), Max Heller, mayor and visionary of Greenville's downtown revitalization (Courtesy of the Upcountry History Museum–Furman University; page 42)

CONTENTS

ACKNOWLEDGMENTS

I undertook this project with one primary goal: to tell the stories of the people who made my adopted home what it is today. I have worked for newspapers in Greenville for more than two decades and as a result have met and interviewed many of the legends (or their descendants) included in this book. My challenge was not in finding enough people to include; my challenge was paring down the list to include a mix of people from all walks of life spanning more than two centuries.

To see *Legendary Locals of Greenville* be transformed from a list of names scribbled on a legal pad into a book that celebrates the contributions of Greenville's famous and the not-so-famous was rewarding.

I am grateful for the overwhelming support and enthusiasm shown by my family, friends, and members of the community. To my family and friends, thank you for your support. To members of the community, thank you for your help.

This book would not have been possible without the willingness of so many people to share their knowledge and their images from the past. They include Heather Yenco, Dana Thorpe, Vince Moore, Robyn Zimmerman, Mark Johnston, Greg Beckner, Hayne Hipp, Brad Halter, Brian S. Kelley, Fred Rollison, Brad Wyche, Ruth Ann Butler, Grier Mullins, Bob Hughes, and David Wilkins. Also, the Greenville Drive, Fluor Corp., the Upcountry History Museum–Furman University, Bob Jones University, the Greenville County Historical Society, the Furman University Special Collections and Archives, the Greenville County Library System South Carolina staff, and the University of South Carolina Political Collections staff.

Thanks also go to Greenville historians who have come before me, especially Judith Bainbridge, A.V. Huff, Nancy Vance Ashmore, and Courtney Tollison Hartness.

Thank you to Erin Vosgien and Jason Humphrey of Arcadia Publishing for their patience and support in seeing the project to completion.

Finally, it is my wish that members of the community will know a little better the stories of the people, past and present, who have made Greenville the city it is today. I know I do.

INTRODUCTION

From the time Richard Pearis ventured into hostile Cherokee hunting territory and set up a trading post to the 21st century renaissance of Greenville's downtown, the Reedy River has been central to Greenville's existence.

Pearis, Greenville's first colonial settler, discovered the Reedy about 1770. In addition to a trading post, his Great Plains Plantation in what is now downtown Greenville had a sawmill, gristmill, and stables. But Pearis did not stay in Greenville long.

During the Revolutionary War, Pearis sided with the Tories and their Cherokee allies against the patriots. The patriots retaliated, raiding his plantation and burning his home, and they hauled Pearis off to jail in Charleston. After he got out, he never returned to Greenville.

After the war, Cherokee land was divided and given to patriot soldiers as their payment for wartime services. Greenville County, originally spelled "Greeneville" for war hero Gen. Nathaniel Greene, was established in 1786 by the South Carolina Legislature.

In 1815, Vardry McBee, referred to as the "Father of Greenville," bought 11,000 acres of the former Cherokee land for $27,557. He built a gristmill near Reedy Falls, the first of many of McBee's Greenville businesses. The foundation of a larger mill McBee constructed in 1829 along the river's edge still exists, the oldest ruin in downtown Greenville. Signs of another one of Greenville's first businesses can still be found along the Reedy as well.

Blacksmiths Ebenezer Gower and Thomas M. Cox started a carriage factory on the river in 1835. Thomas Claghorn Gower joined the company, and H.C. Markley followed. The company became the leading carriage manufacturer south of the Potomac.

In 1851, Furman University relocated to Greenville from Winnsboro, South Carolina. It, too, found the Reedy. The move helped the school founded by Richard Furman to elevate itself to a well-respected center for learning. Four years after Furman's arrival, the Baptists opened the Greenville Baptist Female College.

James C. Furman was among the delegates that approved the Ordinance of Secession in Charleston in December 1860.

Greenville escaped the Civil War's battles, but the war had great impact on the town. Local industries produced supplies and equipment for the troops.

The period immediately following the Civil War was challenging for Greenville. In 1869, Greenville was chartered as a city. A construction boom followed in the 1870s that would shape Greenville for the next century.

Three Bostonians, Oscar H. Sampson, George L. Hall, and George Putnam, leased McBee's old mill. They remodeled and enlarged it for a spinning mill. The Camperdown Mill No. 1 opened in 1874. Sampson leased additional land from Vardry's heirs for Camperdown Mill No. 2. Other mills were established; Charles E. Graham and Charles H. Lanneau organized Huguenot Mills in 1881. In the late 1890s, Francis Poe opened the F.W. Poe Manufacturing Company and built a mill with 10,000 spindles. Otis Prentiss Mills built Mills Mill.

By 1902, there were 14 textile mills in Greenville and the surrounding environs. Textiles would dominate Greenville's economy for the next century, earning the city the moniker of "Textile Capital of the World."

The biggest was built by John T. Woodside and two of his brothers. It expanded twice and, in 1914, with 112,000 spindles, became the largest textile mill in the world under a single roof.

Mill owners such as the Woodsides, Thomas Parker, Bennette Geer, Ellison Adger Smyth, and Francis Poe drove Greenville's development in other ways as well.

Robert Woodside joined his brothers and created Woodside National Bank. In 1923, they built the Woodside Building, the state's tallest building at 17 stories. John Woodside, who declared himself the richest man in Greenville before World War I, also played a central role in the construction of the Poinsett Hotel on Main Street. But John Woodside, along with his brothers, saw their fortunes disappear when the stock market crashed at the start of the Great Depression.

Parker, owner of Monaghan Mill, was known for providing mill workers who lived in the village surrounding the mill with programs and facilities, including the first industrial YMCA. Lawrence Peter Hollis was brought in to run the YMCA.

The years following World War I proved challenging. Cotton prices nosedived because of overproduction and foreign competition. The boll weevil devastated the industry. The General Textile Strike of 1934 brought martial law to the city when National Guardsmen came to the mill villages.

World War II brought some relief, as the Greenville Army Air Base was built and mills cranked back up to supply the troops.

Following the war, even though Greenville referred to itself as the "Textile Center of the World," the call for industrial diversity was made.

Leading the effort was Charles E. Daniel, who built an international engineering and textile firm. Daniel's motto was "Builder of the South," and that he did. He sold companies in the Northeast and Midwest on expanding in the South. Their expansion South fueled the need for technical training. With former Clemson football star Thomas "Black Cat" Barton at the helm, Greenville Technical College was built on an old garbage dump. The school was tasked with providing workers the training they needed to fill the jobs in Greenville's growing industrial base.

While the 1960s brought new industries to Greenville, it was also a time of racial unrest. In 1947, a group of white taxi drivers lynched a young black man, Willie Earle. Earle was accused of killing a white taxi driver, Thomas W. Brown. The entire mob was arrested and brought to trial, but they were acquitted. Lunch counter and library sit-ins ushered in the end of segregation in the city, and lawsuits prompted the integration of Greenville County schools.

In the 1970s, attention turned to Main Street. Mayor Max Heller envisioned a downtown similar to those he saw in Europe. With Tommy Wyche and Buck Mickel, they convinced the Hyatt to build on Main Street.

Over the next decades, downtown revitalization followed, and once again, the river played a big role. The pages of this book tell the stories of some of the people who have shaped Greenville.

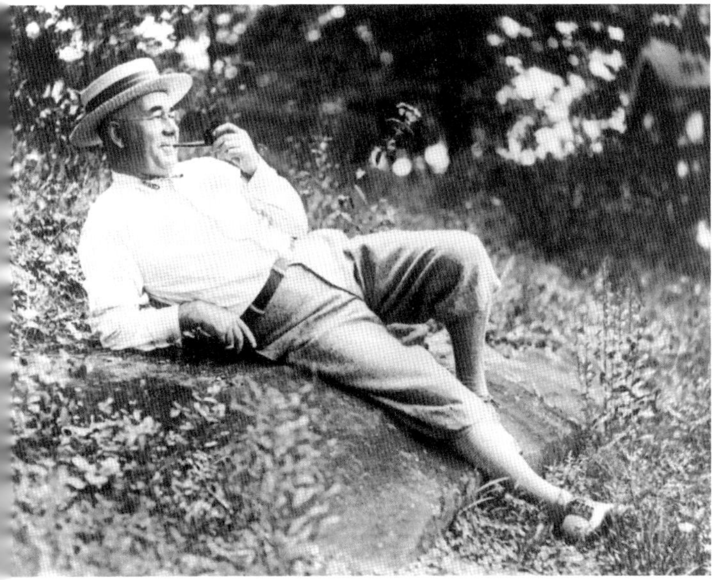

Labor Strife

Labor strife plagued textile mills during and after the Great Depression. Thomas M. Marchant, president of the Victor Monaghan Mill, was president of the American Cotton Manufacturers at the time. When the New Deal introduced labor standards and wage laws, the association came out in support of a 40-hour work week. Marchant is shown here at Caesar's Head in 1931. (Courtesy of the Greenville County Library System.)

CHAPTER ONE

Founders

Swashbuckling frontiersman Richard Pearis could be called Greenville's first man of vision.

He ventured into the Cherokee Indian territory that would eventually become Greenville to start a trading post. Pearis had an advantage over other settlers in that he was accepted in the Indian world, thanks to the son he had with a Cherokee side wife.

But he was far from the only early visionary.

Some of Pearis's early land ended up in the hands of Lemuel J. Alston, a man of wealth and influence who built Prospect Hill, an imposing house that would eventually become Greenville's first hotel.

Elias Earle was a major landowner, too, and a rival of Alston's. Both men wanted Greenville's first county courthouse located on their land. Alston ended up winning out.

The man with the biggest vision and lasting influence on Greenville is Vardry McBee. He is called the Father of Greenville for good reason. After he had bought Alston's property, he donated land for the city's first churches and first schools. An article in *De Bow's Review* in 1852 said about McBee, "Instead of hoarding up his money, and lending it out at interest or investing it in bank stock, he had employed it in the improvement of the county, and in the support of the poor and needy."

There were others that set the foundation for what Greenville would become.

Fountain Fox Beattie was one of Greenville's first merchants. Benjamin Perry's influence came from his position as a newspaper editor and provisional governor of South Carolina. Joel Poinsett, the man whose name adorns the Christmas favorite poinsettia plant, triggered development of the city in which he resided during summers. Poinsett oversaw construction of a road that helped connect the North Carolina mountains to the South Carolina coast and cemented Greenville's place as a trading center.

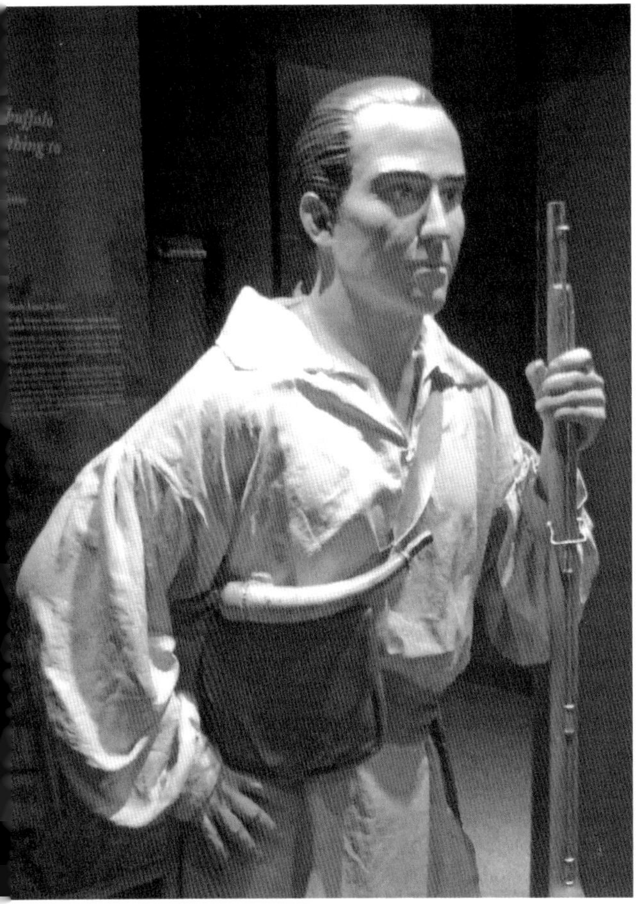

Richard Pearis

Richard Pearis, shown at left in a life-sized replica at the Upcountry History Museum, had an advantage when it came to building trust with the Cherokees that occupied the land that is now Greenville. Pearis, an Indian trader from Virginia, was living with a Cherokee chief's daughter and had a son with her. In 1770, he claimed 12 miles of Cherokee hunting land. In 1773, a court found Pearis guilty of violating a statute that forbade British citizens from owning Indian land. That did not stop him for long. Cherokee leaders granted a deed for the land to Pearis's son George, who subsequently transferred the holdings to his father. Along the banks of the Reedy River in today's downtown Greenville, Pearis set up the Great Plains Plantation. Although the spelling is different, Paris Mountain and Paris Mountain State Park are named after Pearis. (Left, courtesy of John Foxe; below, courtesy of Greenville County Historical Society.)

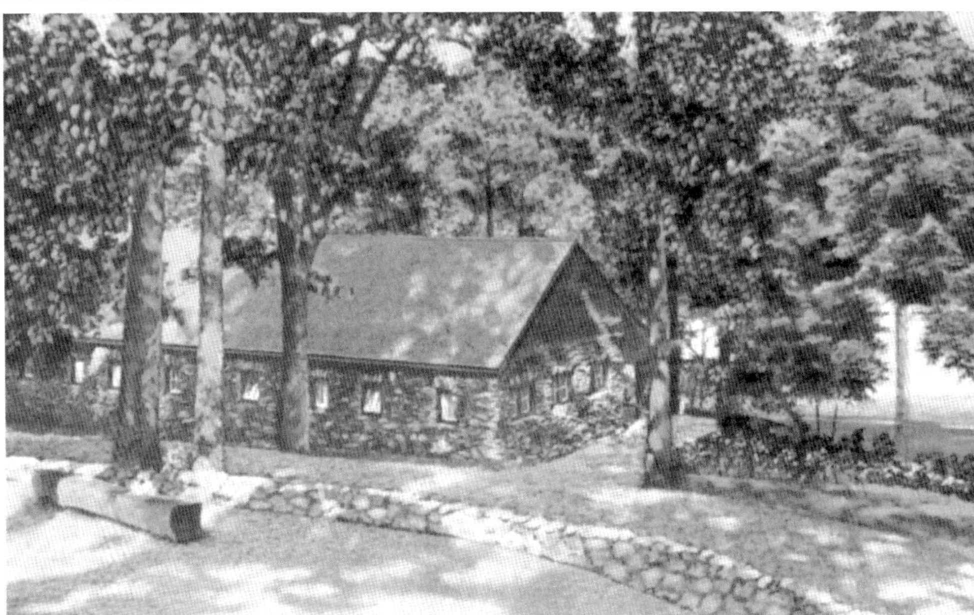

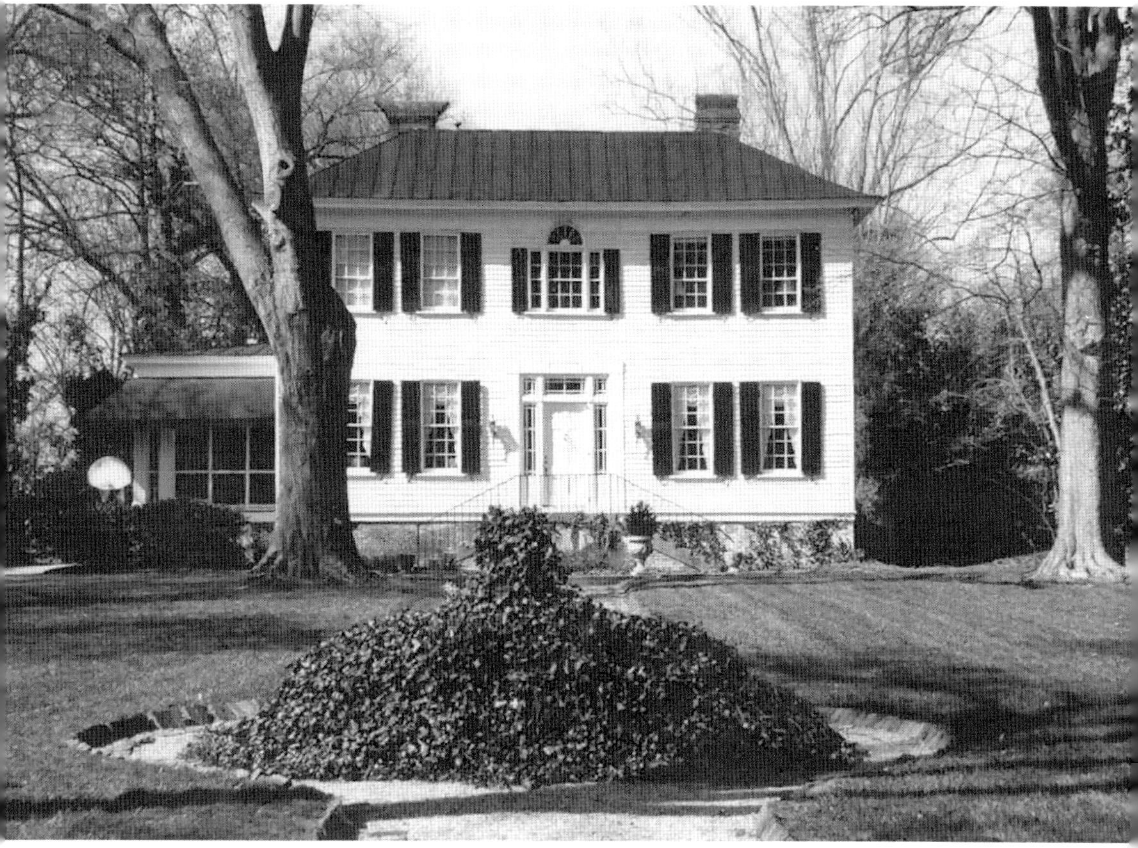

Elias Earle

Some call Elias Earle one of Greenville's most notable early residents. He was considered one of the South's earliest iron masters, according to the biographical directory of the US Congress. Earle served in the South Carolina House of Representatives and Senate before his election to the US House of Representatives. Two of Earle's nephews, Samuel Earle and John Baylis Earle, and two of his great-grandsons, John Laurens Manning Irby and Joseph Haynsworth Earle, also served in Congress. A historic district named after Earle is home to two of Greenville's oldest landmarks—the Earle Town House, shown here, and Whitehall, the summer home of Gov. Henry Middleton built in 1813. (Courtesy of the Greenville County Library System.)

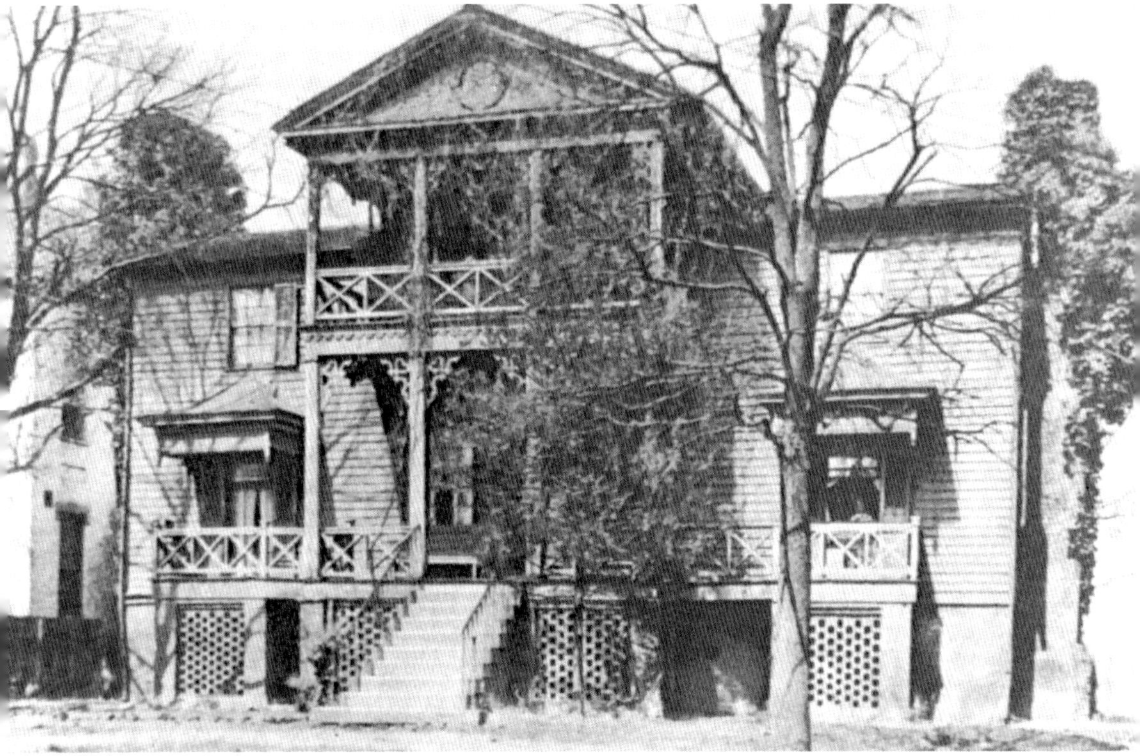

Lemuel J. Alston

Lemuel J. Alston and Elias Earle, two of Greenville's early residents, were rivals, a competition that started when in 1794 the general assembly decided to put Greenville Courthouse on Alston's property instead of Earle's. The rivalry continued when Alston defeated the incumbent Earle and another man, William Hunter, for a seat in Congress in 1806. Alston defeated Earle for reelection in 1808. The two faced each other again in 1810, and Earle won the seat back. Alston sold the land in Greenville he owned to Vardry McBee and moved to Alabama. Alston's home, Prospect Hill, became Greenville's first hotel. (Courtesy of the Greenville County Historical Society.)

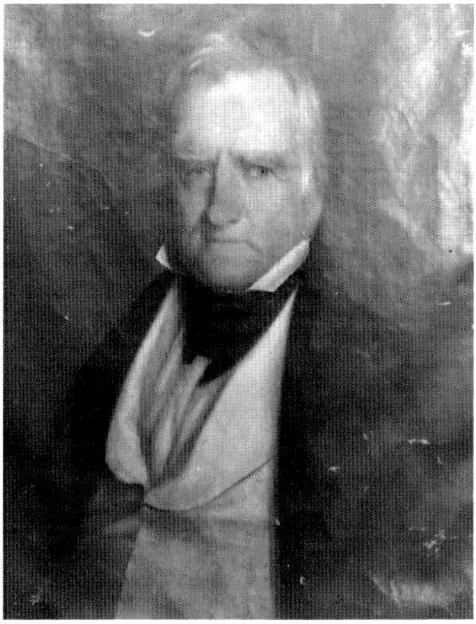

Chancellor Waddy Thompson

Chancellor Waddy Thompson served in the US House of Representatives from 1796 to 1799, as a solicitor and chancellor. He resigned after passage of a constitutional amendment that allowed the removal of officials for infirmity in office. In *Reminiscences of Public Men*, Gov. Benjamin Perry described Thompson's mind as "like a rich forest covered over with briers and brambles, instead of producing flowers and fruits." (Courtesy of Greenville County Library System.)

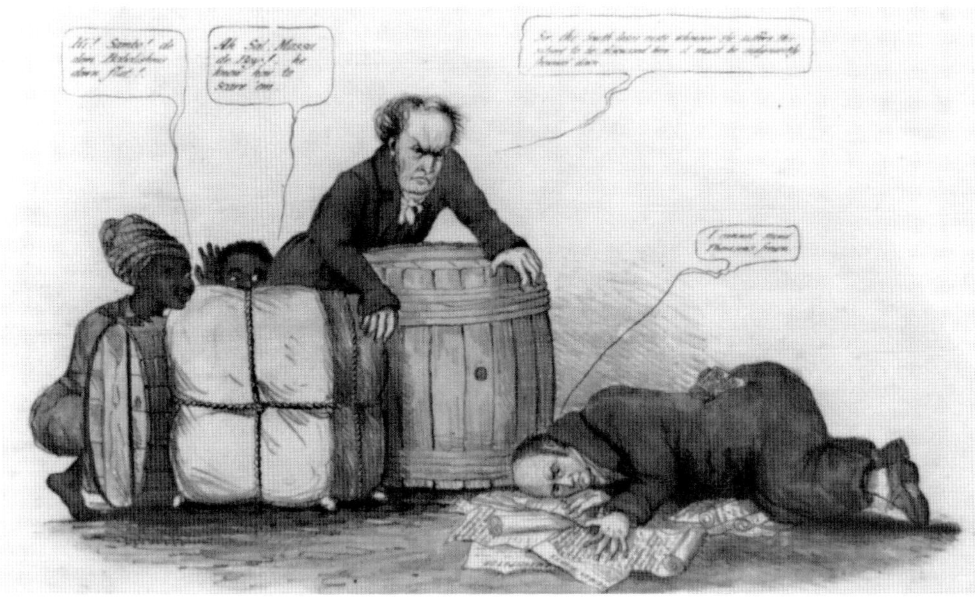

Waddy Thompson Jr.

State legislator Waddy Thompson Jr. once said he would rather live on snowbirds than eat Western pork, and he would rather walk the judicial circuit on foot than ride Kentucky horses. Those words came during an anti-tariff meeting in Greenville in 1828. Thompson later was elected to Congress and served as minister to Mexico in 1842. In December 1839, the House passed a rule forbidding debate, reading, printing of, or reference to any petition on the subject of abolition. In this drawing, titled "Abolition Frowned Down," John Quincy Adams cowers and says, "I cannot stand Thompson's [*sic*] frown." Thompson Jr., glaring at Adams from behind a sack and two casks, says, "Sir, the South loses caste whenever she suffers this subject to be discussed here; it must be indignantly frowned down." (Courtesy of the Library of Congress Prints and Photographs Division.)

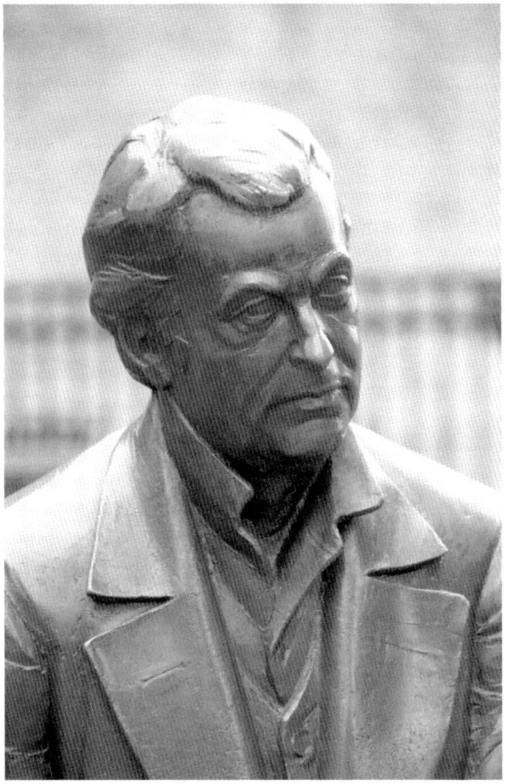

Vardry McBee

Vardry McBee earned the moniker of Father of Greenville because of the significant role he played in the development of the city. Born in Spartanburg, McBee was 12 years old when he dropped out of school after his father lost his fortune following the Revolutionary War. He went to work in a limestone mine for six years.

Later, he moved to Lincolnton, North Carolina, where he operated a saddlery and farmed. McBee served as Lincolnton's clerk of court as well.

In 1815, he bought 11,028 acres—land that now comprises the central part of the city of Greenville, from Lemuel Alston for $27,550. While he still lived in Lincolnton, McBee played a pivotal role in the development of Greenville. He built grist and corn mills along the Reedy River, and he established a tannery, general store, rock quarry, and sawmill. He also built a paper mill and cotton and woolen mills. The foundation wall of one of McBee's mills built at the edge of the upper Reedy Falls remains today and is Greenville's oldest ruin.

On September 2, 1825, McBee donated land to establish an Episcopal church, one of Greenville's original downtown churches. He also donated land for the city's first Baptist, Methodist, and Presbyterian churches.

McBee gave 30 acres of land for male and female academies. He also played a crucial role in Furman University's relocation from Winnsboro to downtown Greenville in 1851.

But one of McBee's most significant contributions to Greenville, where he permanently resided after 1836, could be saving the fledgling Greenville & Columbia Railroad line. Agriculture magazine *De Bows Review* called his purchase of $50,000 in stock "the crowning act of his life." He later served as the railroad's president. The first train arrived at the depot on Augusta Road in December 1853, providing better access to the rest of South Carolina and helping transform Greenville from a resort for Lowcountry residents to a commerce center. Today, there is a statue of McBee in downtown Greenville and a street named after him. (Photograph by Cindy Landrum).

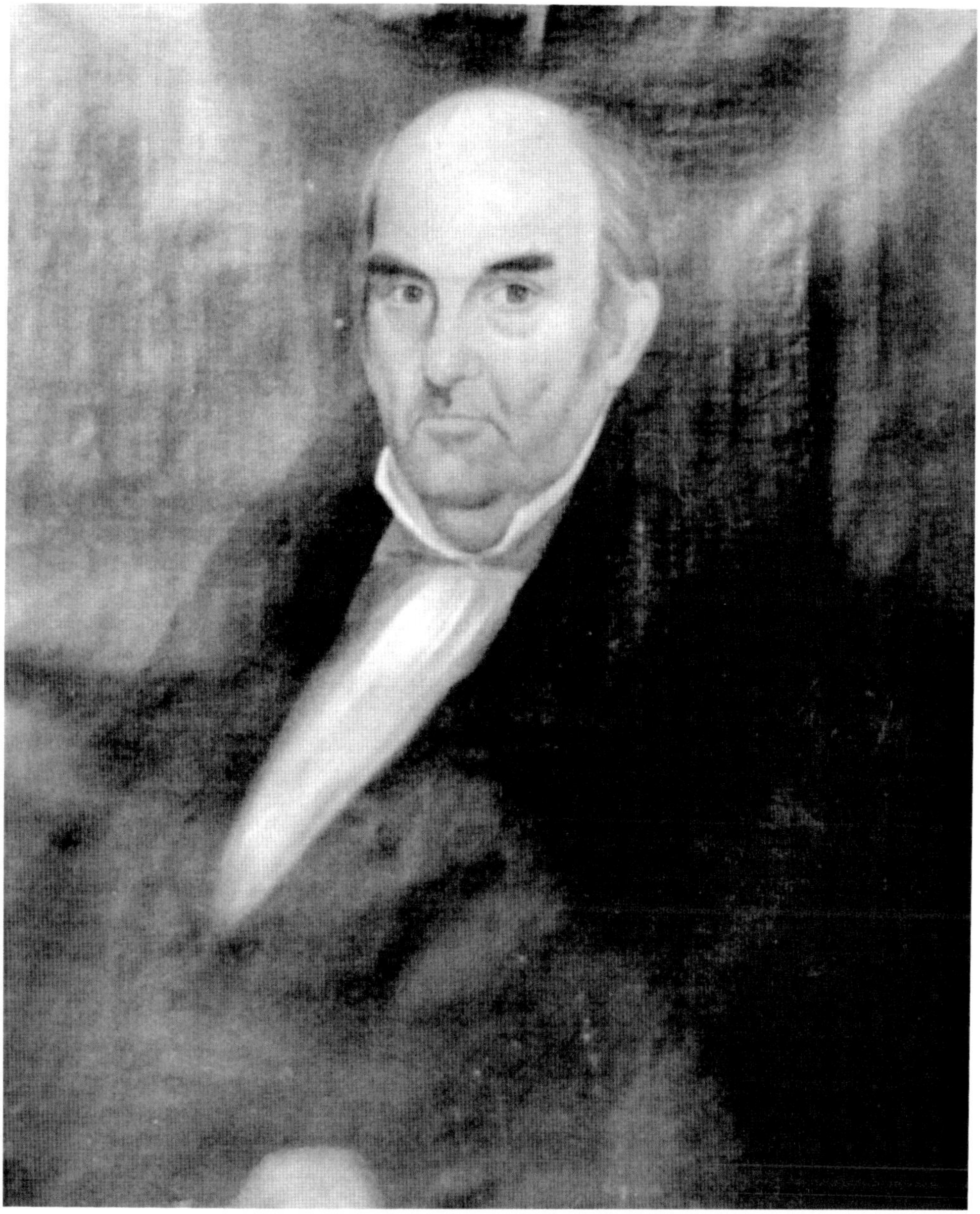

Jeremiah Cleveland

Jeremiah Cleveland moved to Greenville from Asheville, North Carolina, in 1804. He was one of Greenville's first residents and a prosperous merchant who left his children 20,000 acres in South Carolina and Tennessee. He was a trustee of the first female and male academies in the city. His obituary in the *Greenville Mountaineer* in December 1845 said, "When one who has filled so large a space in a community," it was fitting to take notice of his life. Cleveland "was the last man in the world to speak of his own good deeds." The obituary said Cleveland "did good by stealth and blushed to find it fame." (Courtesy of the Greenville County Historical Society.)

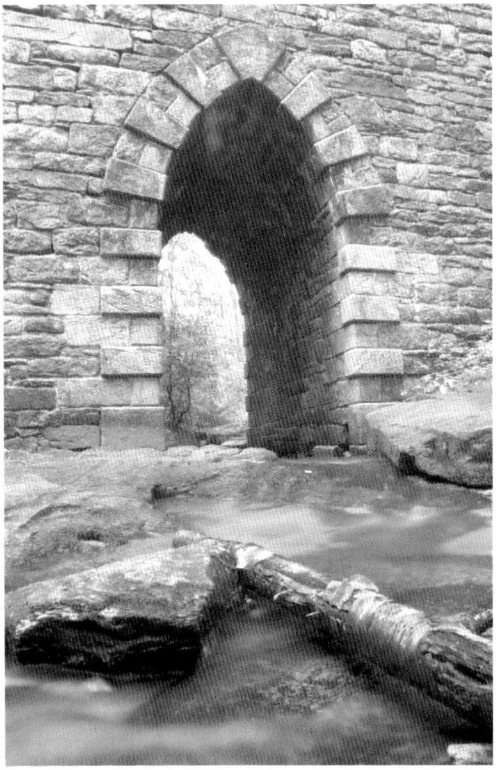

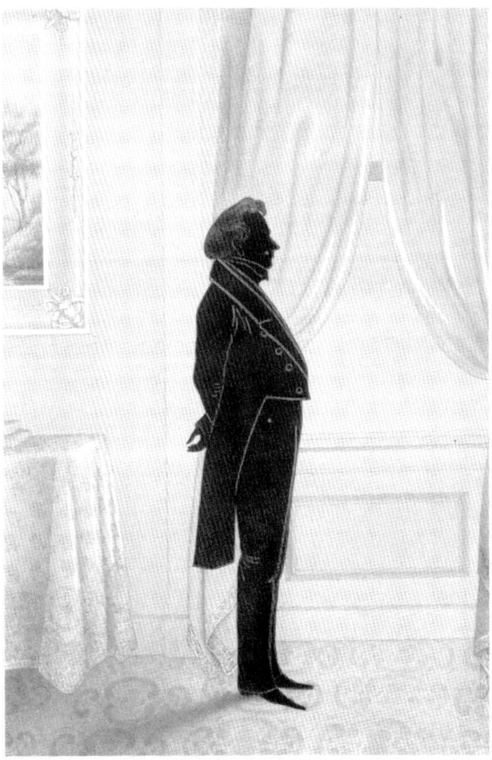

Joel Poinsett

Joel Poinsett is probably Greenville's most famous summer resident, but his name is best associated with a Christmas staple. While he was the first US minister to Mexico in 1825, he saw a plant with red and green foliage. He liked the plant so much that he brought some back to South Carolina. That plant is the poinsettia, a common Christmastime decoration. But that was not Poinsett's only contribution. While head of the South Carolina Board of Public Works from 1817 to 1820, he oversaw the building of a road that connected Charleston with mountain cities in North Carolina. The Poinsett Bridge, believed to be the oldest extant bridge in the Upstate, was part of that road. Poinsett was instrumental in the establishment of the Smithsonian Institution. (Above, photograph by Cindy Landrum; below, courtesy of the Library of Congress Prints and Photographs Division.)

Benjamin F. Perry

As editor of the *Greenville Mountaineer*, Benjamin F. Perry championed Unionist views. When Turner Bynum, the editor of a rival newspaper, made personal attacks on Perry during the Nullification Crisis of 1828–1834, Perry challenged him to a duel. Perry won, fatally wounding Bynum. In *The Leaven of Democracy: The Growth of the Democratic Spirit in the Time of Jackson*, Perry wrote that the event was "the most painful event of my life." Perry was against secession, but when the Civil War came, he supported South Carolina and the Confederacy. "You are all now going to the Devil and I will go with you," he said in 1860. After the war ended, Pres. Andrew Johnson appointed Perry provisional governor of South Carolina. (Courtesy of the Greenville Library System.)

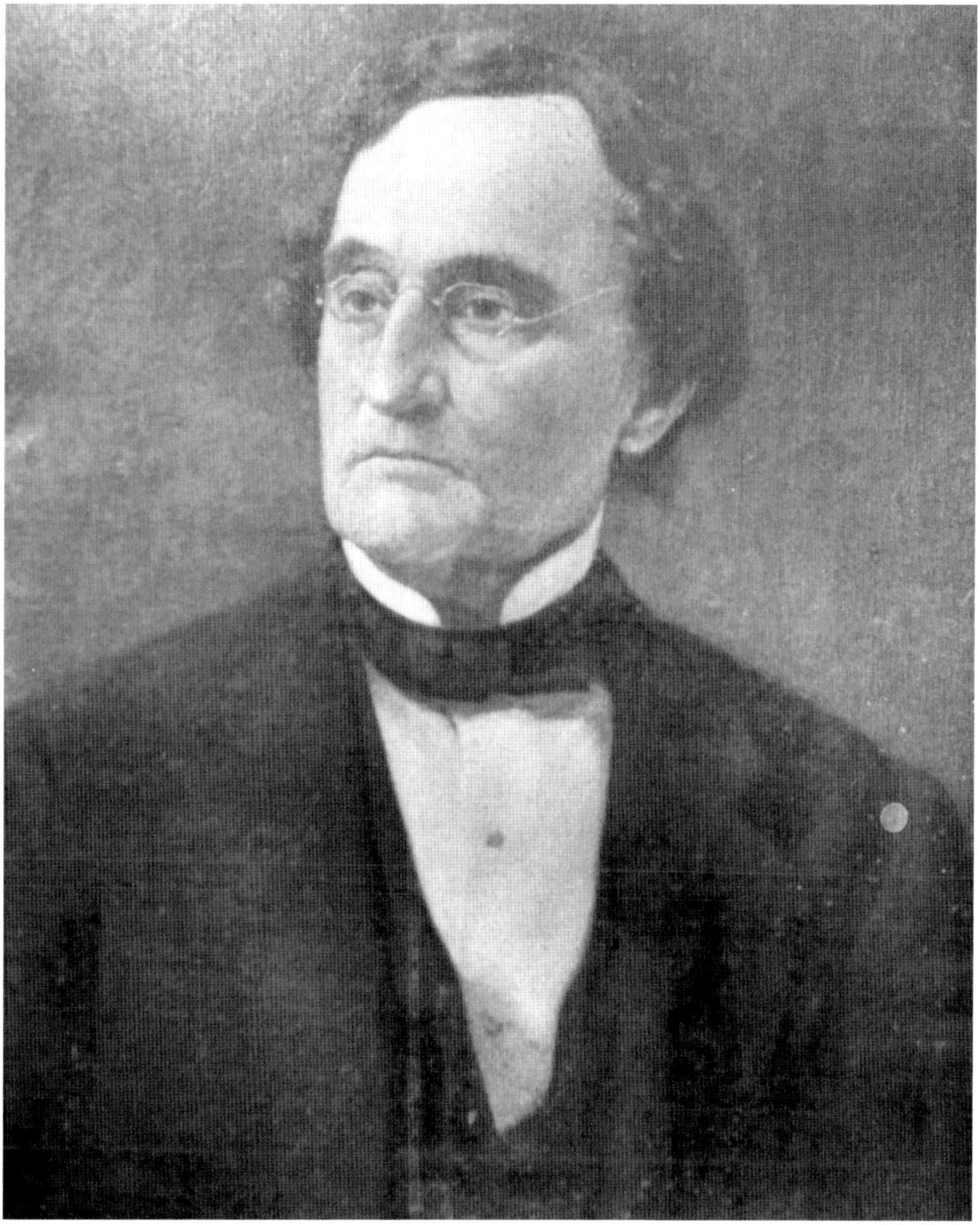

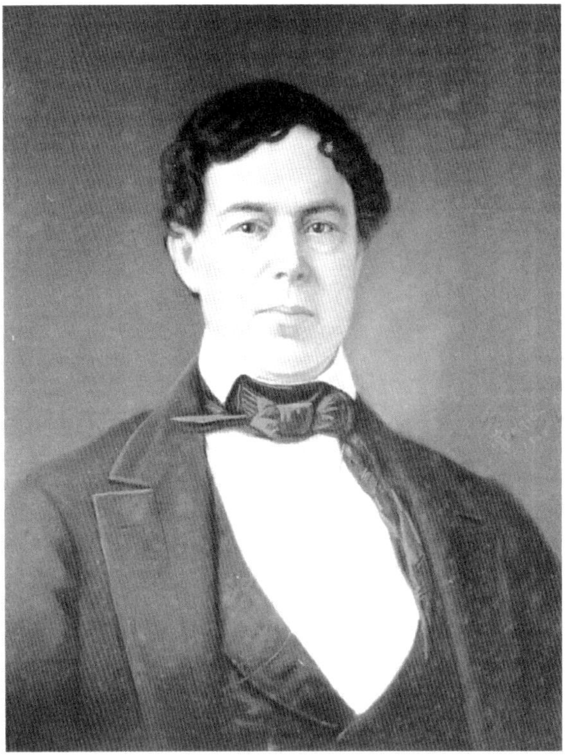

Fountain Fox Beattie

Fountain Fox Beattie moved from Virginia to Greenville in the early 1830s. He was one of Greenville's first merchants and a partner in a general store at the southwest corner of McBee Avenue. The home he built for his bride, Emily Edgeworth Hamlin, was at the center of Greenville's social, cultural, and religious life. Beattie's ancestors occupied the house until 1940. Beattie was one of the first trustees of the Greenville Female College. (Courtesy of the Greenville County Historical Society.)

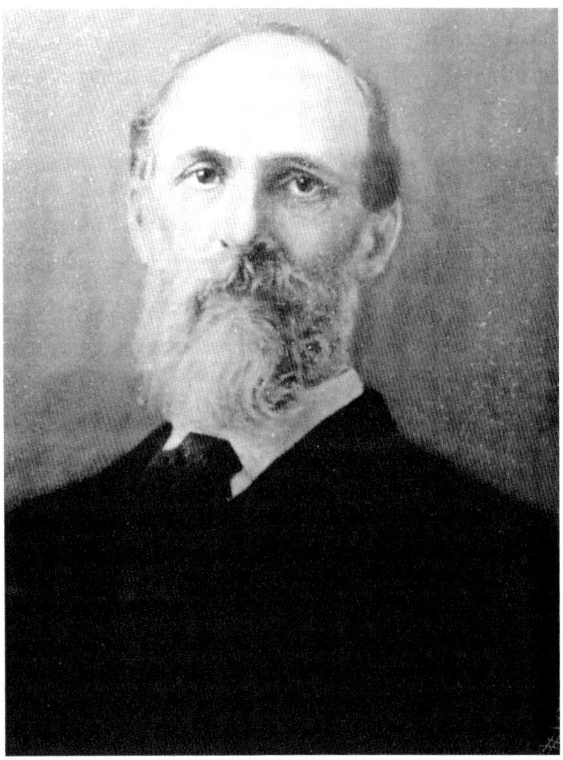

Hamlin Beattie

Before the start of the Civil War, Hamlin Beattie ran an unofficial bank in his dry-goods store. It was beside some bricks in his store that Yankee soldiers—a month after Gen. Robert E. Lee surrendered to officially end the Civil War—found $30,000 sent to him by the state bank in Charleston for safekeeping. In 1872, he started the first National Bank in South Carolina. (Courtesy of the Greenville County Historical Society.)

CHAPTER TWO

Families

Their names are on streets, schools, public buildings, and neighborhood welcome signs. They are Greenville's most famous families.

Although their efforts touched different aspects of Greenville life through generations, they all left lasting impressions.

They have made their marks in many ways. In some cases, they continue to work to make Greenville a better place.

Perhaps no family has had a greater influence on Greenville than the Peace family. Seven generations of the family that made its money in newspapers have called Greenville home. Bony Hampton Peace, one of the second generation, bought the *Greenville News* when it was struggling financially at the urging of his sons.

Family members touched all facets of the community. Family members helped found the Community Foundation of Greenville and their charities. Family members have supported schools, hospitals, and a museum. They worked to develop Falls Park.

Their crowning achievement, however, is the only one in which the entire Peace family was involved—the construction of the Peace Center for the Performing Arts. The facility helped transform downtown Greenville and transform culture in the Upstate. Broadway plays were now as close as the south end of Main Street. Entertainment's most famous stars and shows were now accessible to everybody. And when the Peace Center needed expansion, the Peaces were there to help again.

But the Peaces are not Greenville's only family royalty.

The Wilkins family holds sway in judicial and political circles.

The Gowers are known for their support of education and literacy efforts.

The Wyches are known for their environmental work, preserving hundreds of thousands of acres of land from the Blue Wall to Falls Park.

The Hipps are known for their business leadership and work to groom the leaders of tomorrow.

The Brocks fight for the underdogs and underserved.

The Haynsworths are Greenville legal royalty.

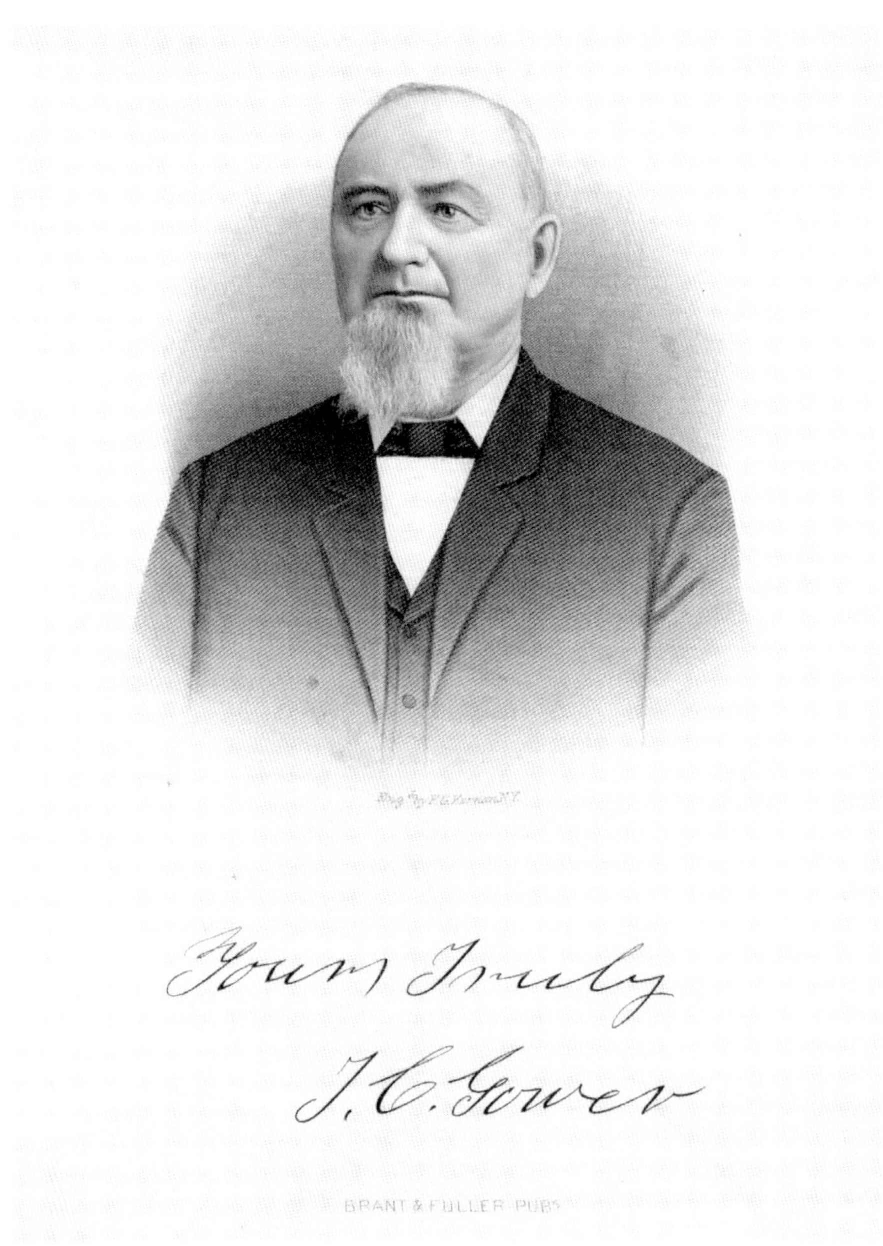

Thomas Claghorn Gower

Thomas Claghorn Gower arrived in Greenville at age 19 to apprentice as a carriage maker. He became one of the men who helped turn the city into a commercial and industrial center. Gower became a partner in Gower, Cox & Gower, which was described by the *Greenville Mountaineer and Patriot* as the largest carriage manufacturer below the Potomac. It was one of the most complete businesses in the Southern states before the Civil War. Gower built Greenville's first streetcar line, and he also operated a tannery, opened Greenville's first builders' supply and coal companies, and bought and developed real estate. Gower's mayoral campaign platform included construction of a bridge over the Reedy River. He led a campaign to establish Greenville's first public school system and was chairman of its first board of trustees. (Courtesy of Grier Mullins.)

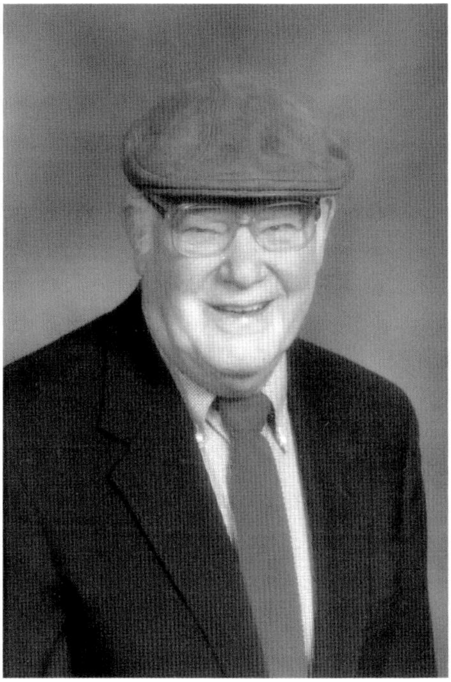

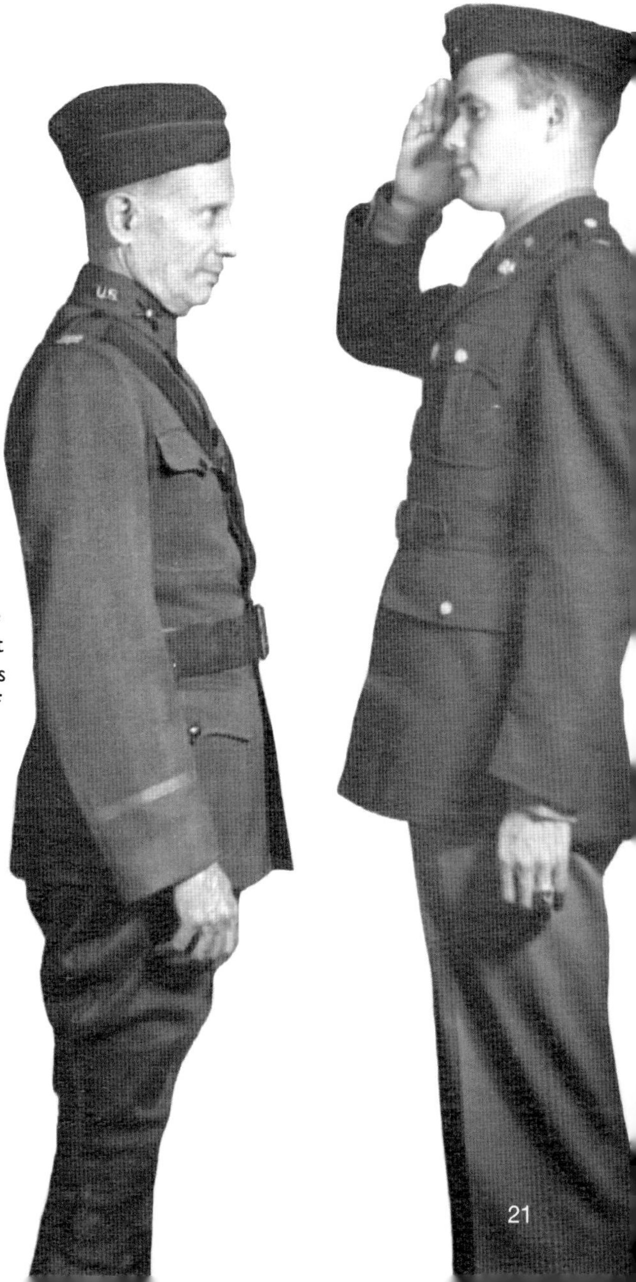

Tom Gower

The great-grandson of Thomas Claghorn Gower, Tom Gower continued the Gower family legacy of public service with two stints on the Greenville City Council. Gower pushed for the elimination of parking meters that generated $100,000 in annual revenue so downtown could compete with shopping malls. Gower opened The Open Book, which at one time was South Carolina's largest independent bookstore. At right, he is shown saluting his father, Charles Gower. (Both, courtesy of Grier Mullins.)

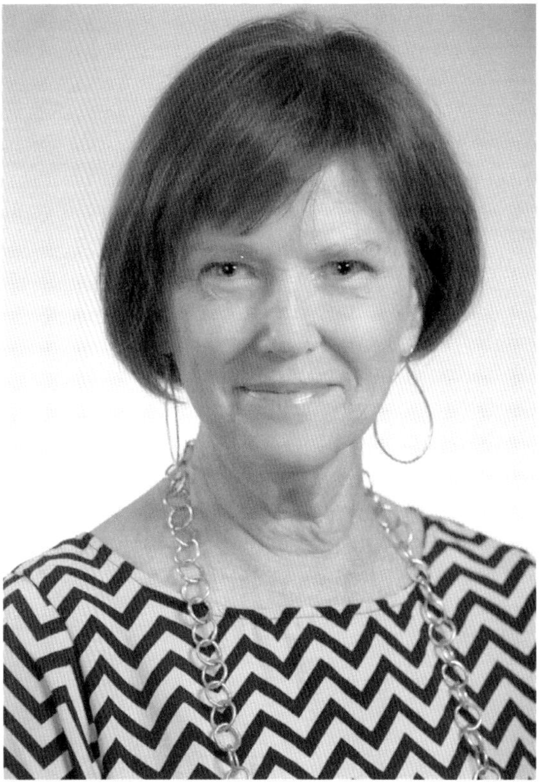

Grier Mullins

Both education and books are dear to Grier Mullins, a former Head Start teacher and PTA president and daughter of the founders of The Open Book. Mullins, executive director of Public Education Partnership Greenville County since 1989, has made strengthening public education her life's work. (Courtesy of Grier Mullins.)

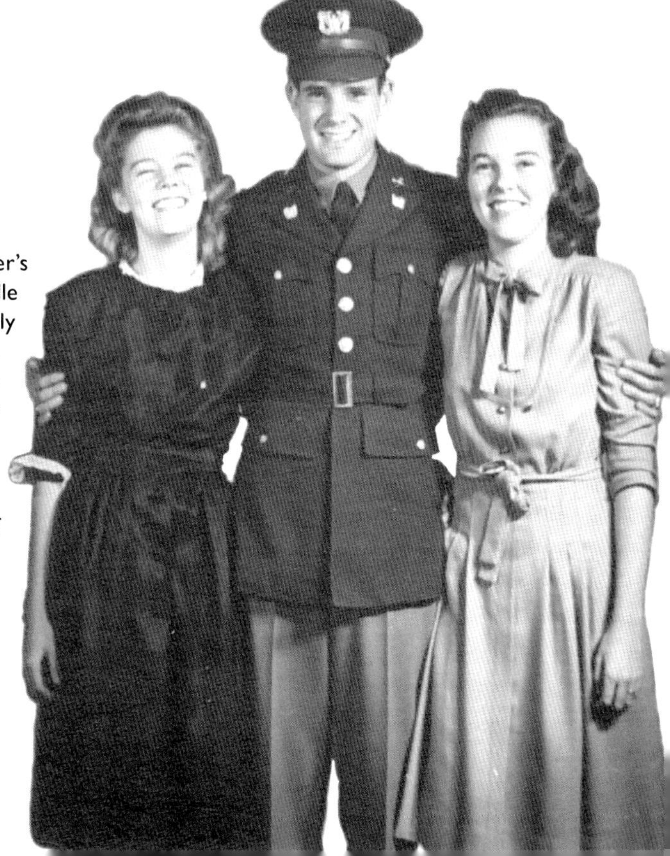

Elizabeth "Ducky" Gower

Elizabeth "Ducky" Gower, Tom Gower's wife, had her turn on the Greenville City Council as well. She spent nearly 20 years as a United Way executive, giving her a unique perspective on the community's needs. Gower, given her nickname as a child by her cousins, is pictured on the right with her twin sister, Margaret Grier Hollis, and her husband, Tom. (Courtesy of Grier Mullins.)

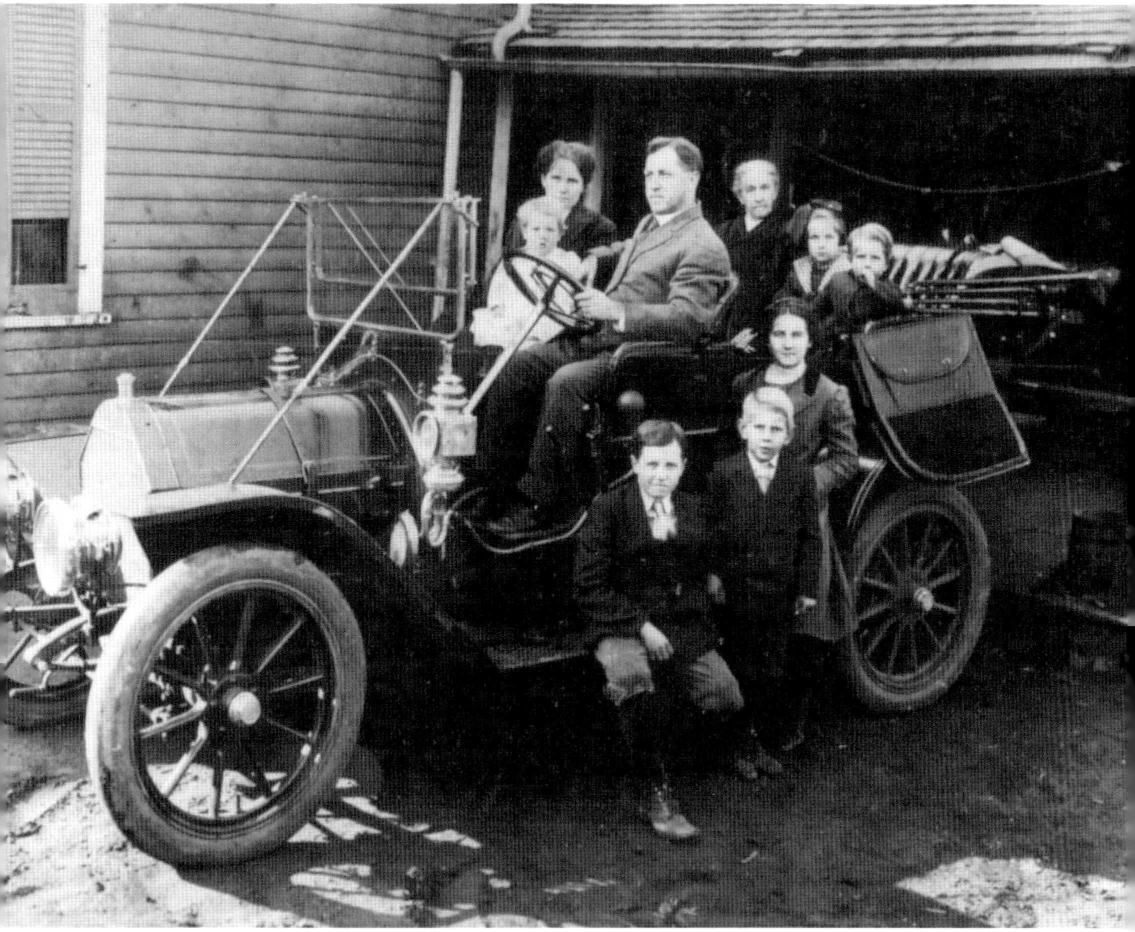

Bony Hampton Peace

Greenville residents would be hard-pressed to find a family with greater influence on the community than Bony Hampton Peace Sr. and his descendants. Bony Hampton Peace Sr. owned a successful commercial printing plant when his sons Roger C. Peace and Charlie Peace urged him to buy the *Greenville News*, the city's financially strapped morning newspaper, in 1919. He later bought the city's afternoon newspaper, the *Piedmont*, in 1927. Peace's first attempt at starting a radio station failed in 1931 when the Federal Radio Commission denied his application to start WGNP after stations in Spartanburg, Toccoa, Georgia, and Miami, Florida, objected. Two years later, Peace and his sons began WFBC, the city's first local radio station. (Courtesy of Betty Stall.)

Roger C., B.H. Jr., and Charlie Peace

Each of Bony Hampton Peace's three sons worked in the family media company. Roger C. Peace got an early start in newspapers by working as a cub reporter for the *Greenville News* while he attended Furman. He became sports editor, then editor, then business manager before becoming publisher. Roger had a reputation for being a reliable and stable leader, warmhearted and unselfish. He served a short stint as a US senator after he was appointed to fill the seat vacated by James F. Byrnes. He decided politics was not for him, and he did not seek reelection. B.H. Peace Jr. was station manager at Greenville's first radio station, WFBC. Charlie Peace served as general manager for the News-Piedmont Co. and president of the Asheville papers after their acquisition. (Courtesy of Betty Stall.)

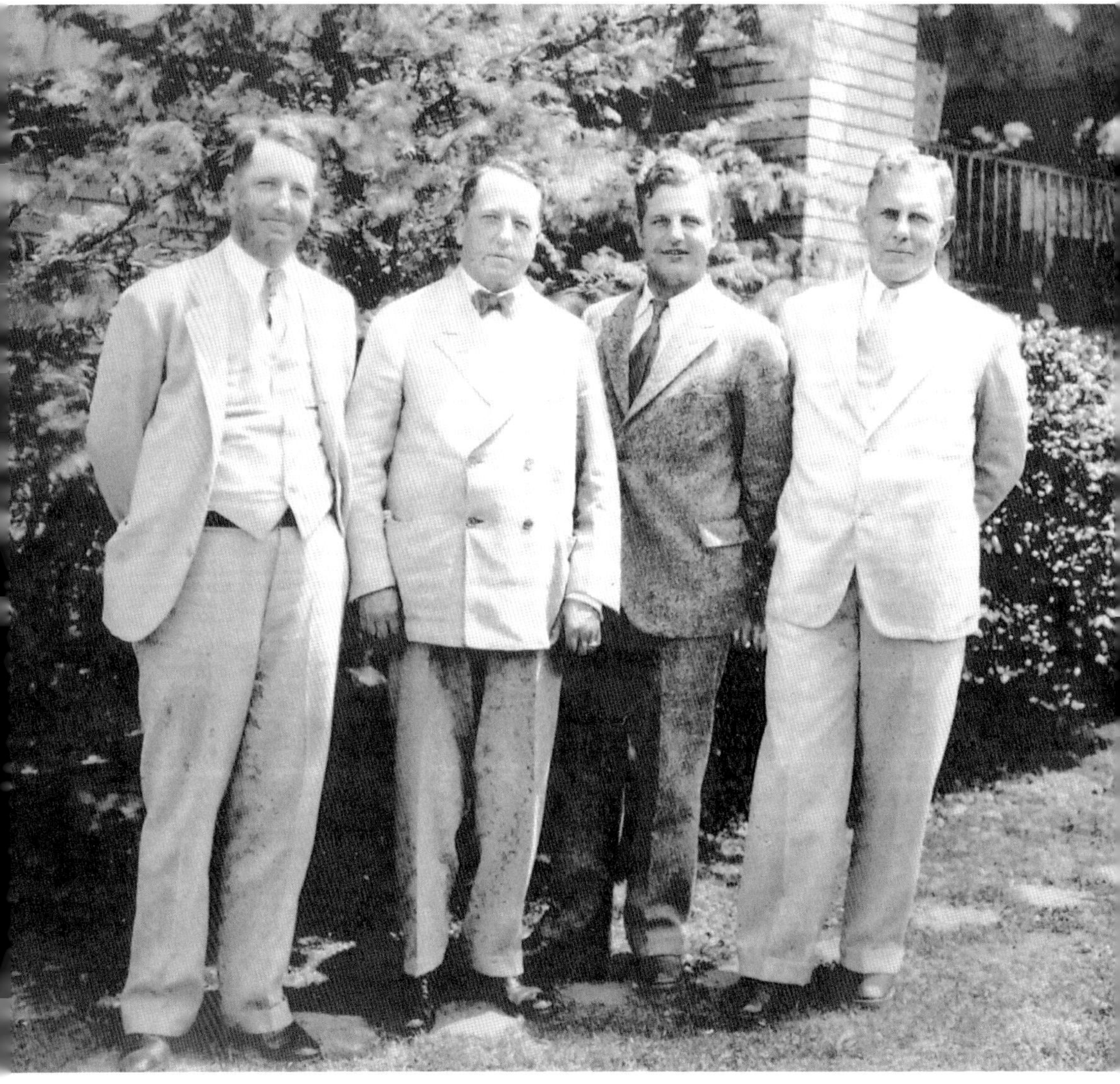

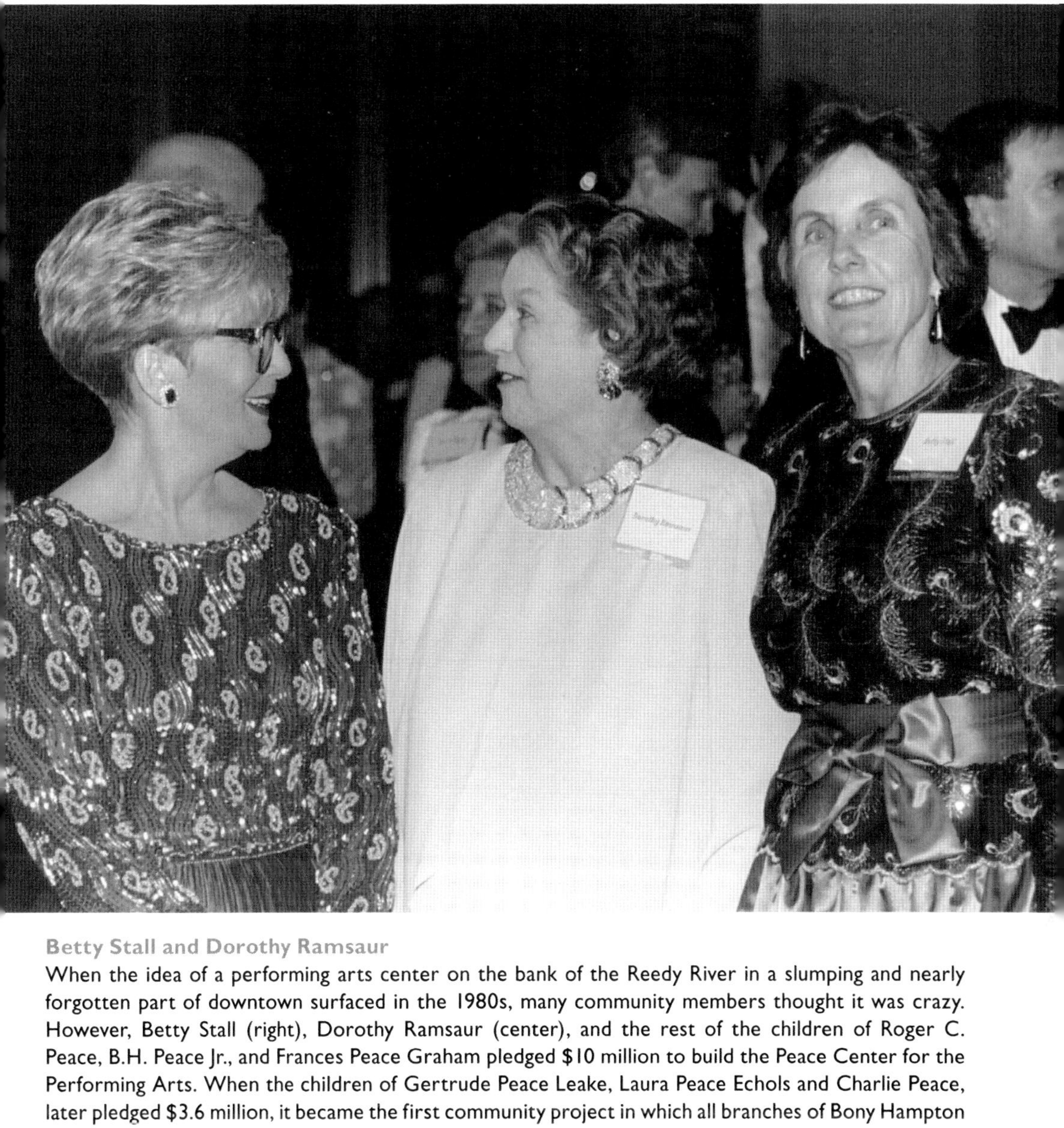

Betty Stall and Dorothy Ramsaur

When the idea of a performing arts center on the bank of the Reedy River in a slumping and nearly forgotten part of downtown surfaced in the 1980s, many community members thought it was crazy. However, Betty Stall (right), Dorothy Ramsaur (center), and the rest of the children of Roger C. Peace, B.H. Peace Jr., and Frances Peace Graham pledged $10 million to build the Peace Center for the Performing Arts. When the children of Gertrude Peace Leake, Laura Peace Echols and Charlie Peace, later pledged $3.6 million, it became the first community project in which all branches of Bony Hampton Peace's family participated. National television talk-show host Sally Jesse Raphael served as emcee at the facility's opening on November 30, 1990. (Courtesy of Betty Stall.)

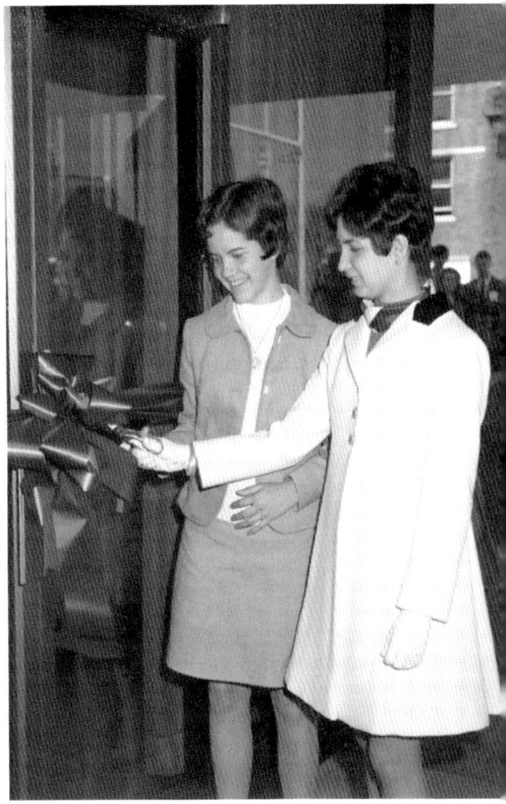

Pedrick Lowrey

Pedrick Lowrey came home from work as a chemist for Coca-Cola Company headquarters in Atlanta, Georgia, one day and told her husband she was going to become a horticulturist. She did and started a landscape design business in Atlanta. She joined the Peachtree Garden Club, the founder of the Southeastern Flower Show. After she had moved to Greenville, Lowrey joined the Carolina Foothills Garden Club, eventually rising to president. Lowrey played an instrumental role in raising more than $3 million for an endowment for Falls Park. Fittingly, the final part of the park is a public garden named in Lowrey's honor, Pedrick's Garden. She is shown on the left with Peace Sterling Sullivan at the ribbon cutting of the *Greenville News*' downtown offices. (Courtesy of Betty Stall.)

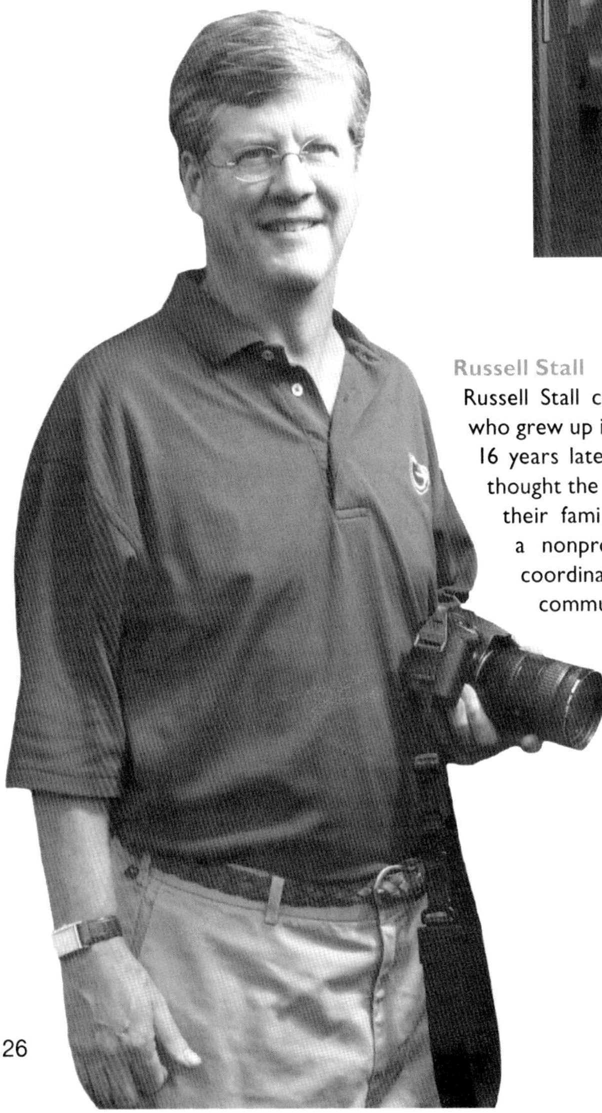

Russell Stall

Russell Stall calls himself a boomerang—somebody who grew up in Greenville, left and came back (albeit 16 years later). He and his wife returned because thought the city was more conducive place to raise their family. Stall founded Greenville Forward, a nonprofit organization that facilitates and coordinates work on Greenville's comprehensive community improvement initiative called Vision 2025. In his off time, Stall works his year-round 4,000-square-foot garden and greenhouse. (Courtesy of Greenville Forward.)

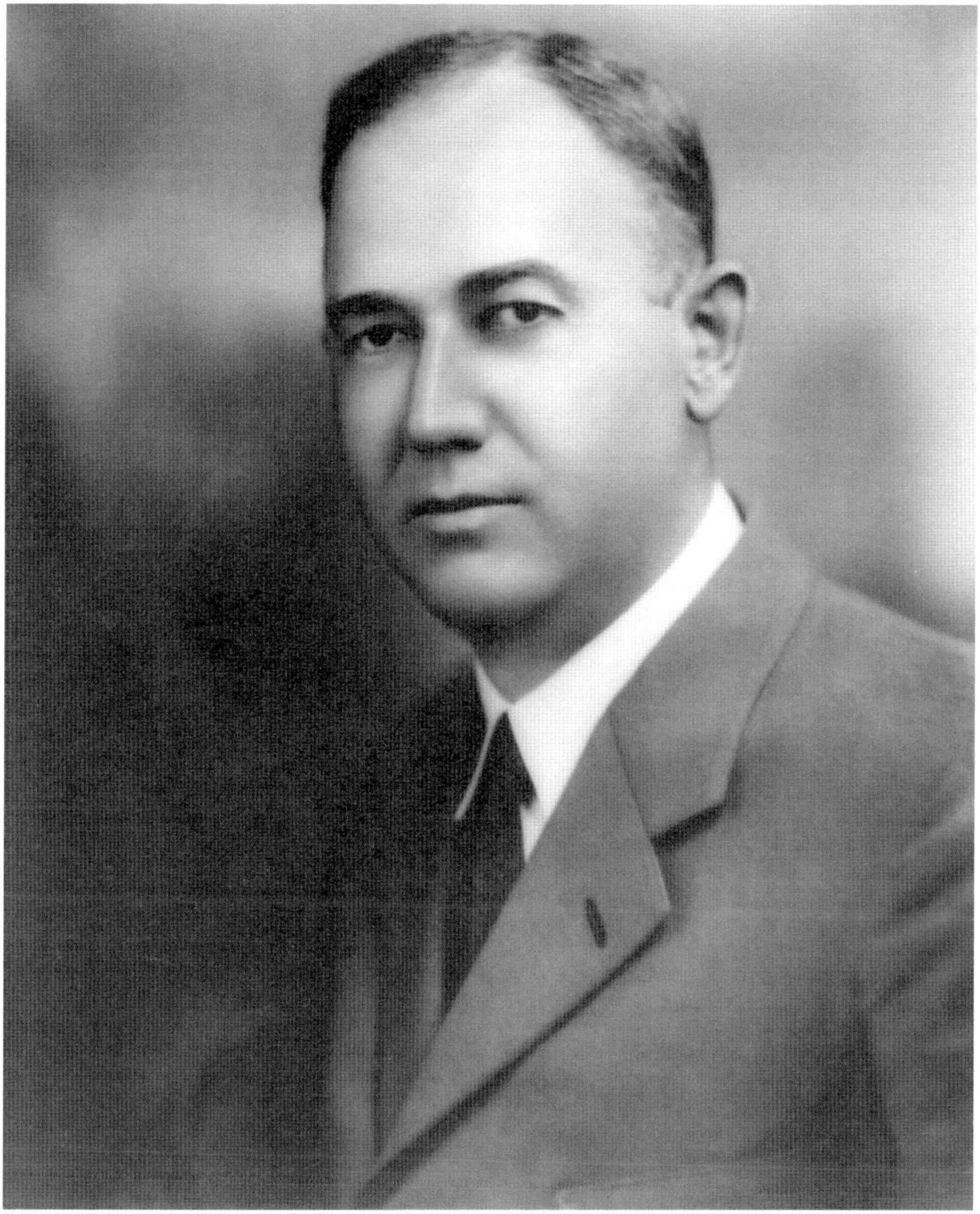

W. Frank Hipp

After a two-year convalescence from tuberculosis, W. Frank Hipp moved to Greenville in 1918 and opened a textile securities investment office. Hipp, who had previous experience as an insurance agent, decided Greenville was ready for a weekly premium insurance company. He established the Liberty Life Insurance Co., a company that offered a life insurance policy for 2¢ a week, perfect for Greenville's mill workers. The company issued $1.7 million in new insurance in 1920. Some of the company's board wanted to add ordinary premium policies and expand into adjoining states, but Hipp refused to alter his vision. The dissenters left. Liberty Life began offering ordinary life insurance in 1922. Thinking radio would be the perfect medium for advertising, Hipp bought WIS, a fledging and struggling station in Columbia, South Carolina. (Courtesy of Hayne Hipp.)

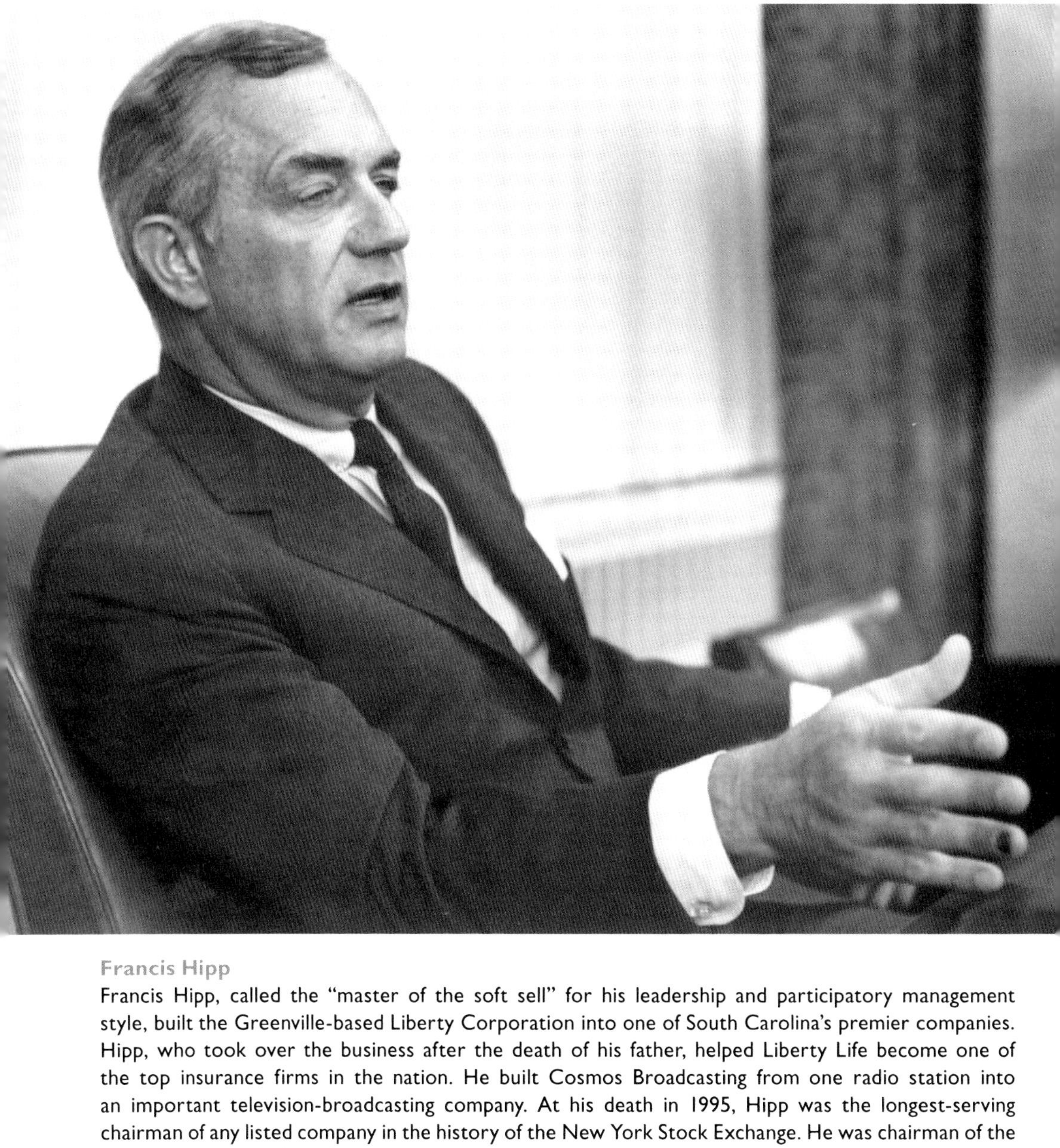

Francis Hipp

Francis Hipp, called the "master of the soft sell" for his leadership and participatory management style, built the Greenville-based Liberty Corporation into one of South Carolina's premier companies. Hipp, who took over the business after the death of his father, helped Liberty Life become one of the top insurance firms in the nation. He built Cosmos Broadcasting from one radio station into an important television-broadcasting company. At his death in 1995, Hipp was the longest-serving chairman of any listed company in the history of the New York Stock Exchange. He was chairman of the State Development Board during a time when new industrial investment in Greenville County soared. (Courtesy of Hayne Hipp.)

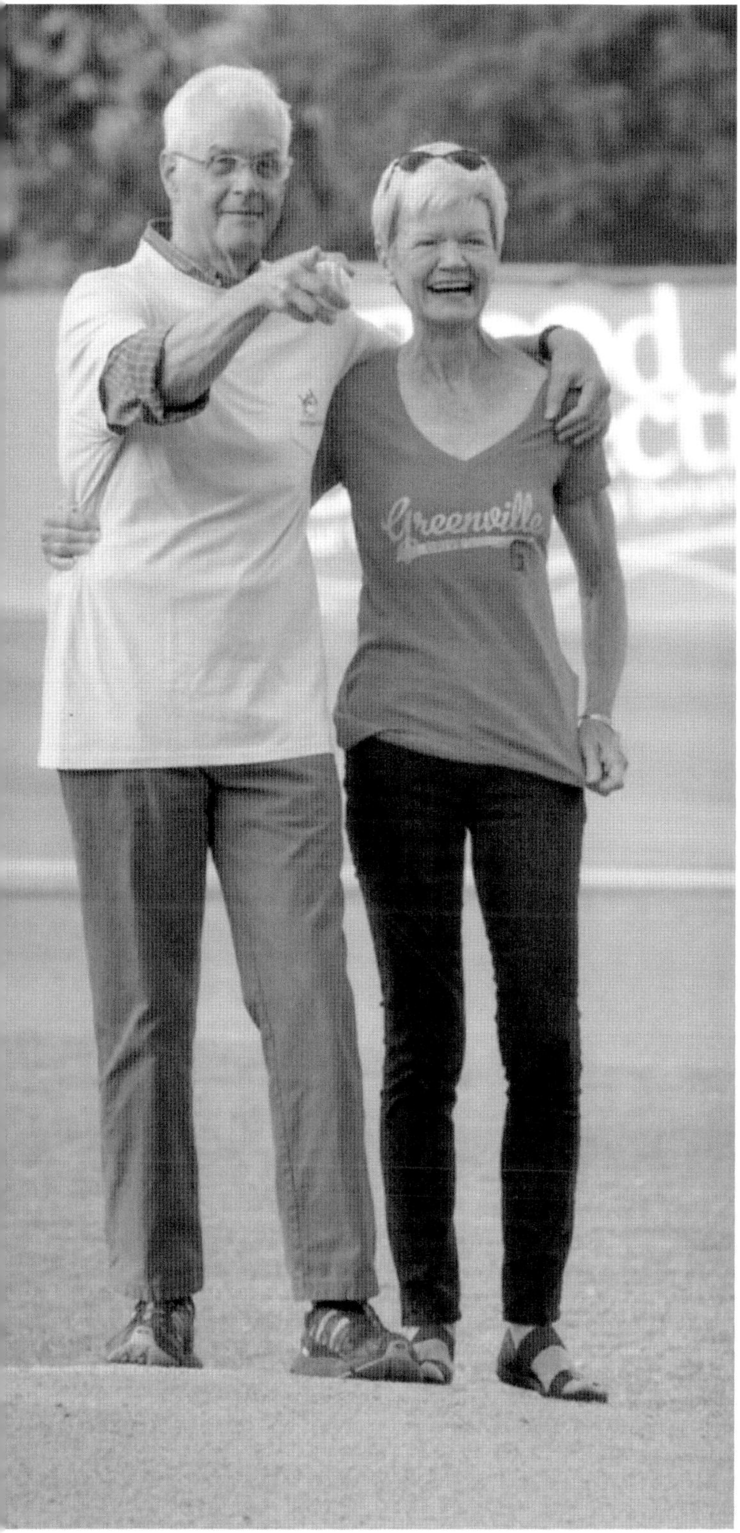

Hayne Hipp and Anna Kate Hipp
Big challenges are not anything new for Hayne and Anna Kate Hipp. Hayne, the former CEO of Liberty Corporation, hiked the entire Appalachian Trail, section by section. Anna Kate, a philanthropist who focuses on education and environmental issues, was instrumental in the development of Falls Park. Together, they founded the Liberty Fellowship, a leadership incubator designed to empower South Carolina and its future leaders to address the state's challenges. The list of Greenville and South Carolina organizations for which one of the Hipps has served on the board is like a laundry list, including the Peace Center for Performing Arts, Friends of the Reedy River, Greenville Health System, South Carolina Chamber of Commerce, Greenville County School District, and the Palmetto Business Forum. (Courtesy of the Greenville Drive and Darrell Snow.)

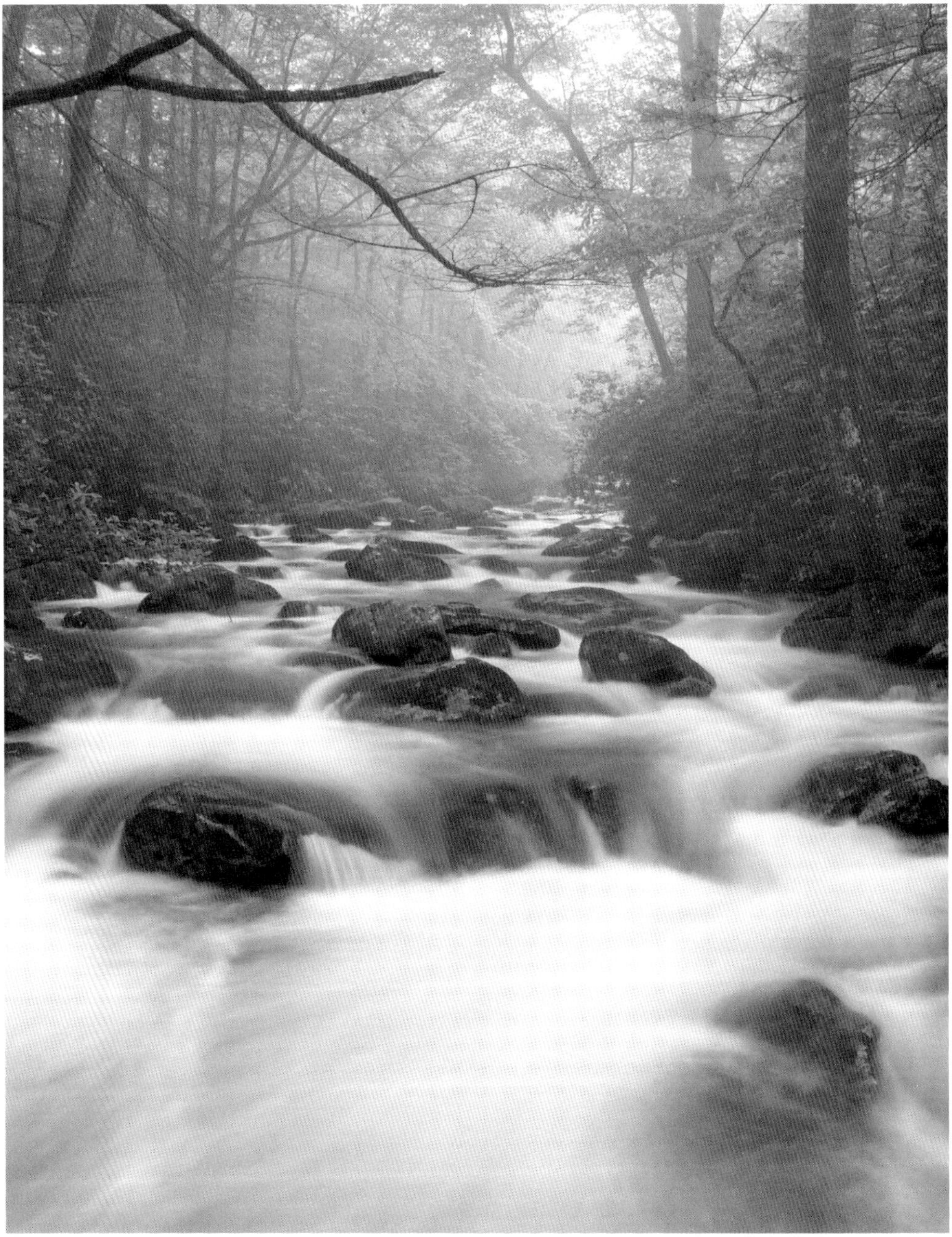

Jones Gap State Park

South Carolina Department of Parks and Recreation director Phil Gaines said it would not be a stretch to credit Greenville attorney and environmentalist Tommy Wyche for the existence of Jones Gap State Park and Caesar's Head State Park. Wyche founded Naturaland Trust, one of the state's first conservation land trusts. (Photograph by Cindy Landrum.)

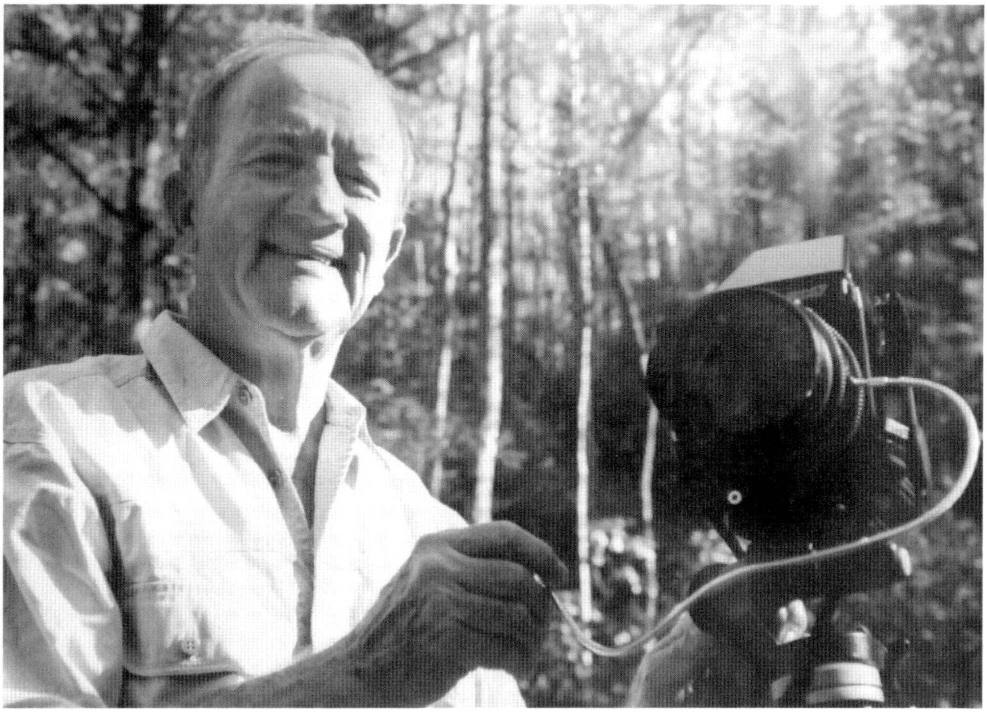

Tommy Wyche
Serve and protect is a motto commonly associated with law-enforcement officers, but it was just as fitting for Greenville attorney Tommy Wyche. He was a catalyst for change in some ways and keeping things the same in others.

Wyche was as tenacious as he was gracious, as committed as he was humble. He spent more than 60 years with the Wyche law firm, the firm founded by his father, joining shortly after he graduated law school in 1949. Wyche built a reputation as a brilliant lawyer and a civic-minded leader who worked strategically and diligently on a project until it came to fruition, even if that payoff was 20 or 25 years down the road.

Wyche played a crucial role in bringing the Hyatt Regency to Greenville, using connections and South Carolina's first-ever horizontal property regime to attract the major hotel as the anchor for downtown's rebirth. He worked to make construction of a performing-arts center on the banks of the Reedy River a reality. On the other side of the Reedy, an asset that was long forgotten and underutilized, he foresaw an artist-friendly mixed-use development RiverPlace and worked to cobble together the land for decades to make it possible.

Those are the changes, but it is his work to ensure a broad swath of land in the foothills and mountains would stay the same that garnered Wyche state and national awards. After a trip in 1972 to Los Angeles, California, where Wyche saw how development devastated mountains in that region, Wyche founded Naturaland Trust. It was one of the first conservation land trusts in the Southeast and responsible for preserving properties in the Jocassee Gorges, Jones Gap State Park, and Caesar's Head State Park. Wyche spearheaded efforts to get the Chattooga River designated as a wild and scenic river.

Wyche, who died on January 23, 2015, was a fervent supporter of the arts, earning the Elizabeth O'Neill Verner Lifetime Achievement Award, the state's highest honor in the arts. He was a state tennis champion as well. All in all, Wyche was a modern Renaissance man. (Courtesy of Brad Wyche.)

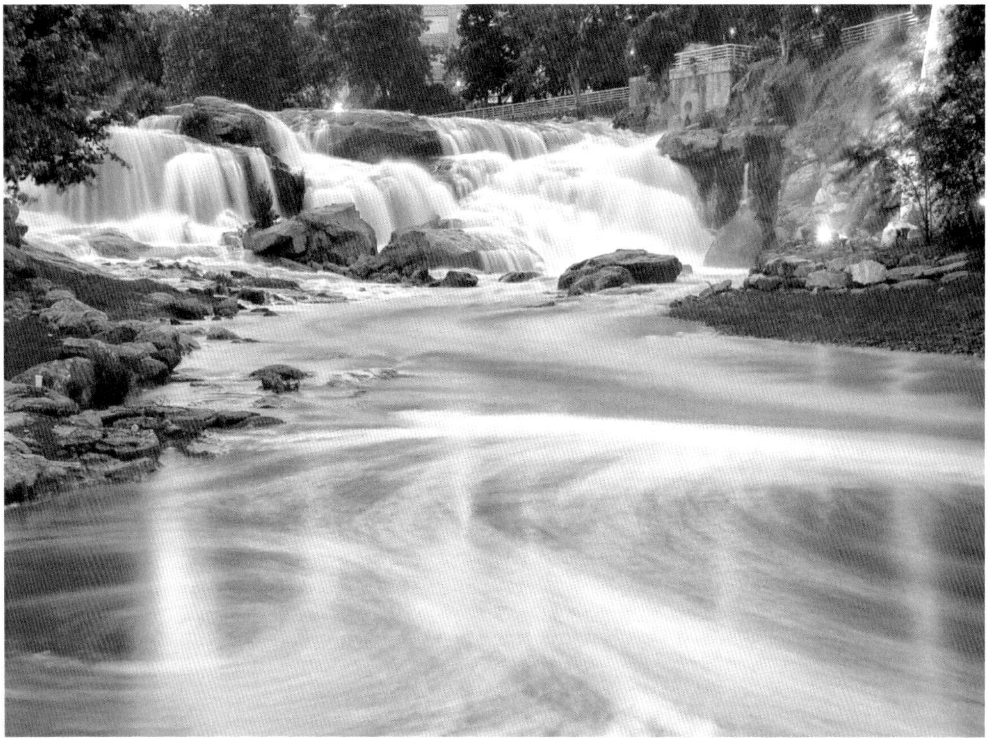

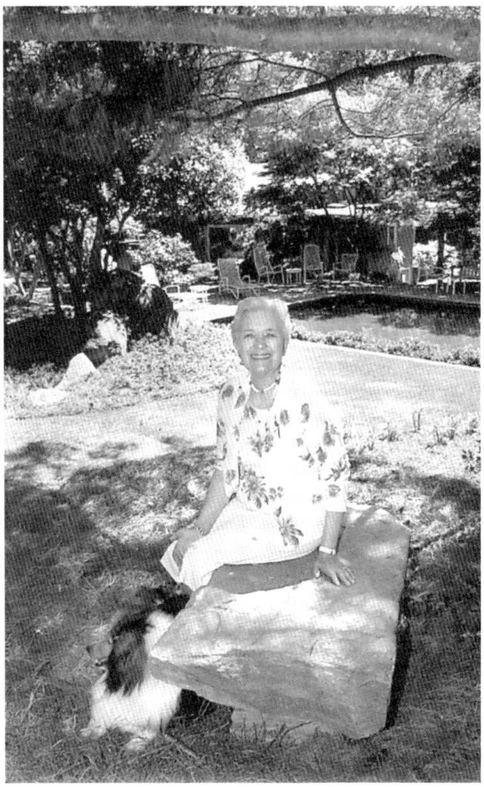

Reedy Falls

When the Reedy River was polluted, stinky, and essentially forgotten, Harriet Wyche knew what an unpolished jewel Greenville had downtown. She and a small group of Carolina Foothills Garden Club members fought for the removal of an ugly concrete vehicular bridge that had obscured the falls. The signature pedestrian overlook to the falls, Liberty Bridge, is now the main attraction of Falls Park. (Photograph by Cindy Landrum.)

Harriet Wyche

Harriet Wyche was the driving force behind Greenville's centerpiece, Falls Park on the Reedy, but that is far from her only accomplishment. Wyche, who died in 2011, was a fierce advocate for the arts as well. The grounds at the home she shared with her high school sweetheart and husband, Tommy Wyche, were featured in *Southern Living* magazine. She was also a master puzzle solver and a devoted Atlanta Braves fan. (Courtesy of Brad Wyche.)

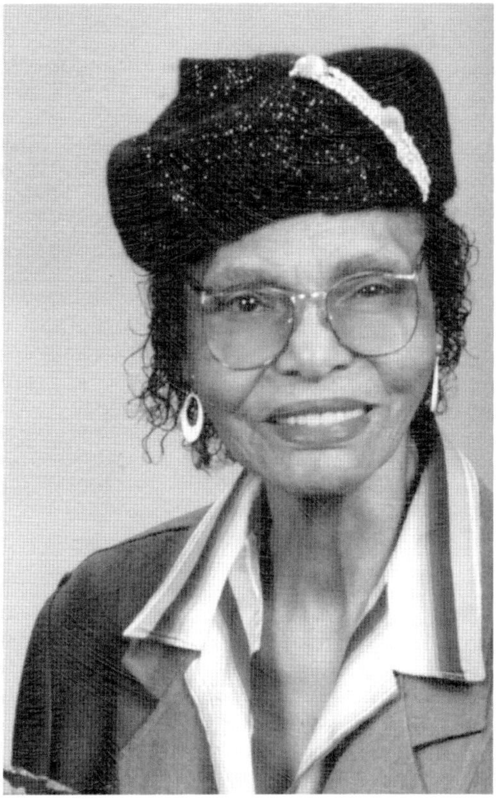

Lila Brock

Unemployment, dilapidated buildings, and empty lots characterized Greenville's Southernside neighborhood in the 1970s. Retired school lunchroom operator and community leader Lila Mae Brock would not let the neighborhood die. She fought to get Southernside Community Center opened, paying the bulk of the first year's bills with her Social Security checks. She pushed for affordable housing to attract families back to the area. (Courtesy of Lillian Brock Flemming.)

Lillian Brock Flemming

Firsts are nothing new to Lillian Brock Flemming. She was one of the first African American women to enroll at Furman University (in 1967) and was one of the first to graduate (in 1971). In 1981, she was the first African American woman elected to Greenville City Council. A former math teacher who now recruits teachers for the school district, Flemming became Furman's first female African American trustee in 1995. (Courtesy of Furman University.)

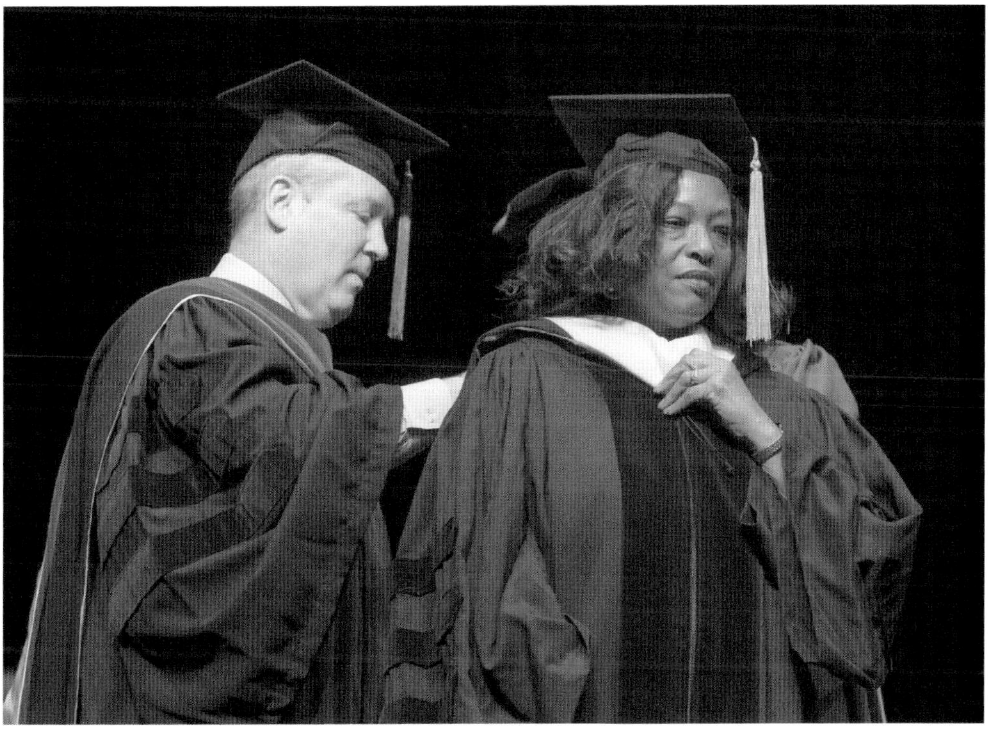

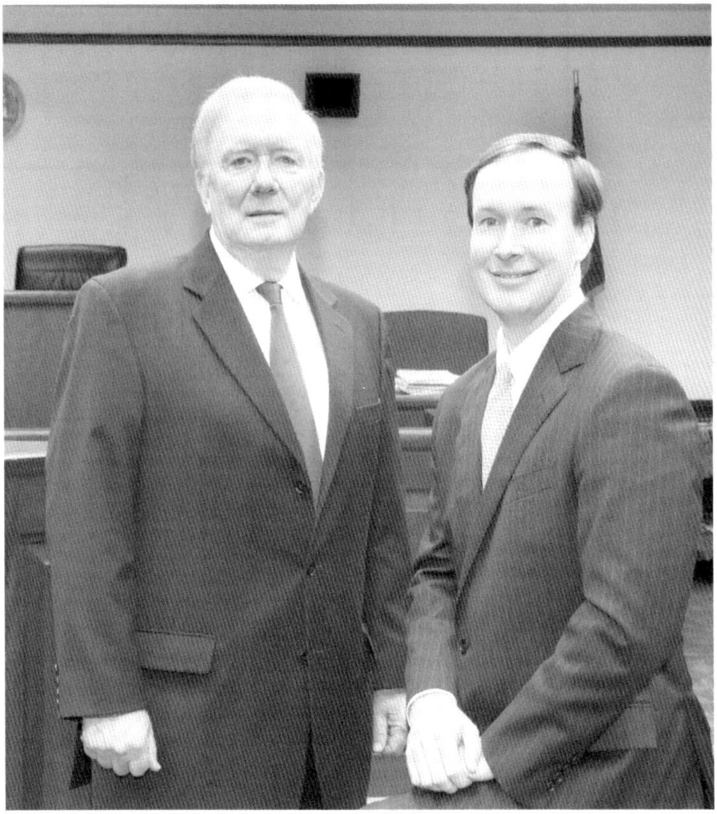

Billy and Walt Wilkins

Billy Wilkins was destined to be in the courtroom. He decided law would be his calling as a boy as he watched his father in action in a Greenville County courtroom.

William "Billy" Wilkins, a masterful trial lawyer who could pack a courtroom with his closing argument, created the nation's first multiagency taskforce as solicitor to take down the Dawson Gang and corrupt cops. Pres. Ronald Reagan appointed him a federal judge, the president's first appointment to the federal bench. As the first chairman of the sentencing commission, he helped create the guidelines used by federal judges today to sentence prisoners. The guidelines, designed to account for the severity of a crime and the defendant's criminal history, replaced an indeterminate system that gave judges broad discretion, from probation to the statute's maximum.

He was chief justice of the Fourth Circuit Court of Appeals and is now a partner with the Nexsen Pruet law firm, one of the largest in the Carolinas. Wilkins was the defense attorney for businessman John Ludwig in one of Greenville's most notorious recent cases. Ludwig avoided prison time after pleading guilty to reckless homicide after his Maserati plowed through a house and left the homeowner who had been sitting on his couch watching television dead.

Billy's son, Walter, was elected Thirteenth Judicial Circuit solicitor in 2010. Prior to that, he was US attorney for South Carolina, noted for his tough stance on gang-related crime. But facing off with gangsters in the courtroom is not scary when compared with some things Wilkins has experienced.

Wilkins and his wife, Donyelle, had just gotten married and were aboard a twin-engine plane bound for the Bahamas and their island honeymoon. But the plane had engine trouble and crashed six miles short of Abaco Island, hurling the couple and eight other passengers into the rough waters. A woman and her niece died in the crash, but the couple helped save her four-year-old and six-year-old daughters. They treaded water and kept the girls afloat for nearly two hours, singing "Amazing Grace" and "Jesus Loves Me" before being rescued by the Coast Guard. (Photograph by Cindy Landrum.)

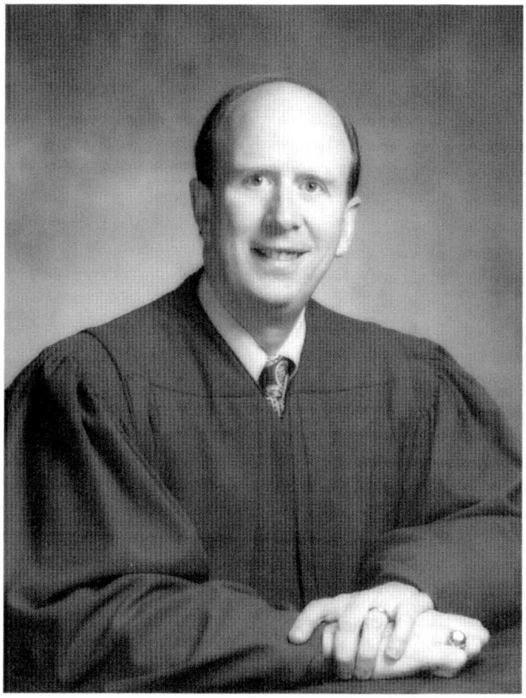

David Wilkins

Nobody predicted David Wilkins's meteoric rise in politics—not even Wilkins himself. When he ran for the state house of representatives in 1980, he never had worked on a campaign before, winning to become one of 18 Republicans in the 124-seat House. In 1994, Wilkins was elected as Speaker of the House in a still-Democrat majority body. Despite being one of South Carolina's most influential politicians, he left to become ambassador to Canada in 2005. He calls it the greatest position he ever held. Wilkins, a lawyer with Nelson Mullins, is Clemson University's board chairman. (Courtesy of David Wilkins.)

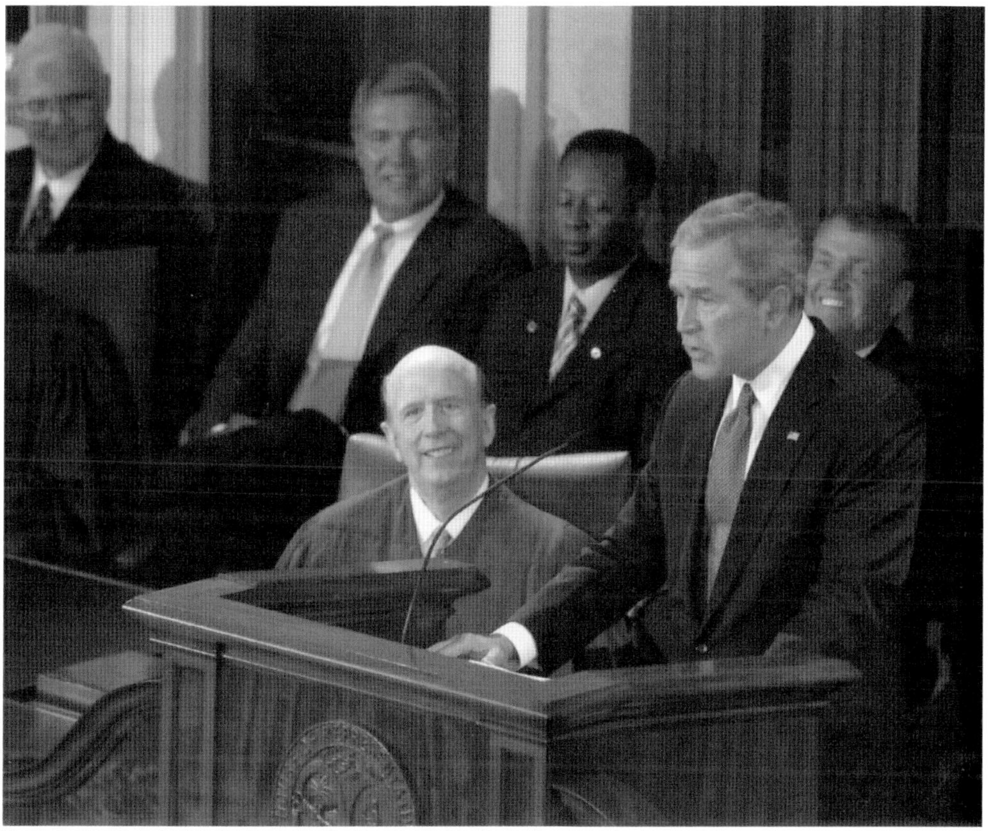

Clement Furman Haynsworth Jr.

Clement Furman Haynsworth Jr. came from Greenville legal royalty, and he would have risen to his profession's pinnacle if it had not been for a power tug-of-war between Congress and then-president Richard M. Nixon.

Haynsworth, who was a fifth-generation lawyer, was appointed a federal court judge by President Eisenhower in 1957. He was 45. Haynsworth was 52 years old when he was named Fourth Circuit Court of Appeals chief judge, making him youngest among the country's 11 chief appeals judges.

Nixon nominated Haynsworth for the US Supreme Court in 1969. But his nomination was derailed by opposition from labor unions, civil-rights leaders, and a ruling that raised financial conflict-of-interest concerns. (Courtesy of the Greenville County Historical Society.)

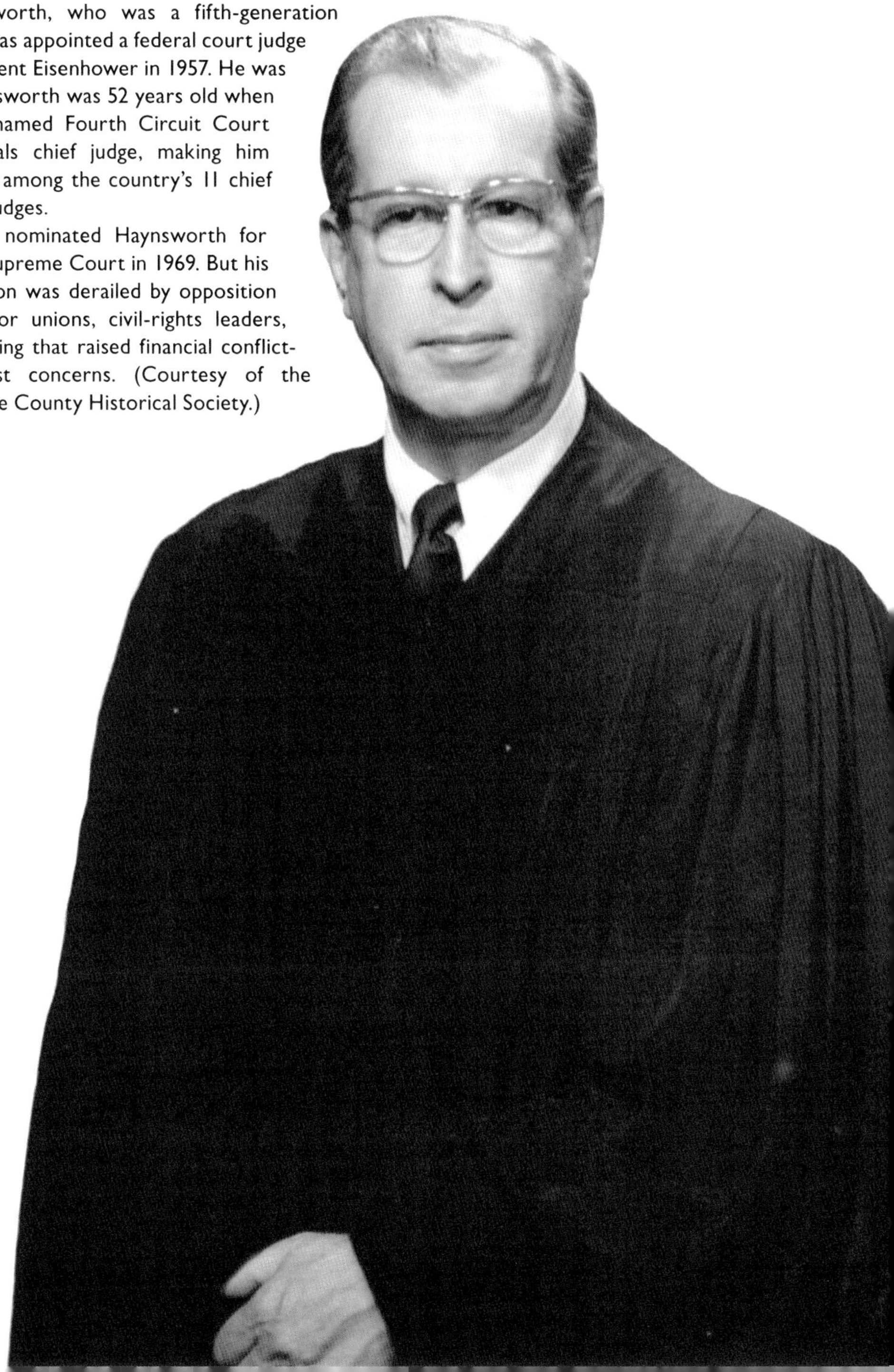

CHAPTER THREE

Politicians and Public Servants

Greenville has always been a city with influential politicians and public servants.

The influence was not limited to the South Carolina Statehouse in Columbia, however. It extended to Washington, DC, and even into foreign countries.

Greenville's political heyday came in the 1970s.

That is when a group of "Young Turks" took over in the state house of representatives, turning the way the state operated upside down. No longer would the power of government be concentrated in the hands of the general assembly. Instead, the Young Turks helped usher in Home Rule, removing the legislature from the running of local governments and school districts.

One of those Young Turks was Richard W. Riley. As governor, he led the transformation of the state's education system by championing the Education Improvement Act, heralded at the time as "the most comprehensive educational reform measure in the United Sates." Riley later served as US secretary of education. The South Carolina Higher Education Hall of Fame inducted him in 2008 and *Time* magazine named him as one of the Top 10 Cabinet Members in the 20th century.

Carroll Campbell Jr. helped the Republican Party take its stranglehold over South Carolina politics.

Locally, when downtown Greenville was dying because of the migration of stores to suburban malls, Mayor Max Heller saw it as a place where people would gather. He decided public service was the way to repay the town that allowed him to escape from Nazi-occupied Austria. Heller led the rebirth of downtown, something from which today's residents are still reaping the benefits.

But the influence of Greenville's politicians and public servants did not stop at the city limits or state borders. There was a national influence as well. During the Watergate scandal, a little-known representative from Greenville, James R. Mann, helped craft the articles of impeachment against former president Richard M. Nixon.

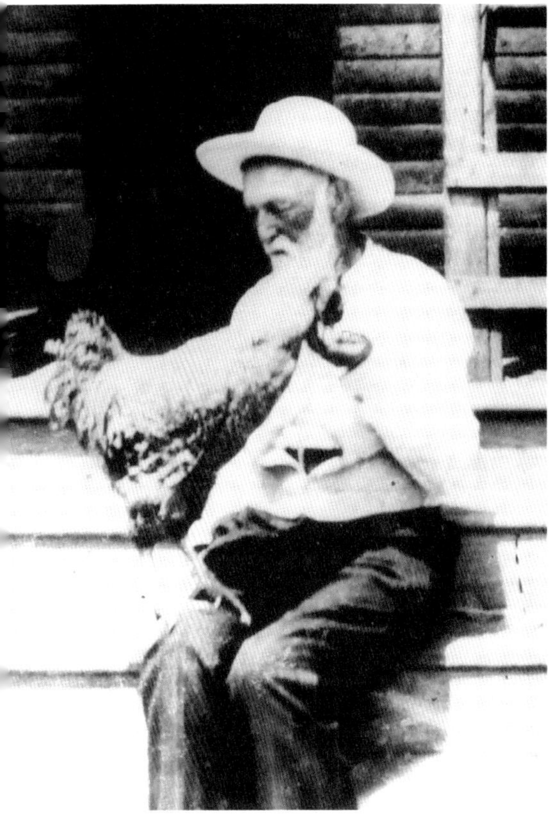

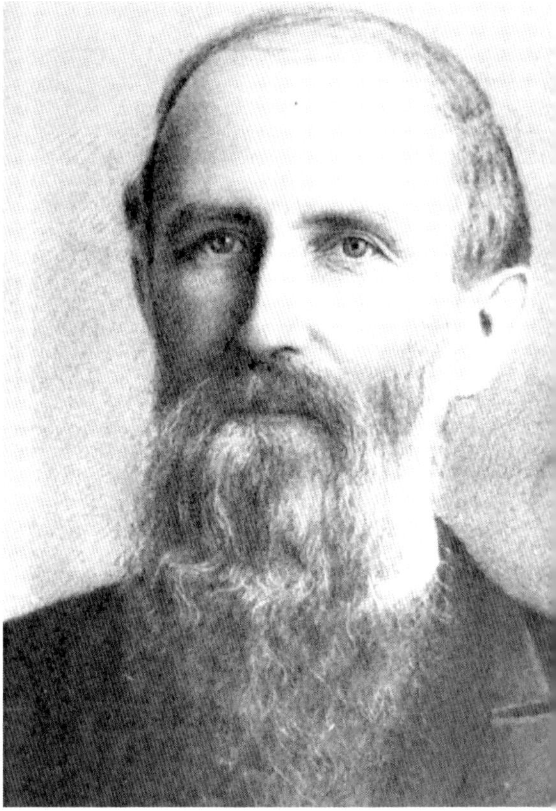

Perry Duncan Gilreath

Perry Duncan Gilreath seldom carried a gun during the 24 years he served as sheriff in the Dark Corner of Greenville County from 1876 to 1900. Instead, he relied on fairness, common sense, and a reputation for keeping his word. Gilreath served as captain of Company F in the Confederate army during the Civil War. Gilreath had farmed near Greenville after the end of the war before he ran for sheriff on the same Democratic ticket that propelled Wade Hampton to governor. The sheriff once talked out a suspect in a revenue agent's death out of his hideout. Because it was late, he fed the man supper and let him spend the night at his home, according to a biography by John H. Gilreath. He took the man to jail the next morning. (Both, courtesy of the Greenville County Library System.)

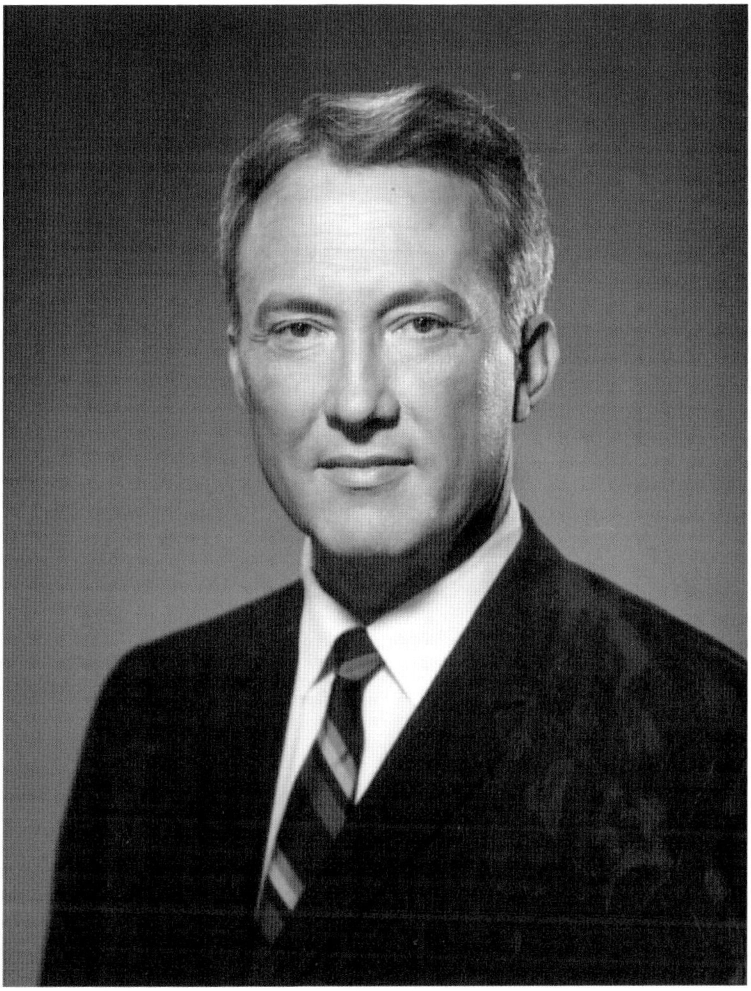

James R. Mann

James R. Mann, a conservative Democrat in a state that overwhelmingly supported Pres. Richard M. Nixon, never held a leadership position during his five terms in the US House of Representatives. But the attorney from Greenville helped craft the articles of impeachment against President Nixon.

During 1974's House Judiciary Committee hearings on the break-in at the Democratic National Headquarters and the cover-up that led to the president, Mann had one of the most memorable quotes: "We would strive to strengthen and preserve the presidency. But if there be no accountability, another president will feel free to do as he chooses. The next time, there may be no watchman in the night."

After the committee had voted to impeach, Mann reworked the articles into something that Republicans and Southern Democrats could support. Nixon resigned before the full House voted.

Mann earned a bachelor's degree from the Citadel and then enlisted in the Army during World War II. After his discharge from the Army with the rank of lieutenant colonel, he started practicing law with his father, a former Greenville mayor. Mann served two terms as Greenville and Pickens Counties' chief prosecutor and twice as president of the Greenville Chamber of Commerce.

A former college athlete, Mann participated in the Senior Olympics. In 2008, he became one of the first inductees into the South Carolina Senior Olympics Hall of Fame. Mann died in 2010. (Courtesy of the Greenville County Library System.)

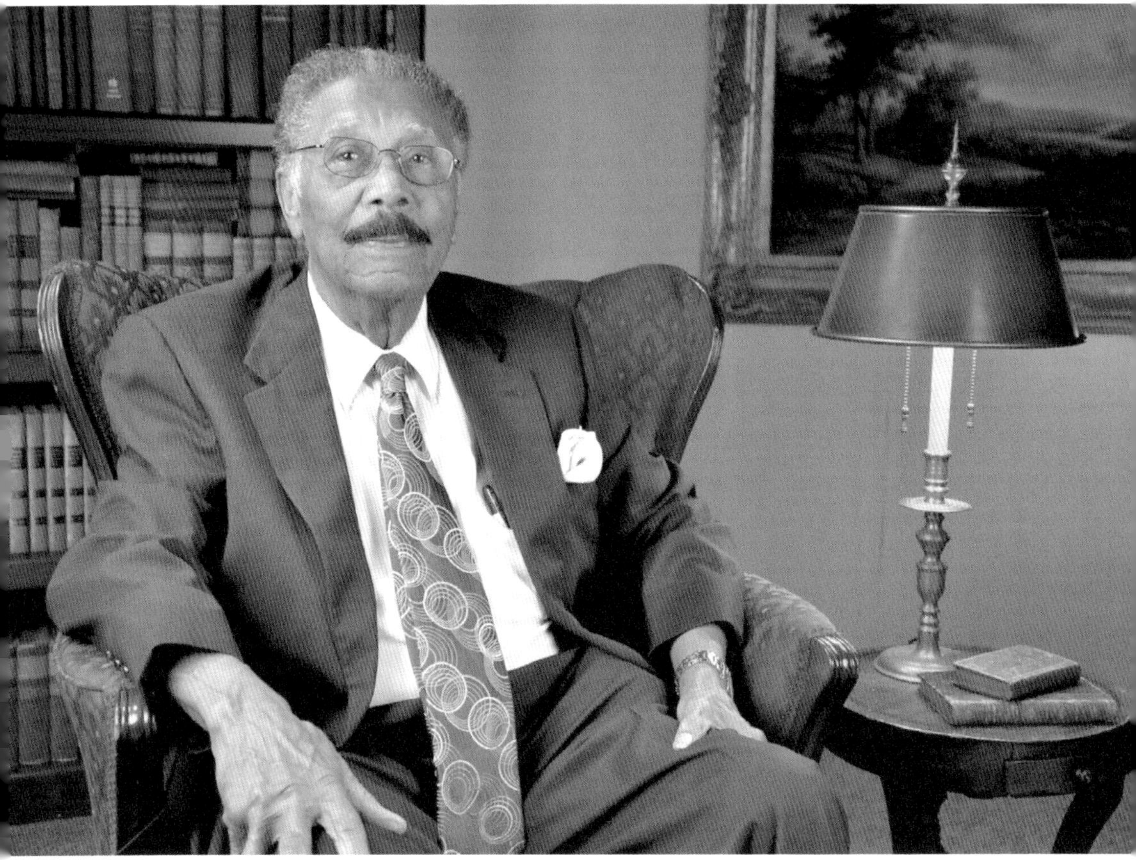

Ralph Anderson

When Ralph Anderson delivered mail to dilapidated homes on his mail route, he knew that the conditions did not match the dreams of home ownership for some of the people who lived there. But he did not have the personal resources or leverage to help, and federal law prevented him from holding elected office while a federal employee. Anderson, who worked for the postal service for 30 years, the last 10 as postmaster in Clemson and Greer, sought public office after his retirement. He started on the Greenville City Council, where he successfully pushed to use community development block grants to help lower-income residents buy homes. Anderson, who played football and basketball player at Sterling High and quarterbacked at Allen University, also served in the South Carolina House of Representatives from 1991 to 1997 and the Senate from 1997 to 2013. (Courtesy of Tim Brosnan.)

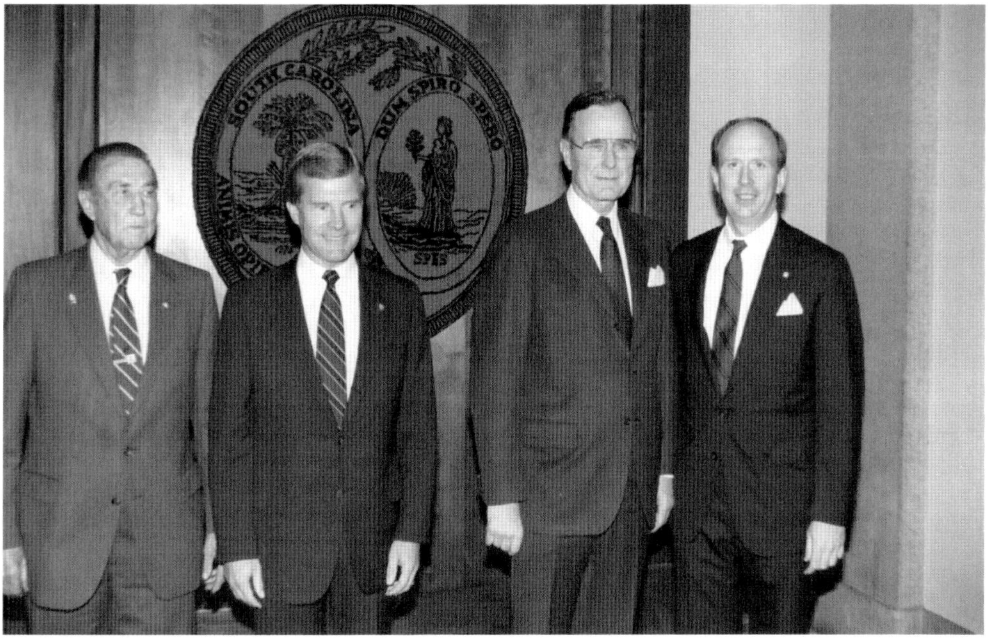

Carroll Ashmore Campbell Jr.

Carroll Ashmore Campbell Jr., a streetwise teenager who once dropped out of high school, became the yardstick by which South Carolina measures its governors, especially when it comes to economic development.

Rising up from a modest upbringing with an alcoholic mother and a blue-collar father, Campbell became a political force both on the state and national levels. Campbell was a master politician and the principal architect of the state's Republican takeover. He recruited BMW's first North American manufacturing plant to Spartanburg County, a move that sent ripples throughout the economy as automotive suppliers joined the international automaker in the Upstate.

Campbell was just as important at the national level. As a young congressman, Campbell bucked other Republican Party leadership when he backed Ronald Reagan in South Carolina's first-ever Republican presidential primary in 1980. Reagan won South Carolina, the first of a series of decisive victories in the South.

But Campbell's political rise did not come without its controversies. He led an anti-busing march in 1970 as South Carolina schools were being integrated.

Later, allegations surfaced that Campbell's 1978 US House of Representatives campaign used telephone "polls" to point out that his opponent, Greenville mayor Max Heller, was Jewish. A late challenger, who said Heller was unfit for the seat because he did not worship Jesus Christ, entered the race. Allegations arose later that the Campbell campaign had a hand in the late candidate entering the race. Campbell denied it, but those claims were said to have cost Campbell a shot at the vice-presidential nomination in 1996.

In 2001, he wrote a letter to South Carolina residents to inform them that he was in the early stages of Alzheimer's disease. "One of my most cherished blessings was the honor of serving you in the State Legislature, Congress, and the Governor's Office. I want to thank you, the people of South Carolina, for all that you have meant to my family and me," the letter said. He died in 2005 from a heart attack.

Before he entered politics, Campbell was a successful businessman, operating parking lots and fast-food restaurants. Campbell, who graduated from McCallie School, a private school in Tennessee, later earned a master's degree in political science while he served as a congressman. Shown above from left to right are Strom Thurmond, Campbell, Pres. George H.W. Bush, and David Wilkins. (Courtesy of David Wilkins.)

Max Heller

Max Heller's journey to Greenville is a classic American immigrant success story.

Using a German-American dictionary, Heller wrote a letter in 1938 to a Greenville woman he met while they were on a European tour asking for help escaping Nazi-occupied Austria. She found him a sponsor, and he came to Greenville with $1.80 in his pocket.

He started working as a janitor at Piedmont Shirt Co. and then moved up to general manager. He started his company, the Maxon Shirt Co., in 1948. The company, which started with 16 employees, had expanded to 700 by 1962.

But Heller made his biggest impact after he sold his company and devoted his life to public service and repaying the community that had been so good to him.

Heller, elected mayor in 1971 and referred to as the "Father of Greenville," was the visionary behind downtown Greenville's rebirth. Main Street had become a collection of vacant buildings and empty streets, as businesses fled to suburban shopping malls. At a time when many cities were abandoning their downtowns, Heller envisioned one where people could gather. His vision for Main Street turned a four-lane road into a two-lane tree-lined street with flower planters, reminiscent of Europe. He, along with other community leaders, convinced the Hyatt Regency to open a hotel downtown.

After his second term as mayor ended, Heller decided to run for Congress. He lost to future South Carolina governor Carroll Campbell in a race that turned ugly. The defeat did not end his public service, and he chaired the South Carolina State Development Board.

But while his love for Greenville was vast, his love for his wife, Trude, was even greater. The couple first met at an Austrian resort when Max was 18 and Trude was 14. He said they would get married one day. Trude Heller was able to escape the Holocaust, too, and the two reunited. They married, and their fairytale love story lasted nearly 69 years, until Max Heller's death in 2011. Heller is pictured on the right. (Courtesy of the Upcountry History Museum–Furman University.)

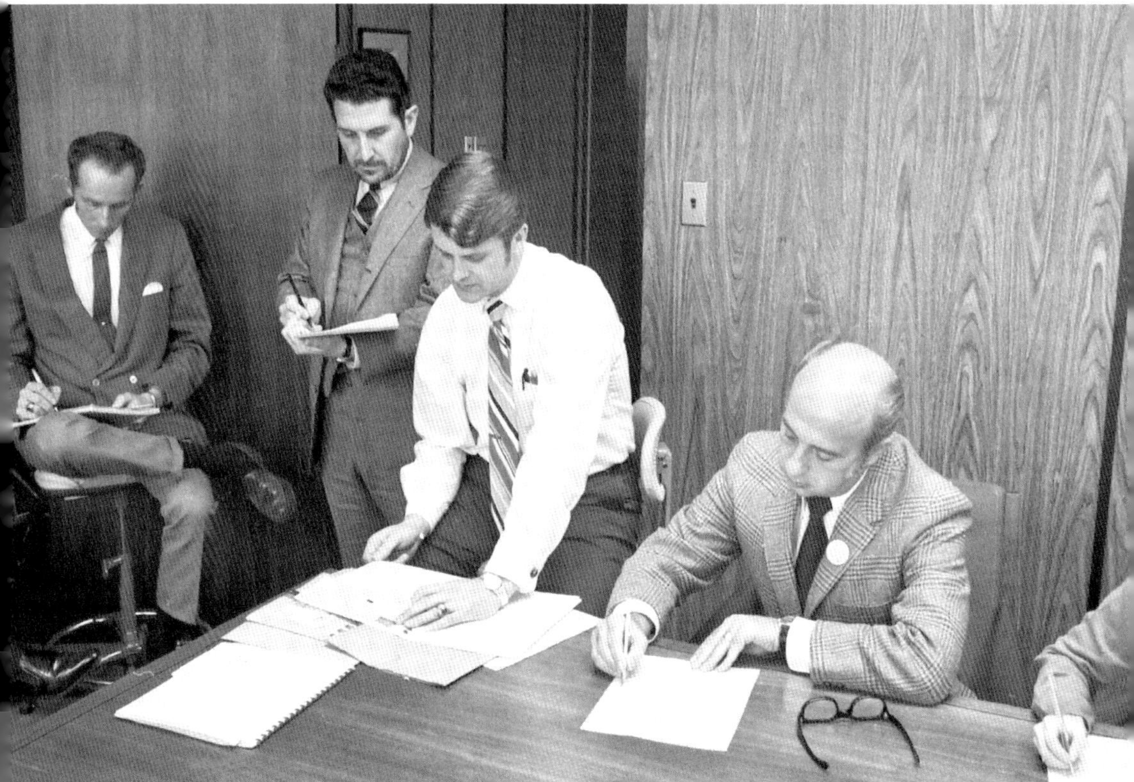

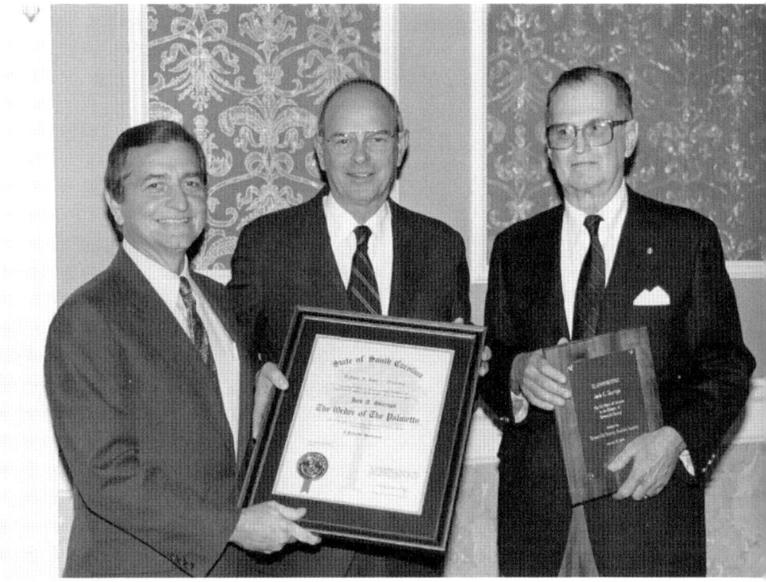

Nick Theodore

Nick Theodore, pictured on the left, is proud to have been a member of the Young Turks, 10 legislative upstarts in the 1960s and 1970s who dared to take on the South Carolina General Assembly's entrenched leaders. His father, citing his Greek heritage, would rather they had a different nickname. The Young Turks stripped power from the legislature and gave it to local governments through Home Rule. (Courtesy of the Greenville Health System.)

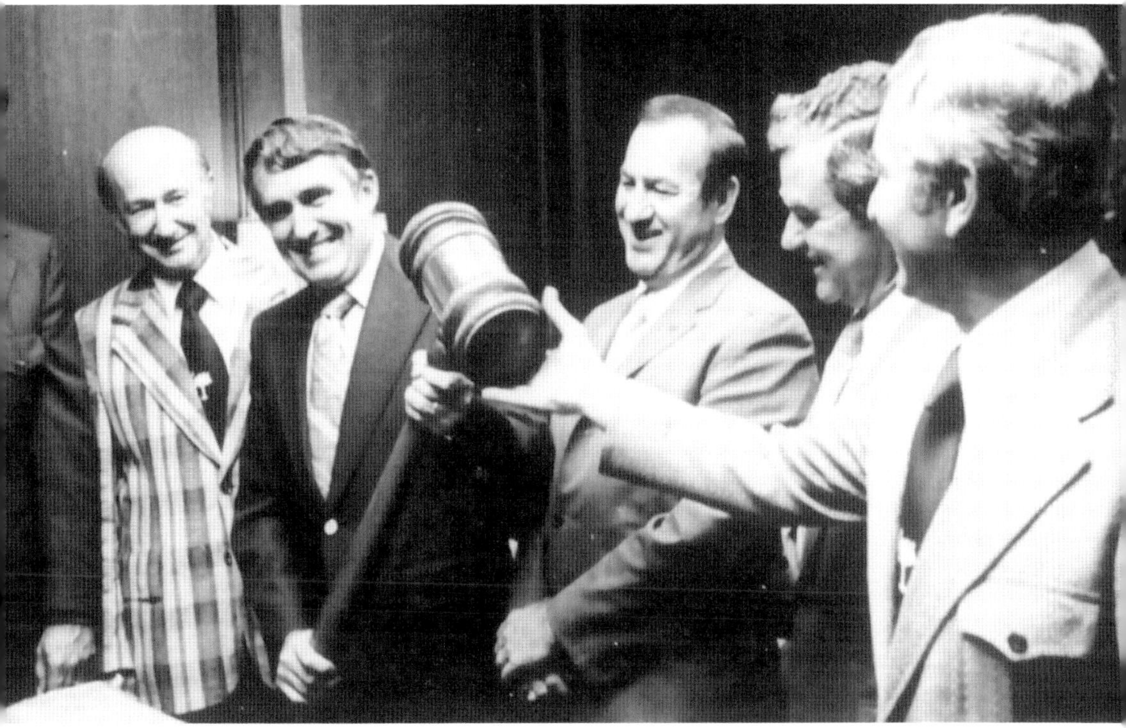

Rex Carter

Even bigger than Rex Carter's dreams was his determination to make them happen. After World War II, Carter found classroom space, but no housing, at Erskine College. He slept in the gym for six weeks. Carter ran for the legislature, campaigning in a 1939 Ford before the advent of four-lane highways and air conditioning. He won 14 terms, rising to Speaker of the House. Pictured from left to right are Victor Pyle Jr., Beattie Huff, Rex Carter (with gavel), Herb Granger, Jack Garrett, and Nick Theodore. (Courtesy of Nick Theodore.)

Richard W. Riley

Former South Carolina governor and US secretary of education Richard W. "Dick" Riley has never let a challenge get in the way of an accomplishment.

Riley was the senior-class president, star tailback, and football team captain at Greenville High School. After graduating from Furman University with honors, Riley was commissioned as an officer in the US Navy. He was overseas when he contracted rheumatoid spondylitis, a rare degenerative spinal disease that left him with a fused spine. Riley refused to allow the disease to stop him. Former South Carolina Supreme Court chief justice Alex Sanders said that while the disease left Riley with weakened backbone, it gave him a strengthened will.

As governor, Riley mobilized support for the Education Improvement Act and its penny sales tax in 1984, considered by many to be the single most important pieces of education legislation ever passed in South Carolina. The *Christian Science Monitor* called Riley "one of the great statesmen of education in this century."

His contributions to education were not limited to South Carolina, however. Riley served two terms as US secretary of education under Pres. Bill Clinton. During that time, Riley pushed for improved academic standards, improved instruction for poor and disadvantaged students, and expansion of college grant and loan programs.

David Broder, the late political columnist for the *Washington Post*, called Riley "one of the most decent and honorable people in public life."

Riley's reputation led Clinton ask if he would accept a nomination in 1993 for a seat on the US Supreme Court, although Riley had never been a judge.

Riley's father, Ted Riley, who was also a Greenville attorney, urged him to accept, saying it was the epitome of any lawyer's career. Others, from his law partner Claude Scarborough to Sen. Strom Thurmond, told him to accept the nomination. His wife, Ann "Tunky" Riley, told him to go where he would make the biggest difference. He turned down the nomination to remain the US secretary of education. A year later, Clinton asked again, and Riley declined.

His involvement in education did not end with that second term, however. He still works on education issues through Furman's Riley Institute. Riley (center) is pictured in 2014 with Clinton (left) and Betty Farr (right). (Courtesy of Furman University.)

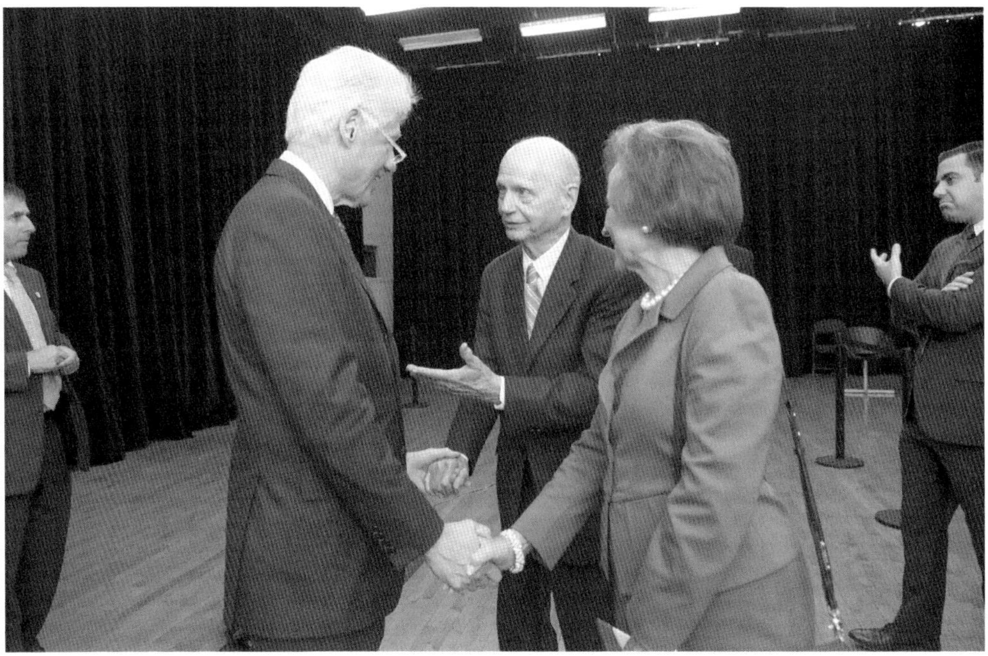

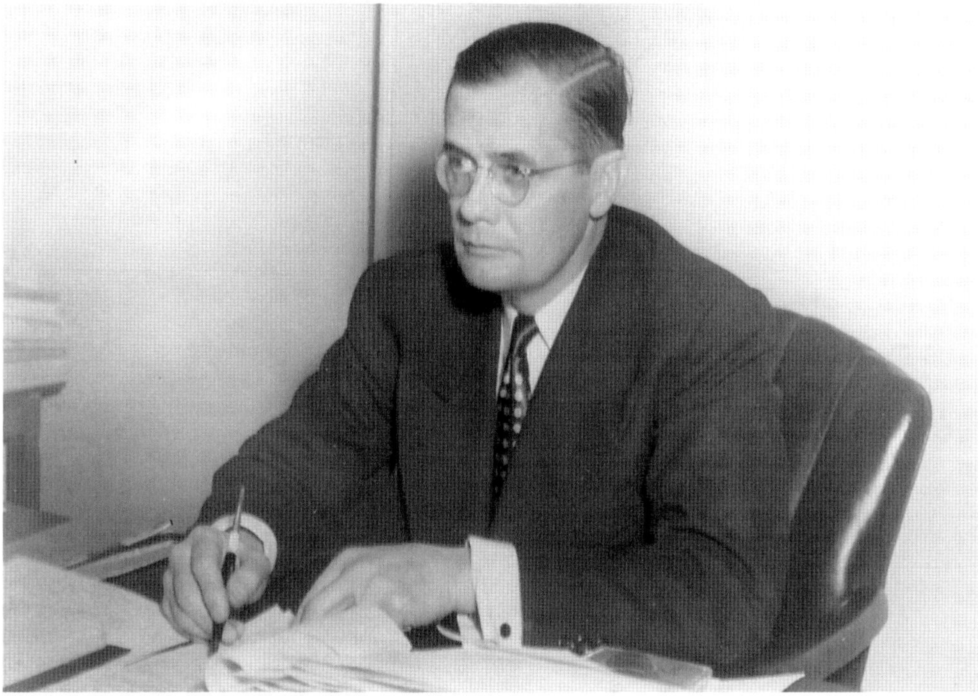

Kenneth J. Cass

Kenneth Cass's trademark look included a worn purple Furman Paladin ball cap, fitting for a man who captained the football and baseball teams there during his senior year in 1930 and is a member of the university's athletic hall of fame. But the athletic field is not the only place Cass made his mark on Greenville. Cass, a Greenville High School graduate who operated a tire company at the corner of East Court and Falls Streets, served as mayor during a pivotal time for the city. During Cass's 14 years as mayor from 1947 to 1961, the city annexed Augusta Road, Overbrook, Northgate, and parts of Laurens Road into its boundaries. The Church Street Bridge and Greenville Memorial Auditorium were built despite initial opposition. The city changed its government to a city manager form. Bob Jones University chose to move to Greenville, while Furman University decided to leave downtown for a new site six miles away. (Both, courtesy of the Greenville County Historical Society.)

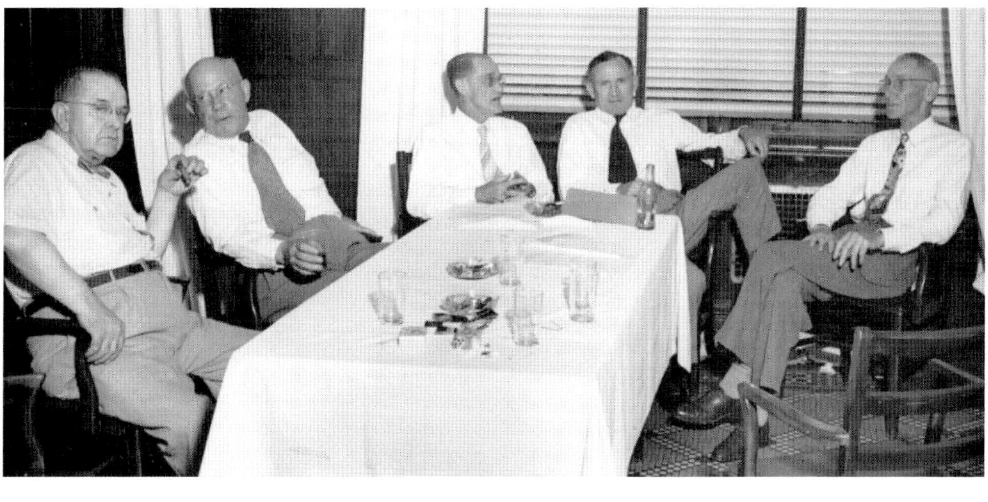

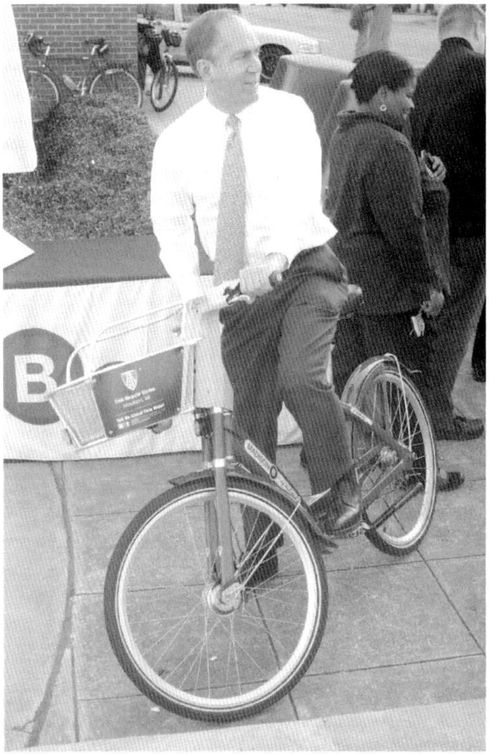

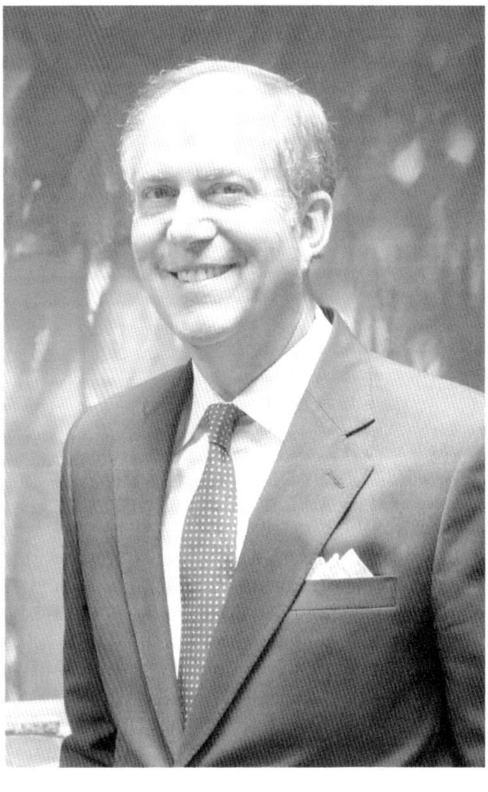

Knox White

Knox White's roots in Greenville run deep. White is a member of an old and prestigious family. He practices immigration law in a firm that traces its beginning back to 1887 with White's maternal great-grandfather. He is the longest-serving mayor in Greenville's history. White had returned to Greenville after serving on the congressional staff of the late Carroll Campbell. Two of Campbell's political operatives pulled him into their car one morning in 1983 and would not let him go until he had agreed to run for a vacant seat on the Greenville City Council. Running on a "neighborhoods first" platform in 1995, he upset incumbent mayor Bill Workman. As mayor, White has spearheaded the transformation of downtown into one of the best in the United States. (Above, courtesy of the *Greenville Journal*; below, photograph by Cindy Landrum.)

CHAPTER FOUR

Service and Sacrifice

There are different forms of service and sacrifice.

Sometimes service and sacrifice comes on the battlefield, both in the air and on the ground, during wars and threats of war.

Greenville has had its fair share of those, including Maj. Rudolf Anderson Jr., the only casualty of the Cuban Missile Crisis. His unarmed U-2 reconnaissance plane was shot out of the sky over Cuba by a Soviet missile. His death probably saved millions of lives, as it prompted the United States and the Soviet Union to pull back from the brink of World War III.

Paul Adams, a black man who was not allowed to go to the air base when he was growing up because of segregation, became a Tuskegee Airman, the group that broke racial barriers in World War II as the US military's first black aviators.

But for some, service and sacrifice comes at home.

Hattie Logan Duckett opened a home and social service center for black women. It is now the Phillis Wheatley Center and serves women and men of all ages.

For Dorris "Dee Dee" Wright and the rest of the Greenville 8, it was summoning up the courage to walk into the city's whites-only library and peacefully refusing to leave. It was one of the many protests in Greenville during the fight for civil rights.

For Edward D. "Ned" Sloan, service and sacrifice comes each time he files a lawsuit against a governmental body, determined to make sure they follow the law. Sometimes, the cost comes out of his pocket.

Heroes are people who achieve the extraordinary and those who lend a hand when it is needed. While the way they serve and sacrifice varies, the result is still the same. Greenville and its people are better for their efforts.

In Greenville, volunteering is not just a way to spend free time—it is a way of life.

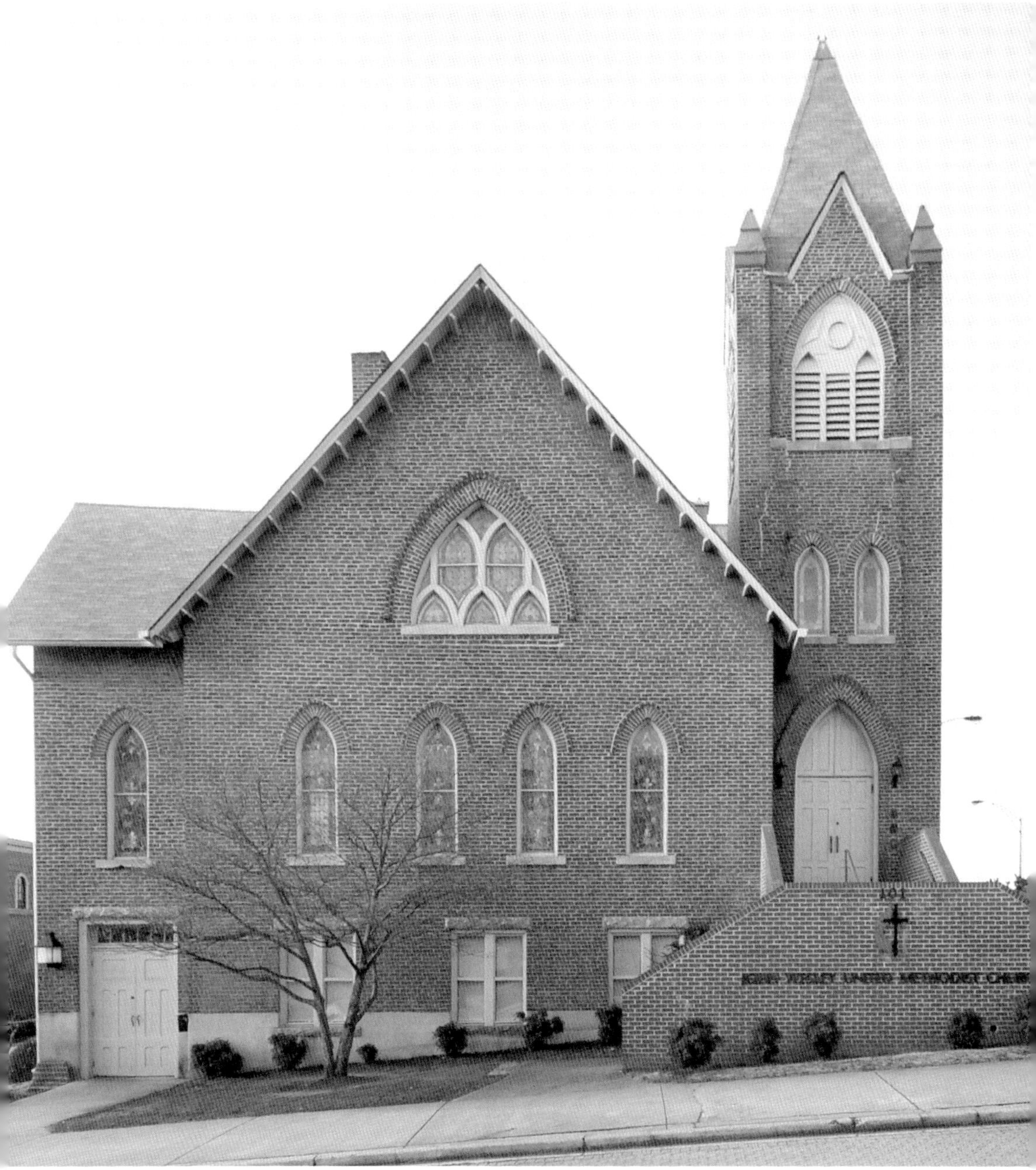

James R. Rosemond

Sharon Church raised $500 of the $800 needed to buy the freedom of "slave preacher" Jim from his owner, Vardry McBee, before the outbreak of the War between the States. After the Civil War ended, the man who would take the name of James R. Rosemond earned his freedom through emancipation. Rosemond organized several black churches in Greenville, Anderson, and Pickens Counties. Before his death in 1902, Rosemond had established 50 churches in the Upstate. John Wesley United Methodist Church was one of the first he organized and one of the first separate black congregations in the state, according to the National Register of Historic Places. (Photograph by Cindy Landrum.)

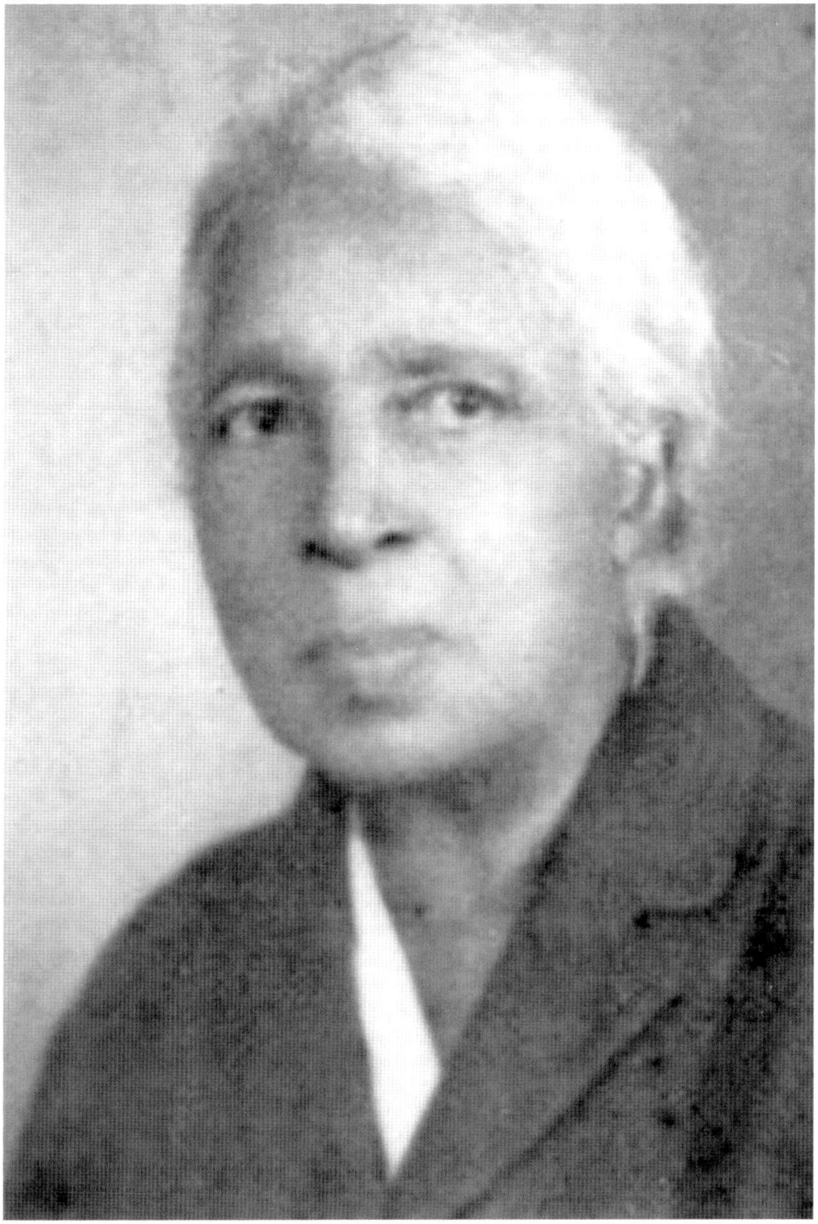

Hattie Logan Duckett

Hattie Logan Duckett had a propensity for helping people. Greenville historian Judith Bainbridge wrote that Duckett's Greenville home turned into a place of refuge for stranded black travelers, abused women, and people in need. After a trip to Cleveland, Ohio, to see a friend who had opened a home and social service center for young black women, Duckett returned to Greenville determined to open something similar in her hometown. She raised $3,500 and bought a small house. With the help of Thomas Parker, a white textile and business leader, Duckett opened the Phillis Wheatley Center, which offered meeting space, a gym, a chorus, and sewing classes. The city's first public library for blacks opened there. Duckett died in 1956, but the Phillis Wheatley Center is still operating. (Courtesy of Greenville Cultural Exchange Center.)

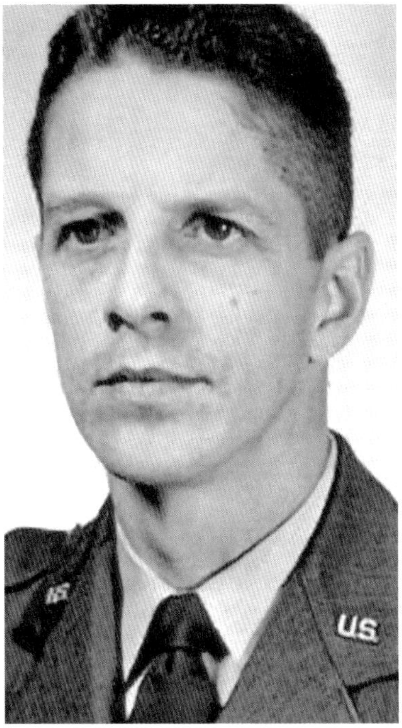

Maj. Rudolf Anderson Jr.

Maj. Rudolf Anderson Jr. was not originally scheduled to fly a spy plane over Cuba on October 27, 1962. But after another pilot reported being shot at two days earlier, Anderson lobbied to be the pilot on the next flight. Anderson became the Cuban Missile Crisis's only casualty after a surface-to-air missile exploded near his unarmed spy plane.

The incident was crucial to ending the Cuban Missile Crisis, a tense 13 days that put the United States and Soviet Union at odds and the world on the brink of war.

Anderson was an Eagle Scout and attended Greenville High School, where he managed the football team. He loved to make model airplanes. He attended Clemson University and graduated in 1948 with a textile degree. At Clemson, Anderson served in the Air Force ROTC.

He served in Korea and earned two Distinguished Flying Cross citations. Anderson received a Purple Heart, the first-ever Air Force Cross and the Distinguished Service Medal. There is a memorial to Anderson in Cleveland Park, and his father helped pick out the site. (Right, courtesy of US Air Force; below, photograph by Cindy Landrum.)

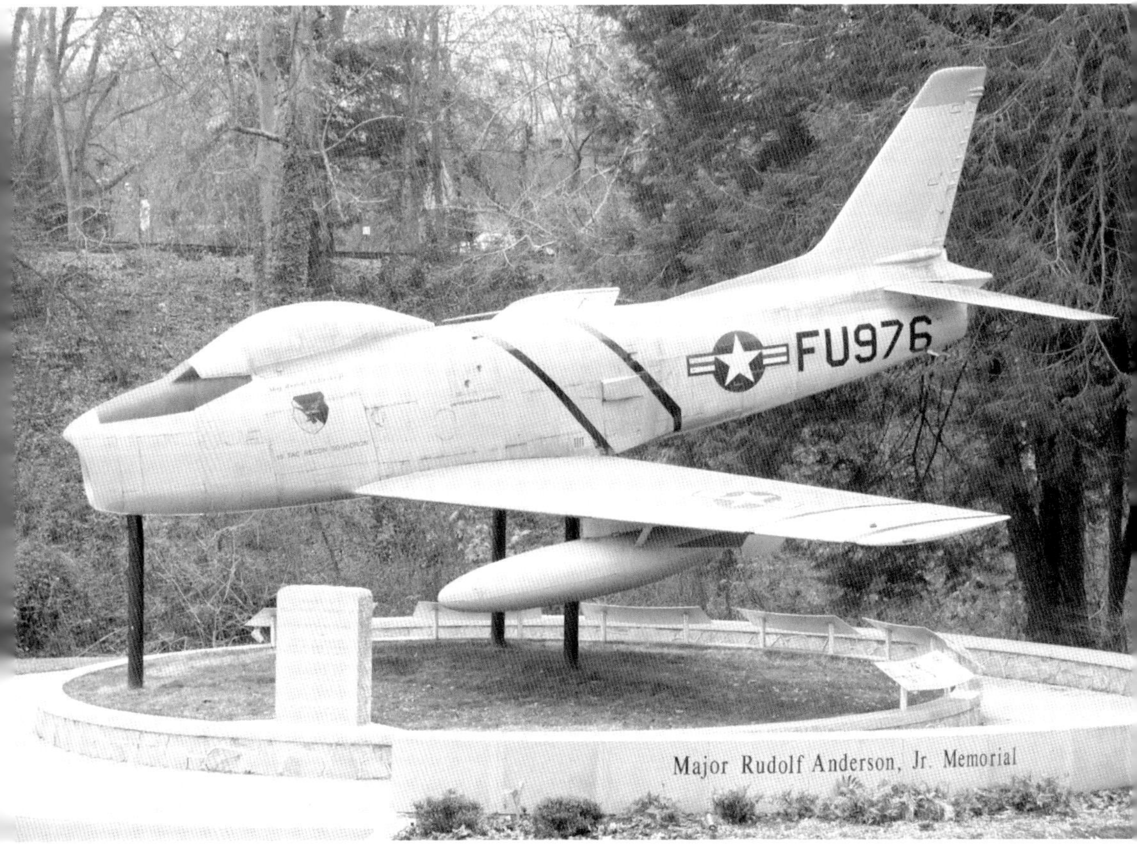

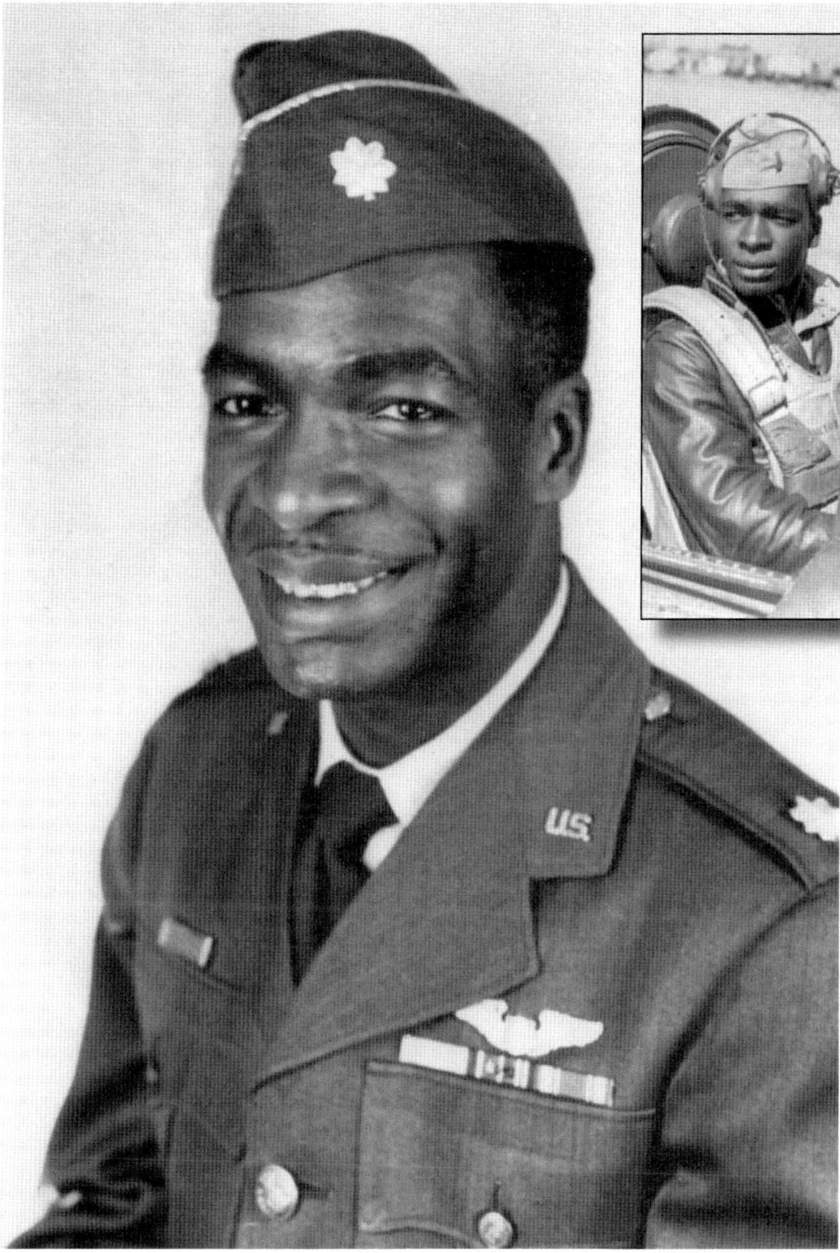

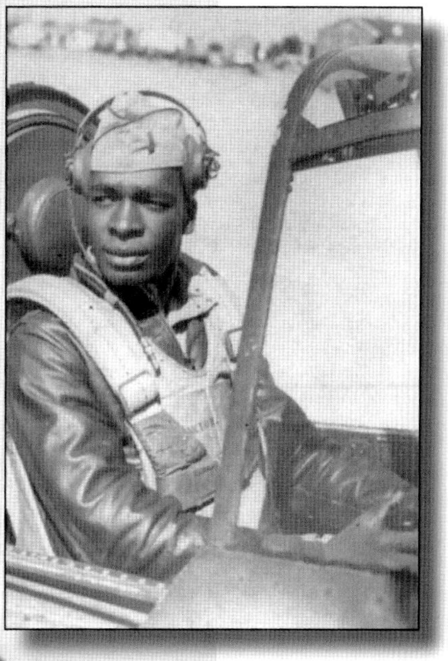

Paul Adams
Paul Adams did not let obstacles get in the way of achieving his boyhood dream of becoming a pilot. Adams was a member of World War II's famed Tuskegee Airmen, a group that broke racial barriers as the first black pilots in the US military. Growing up, Adams, a Sterling High School graduate, was not allowed on Greenville Army Air Base. However, during the war, the group flew 1,500 missions in North Africa and Europe with the 332nd Fighter Group. The group, known as the Red Tail group for their planes' paint scheme, was later the subject of a Hollywood movie starring Terrence Howard and Cuba Gooding Jr. Adams later became one of the first black public school teachers in Lincoln, Nebraska, and he taught industrial arts. (Both, courtesy of the Greenville Cultural Exchange Center.)

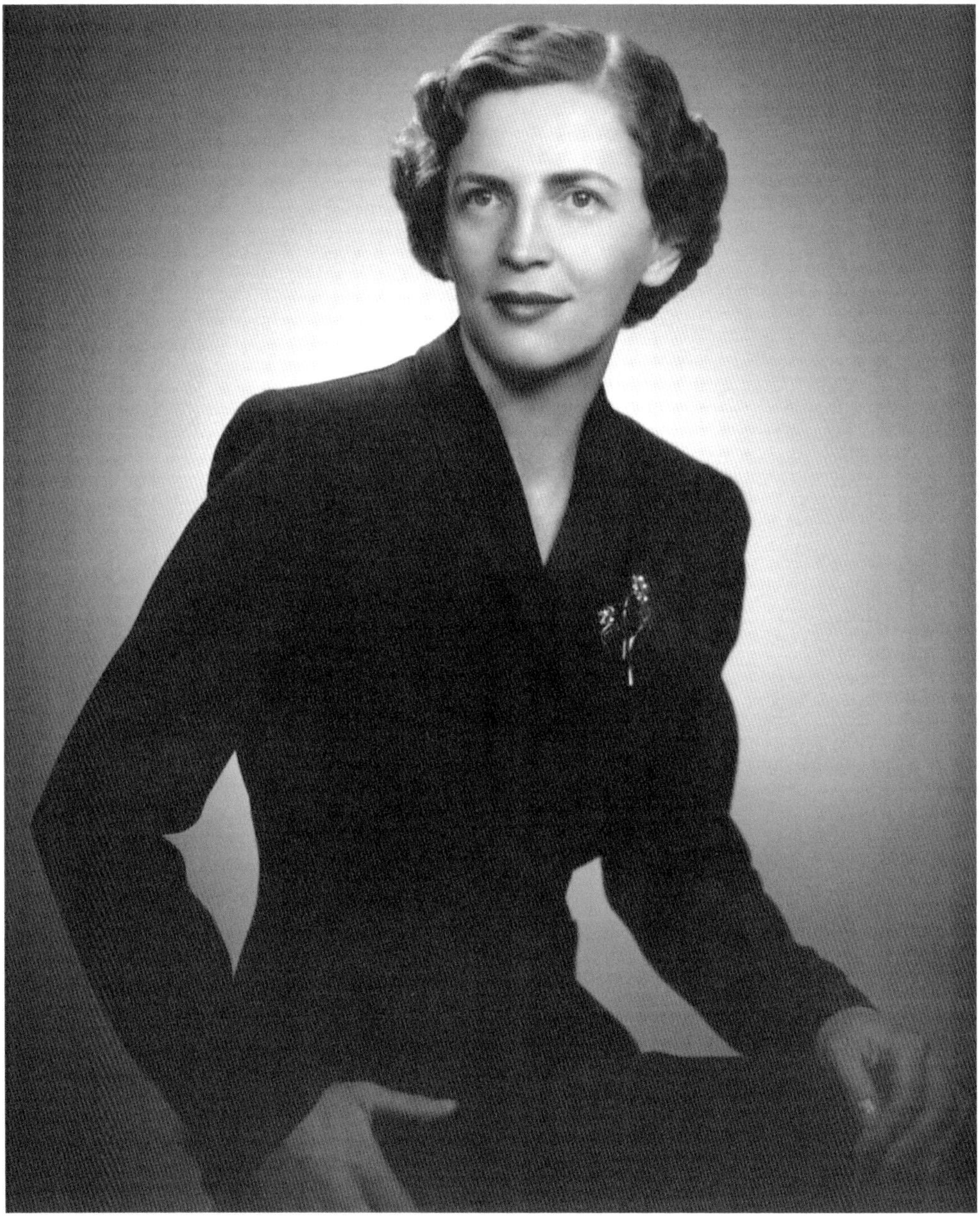

Ruth Alexander Nicholson

Civic participation was something ingrained in Ruth Alexanderson Nicholson. Her father was a country doctor and farmer, and he was the vice-presidential candidate on a ticket with Al Smith, running against Woodrow Wilson in 1918. Her mother was a schoolteacher and postmistress. Nicholson moved to Greenville in 1946, six years after she earned a nursing degree from Duke University and five years after marrying Dr. David Wilson. When their fourth child was a year old, her husband died unexpectedly. She returned to nursing, spending 30 years with the Greenville Hospital System, including as head of medical education. Nicholson served as president of the Greenville Community Foundation, doing much of the foundation's work out of her basement before the foundation could afford staff members. (Courtesy of the Greenville County Library System.)

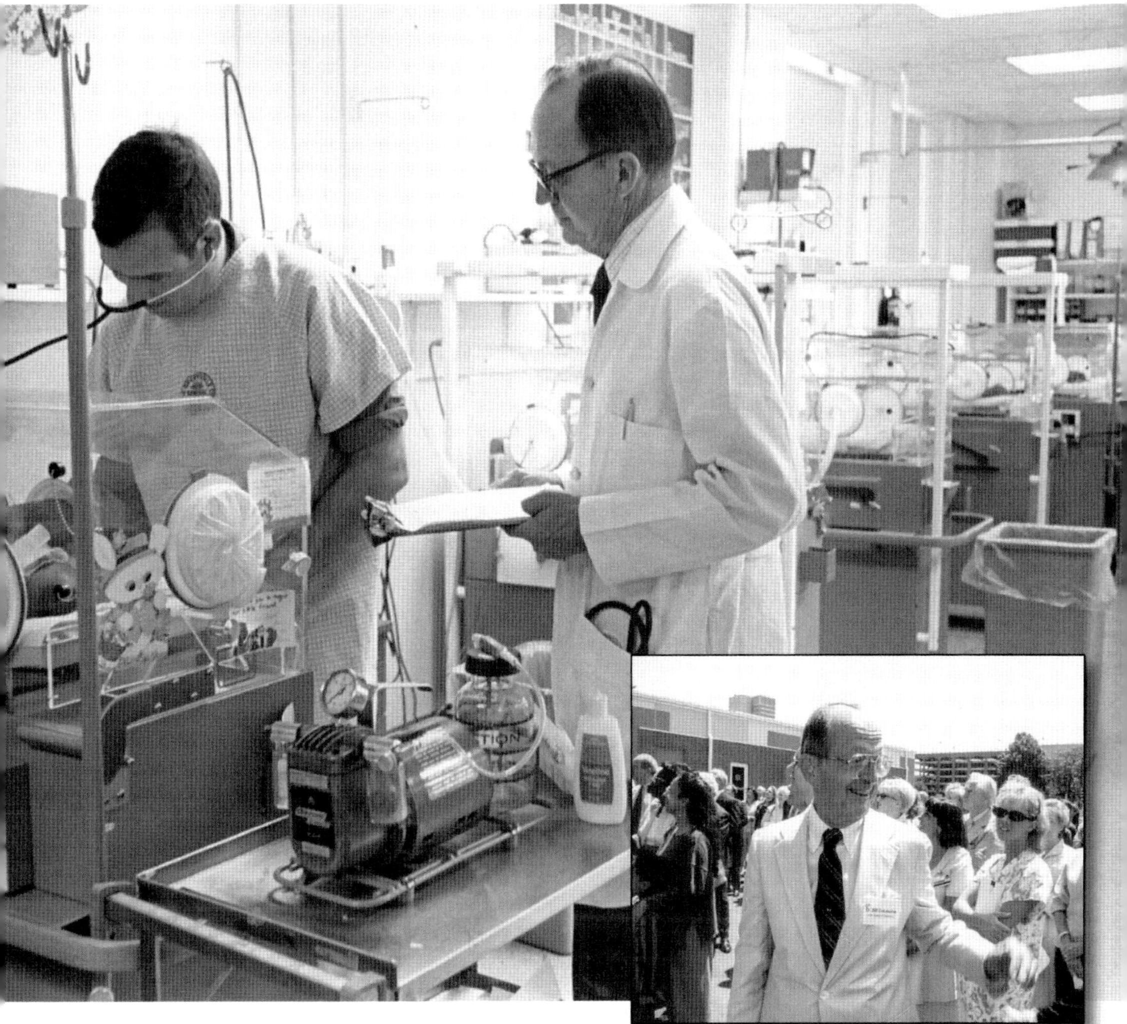

Dr. William R. DeLoache

Dr. William R. DeLoache spent a lifetime meeting the medical needs of Greenville's children. After serving in the US Army Medical Corps, he formed the Christie Pediatric Group in 1953 with some fellow Vanderbilt University students. It was Greenville's first group medical practice. Two decades later, after unsuccessfully trying to recruit a neonatal doctor to establish a neonatal unit in Greenville, he decided to do it himself. He became an intern again at age 52. After completing a residency in Pittsburgh, Pennsylvania, DeLoache returned to Greenville and established its neonatal intensive-care unit. He retired in 1987 but did not stop working. He cochaired a campaign that raised the money to open a comprehensive facility geared toward children with special needs. (Both, courtesy of Greenville Health System.)

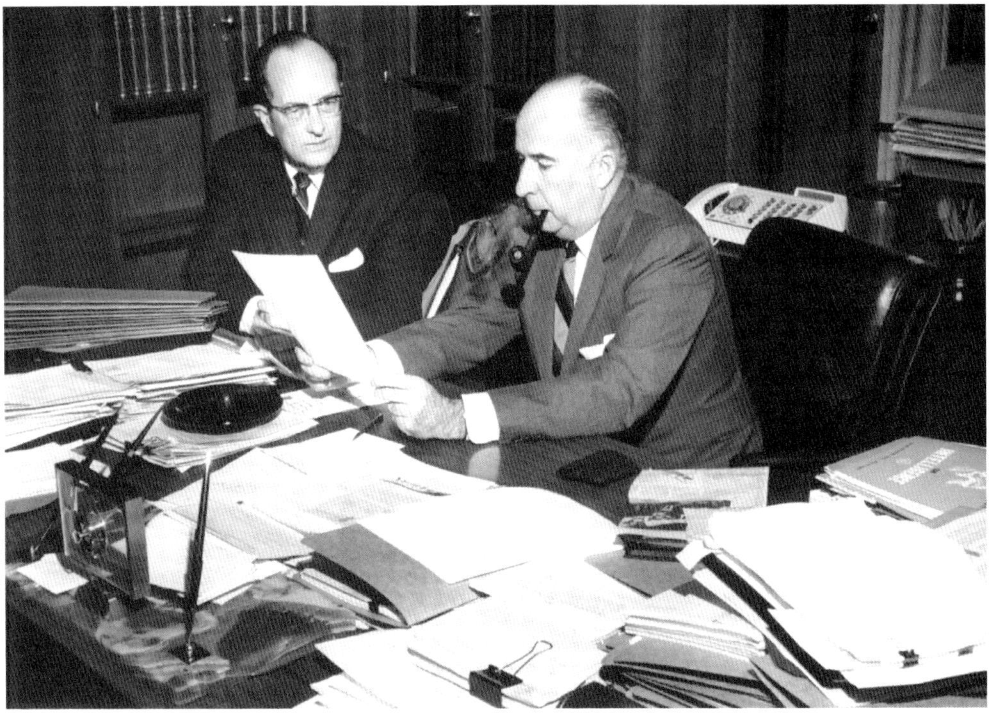

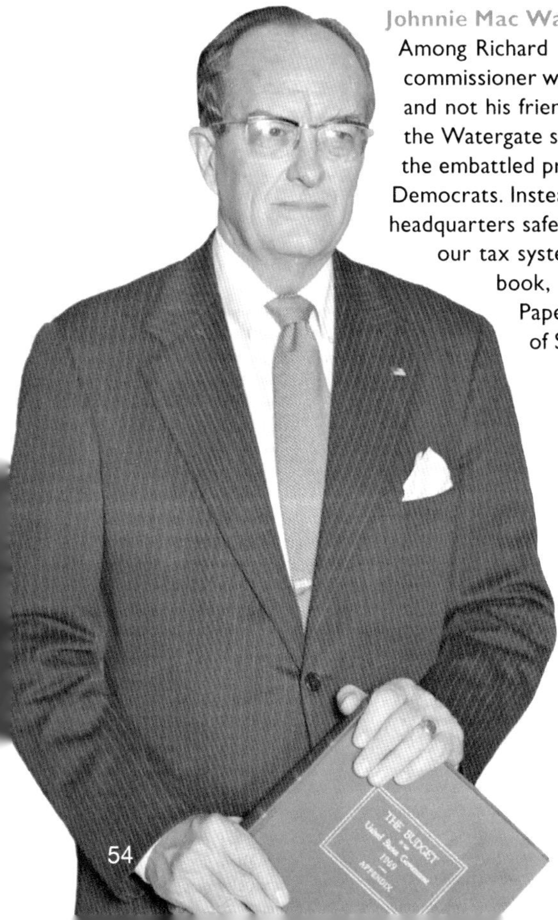

Johnnie Mac Walters

Among Richard Nixon's requirements for an Internal Revenue Service commissioner was somebody willing to go after the president's enemies and not his friends. He did not get that with Johnnie Mac Walters. As the Watergate scandal raged in Washington, Walters refused to act on the embattled president's "enemy list," comprised mostly of prominent Democrats. Instead, he sealed the list in an envelope and put it in his IRS headquarters safe. "By refusing to implement the request, we preserved our tax system and also kept me out of jail," Walters wrote in his book, *Our Journey*. (Both, courtesy of Johnnie M. Walters Papers, South Carolina Political Collections, the University of South Carolina.)

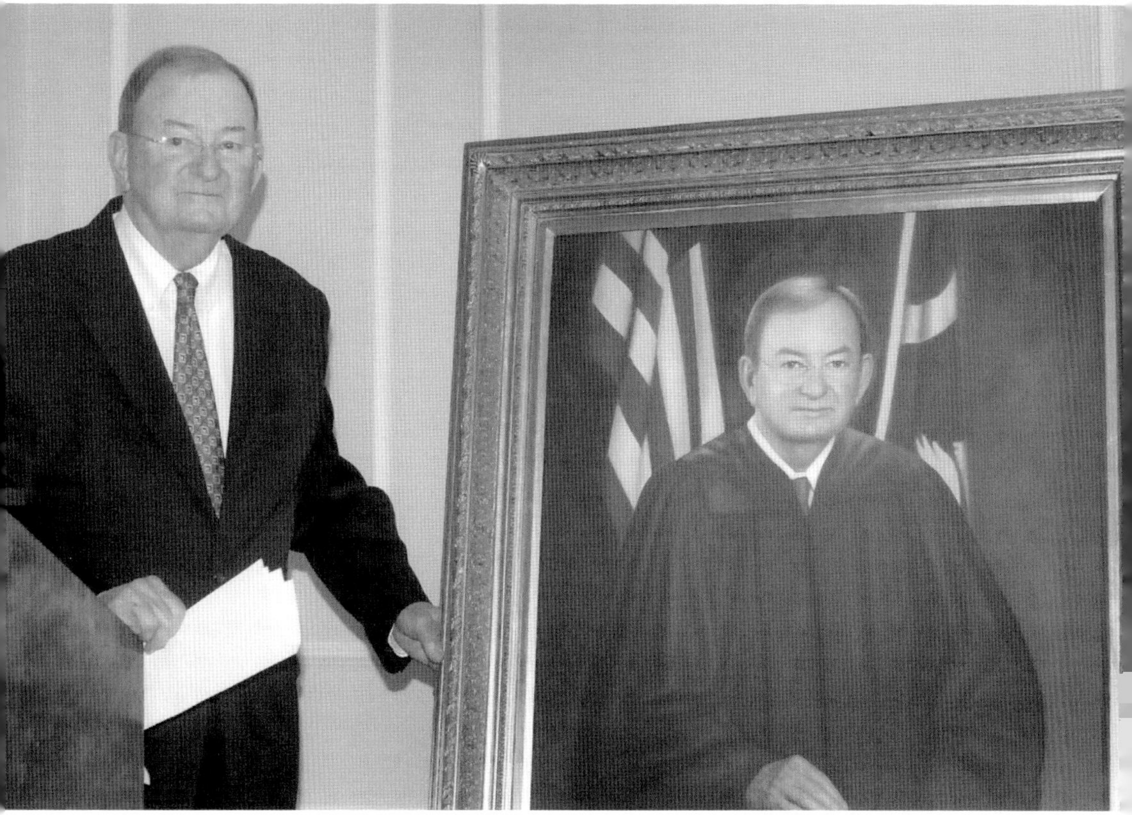

Judge C. Victor Pyle Jr.

Circuit Court Judge C. Victor Pyle Jr. is best known for a 1983 Anderson County rape case in which he gave the three defendants the option of surgical castration instead of prison. The sentence garnered national and international attention, and the US Supreme Court overturned the sentence, saying it was cruel and unusual punishment. Pyle called the case the worst rape case he had ever heard. He received letters from all over the world, 9 out of 10 agreeing with his sentence. Pyle practiced law with his father from 1959 to 1976, fulfilling a childhood dream of becoming an attorney. He served as a Greenville municipal judge from 1965 until his election to the state house of representatives. Pyle became a circuit court judge in 1979. (Courtesy of the *Greenville Journal.*)

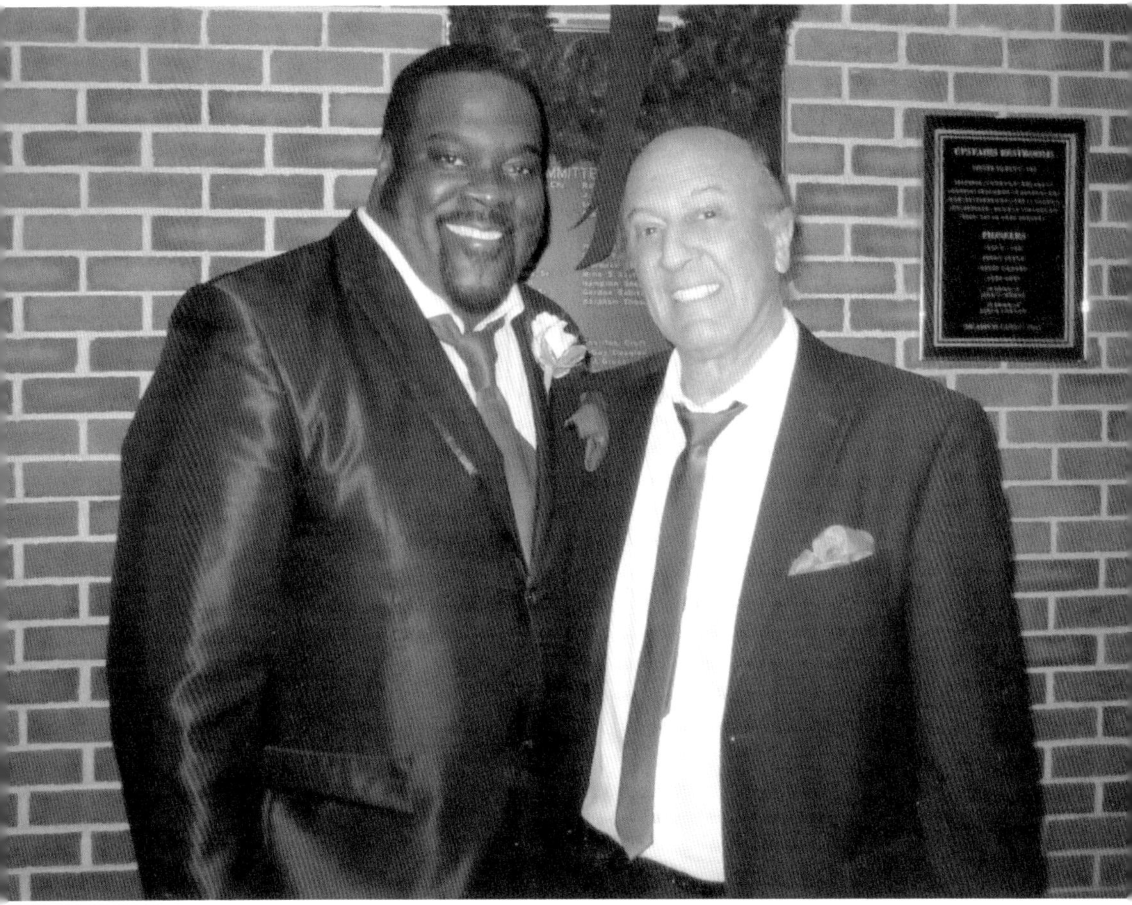

Phillip Boykin and Emile Pandolfi

Phillip Boykin (left) and Emile Pandolfi have both made their marks on the music world. Boykin is a Tony Award–nominated actor who got his start on the stages at the Phillis Wheatley Repertory Theatre. He attended the Greenville County Schools' Fine Arts Center and the South Carolina Governor's School for the Arts and Humanities summer program. He received the nomination for his portrayal of Porgy in *Porgy and Bess*. Pandolfi tought himself to play music by ear and is a pianist noted for his renditions of show tunes. A Greenville High School graduate, he performed at the 1984 Summer Olympics. (Courtesy of Springfield Baptist Church.)

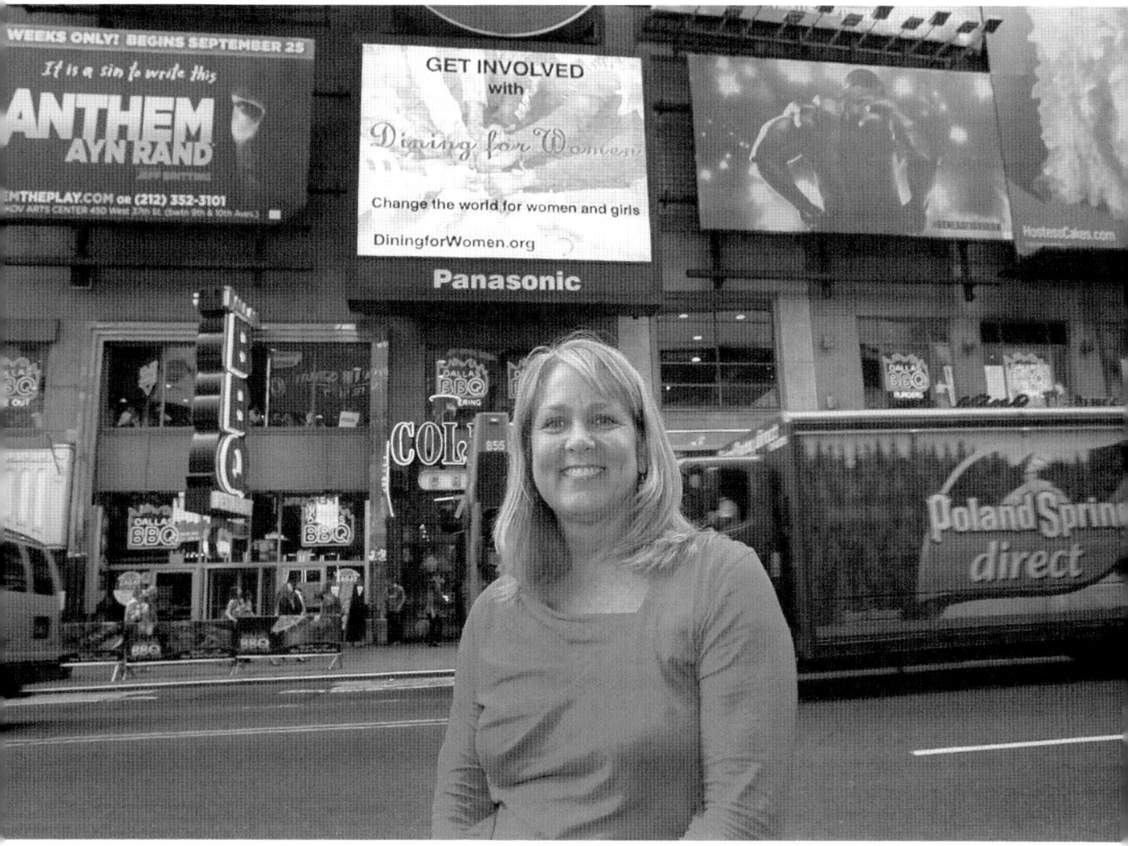

Marsha Wallace

When Marsha Wallace changed the way she celebrated her birthday in 2003, she began to change the lives of women in developing countries. Instead of the usual dinner out with friends, Wallace asked the women to bring a dish to share and to bring the $30 they likely would have spent and instead make a donation to Women to Women International. The group pooled $700, and the women decided to do it every month. One of the women offered to research organizations providing help to women in developing nations. Wallace decided to form a nonprofit, Dining for Women, so the women would not have to write individual checks. Dining for Women is now an international nonprofit that raised $3.25 million between 2003 and 2014. The National Underground Railroad Freedom Center named Wallace an Everyday Freedom Hero in 2014. (Courtesy of Dining for Women.)

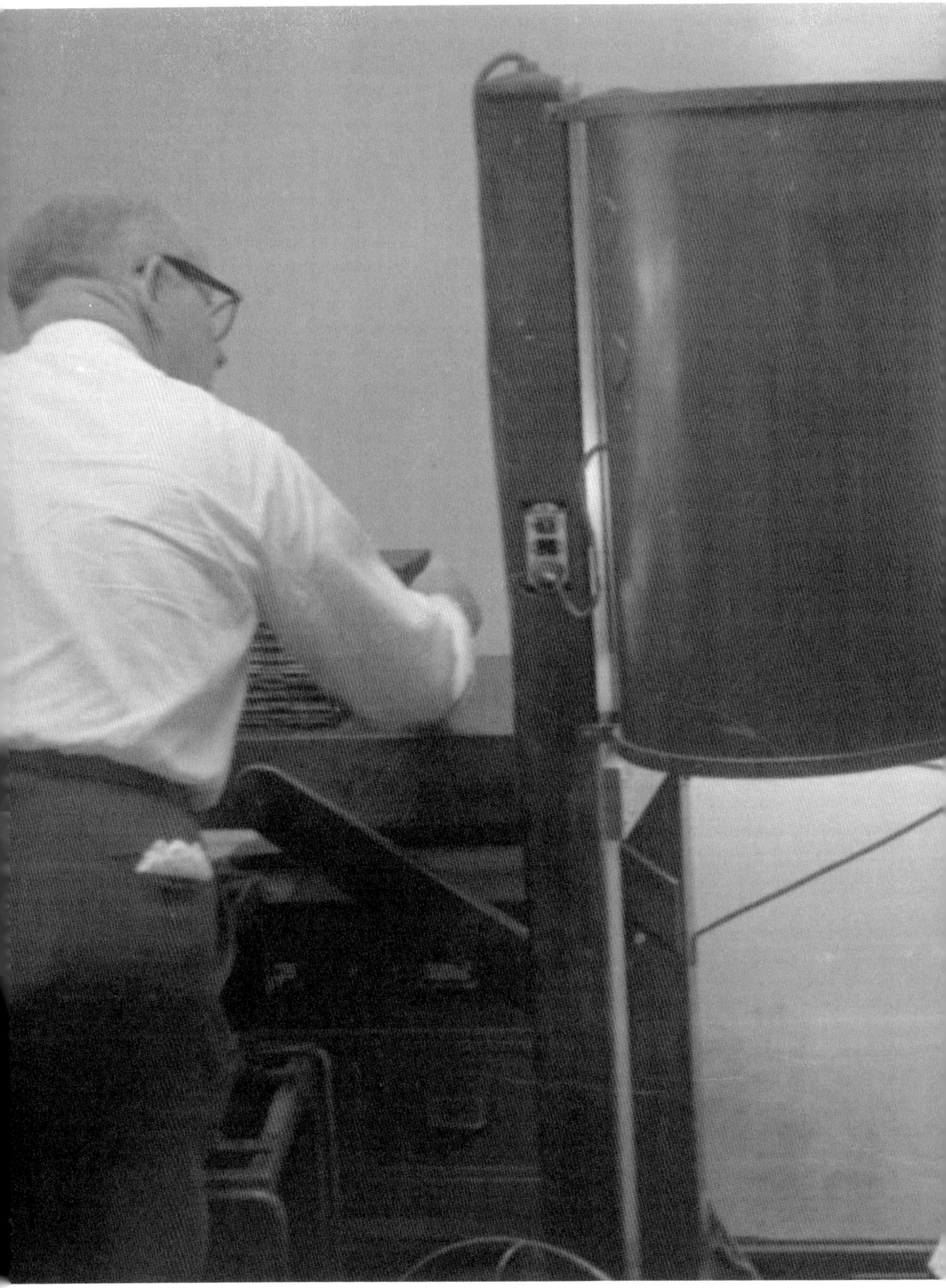

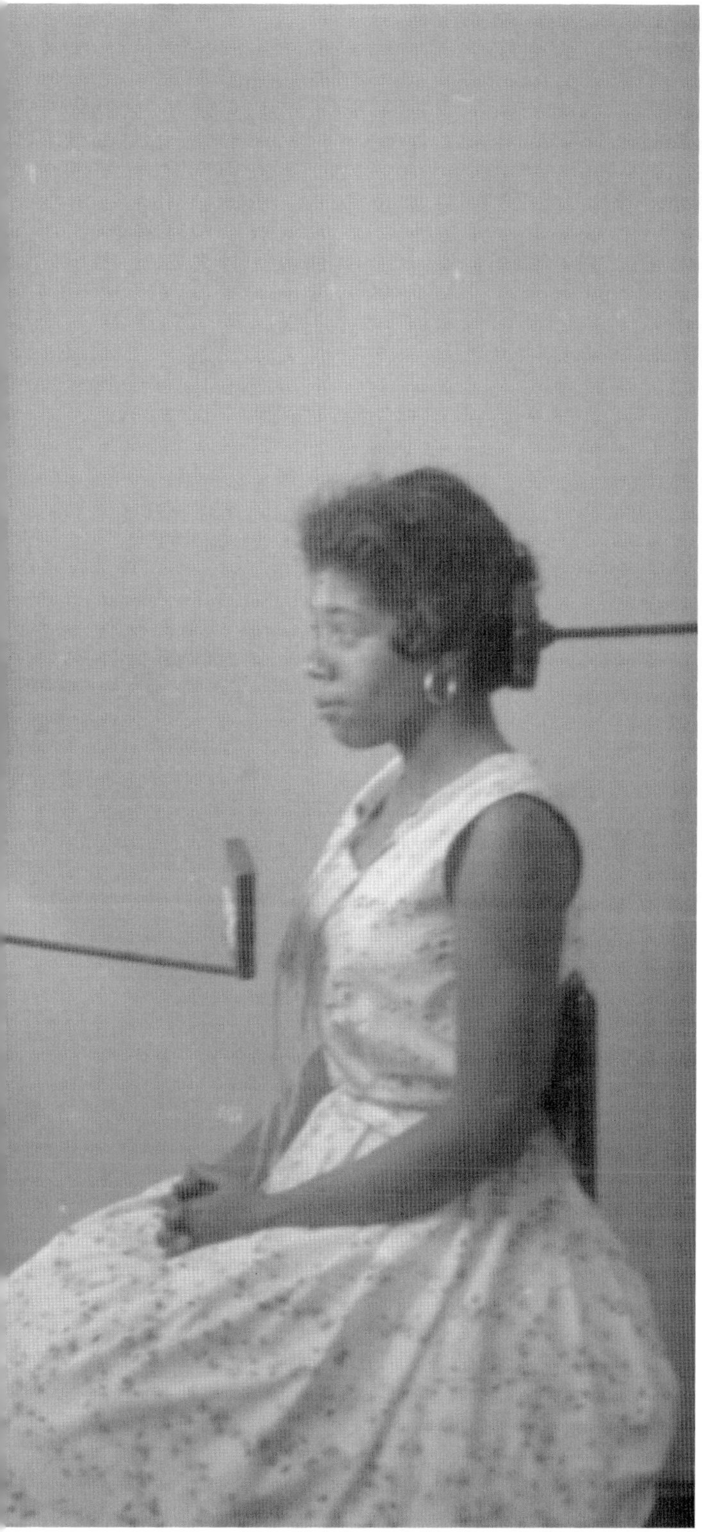

Dorris "Dee Dee" Wright
Dorris "Dee Dee" Wright was among eight black youth arrested on July 16, 1960, for a sit-in at the whites-only Greenville County Public Library. Wright recalled being placed in a filthy jail cell and being served stale cornbread and water in a dirty tin cup. A July 18, 2005, *Chicago Sun-Times* article said death threats came shortly after her release, prompting her mother to move the family to New York. (Courtesy of the James G. Wilson Collection, Upcountry History Museum–Furman University.)

The Greenville 8

They are the Greenville 8, eight black students who walked into the whites-only Greenville Public Library on July 16, 1960. Each pulled a book off the shelf and sat down to read. They refused to leave, knowing that it would be just a matter of time before the police arrived. They were arrested. Later that month, a lawsuit was filed in federal court to integrate it and the city's "black" public library. The facilities closed on September 2, and the lawsuit was dismissed a few days later. An integrated library reopened on September 19. The Greenville 8 are, from left to right, (first row) Joan Mattison Daniel, Elaine Means, Margaree Seawright Crosby, Dorris Wright and Hattie Smith Wright; (second row), Jesse Jackson and Benjamin Downs; (third row) Willie Joe Wright, attorney Willie T. Smith Jr., and attorney Donald Sampson. (Courtesy of the James G. Wilson Collection, Upcountry History Museum–Furman University.)

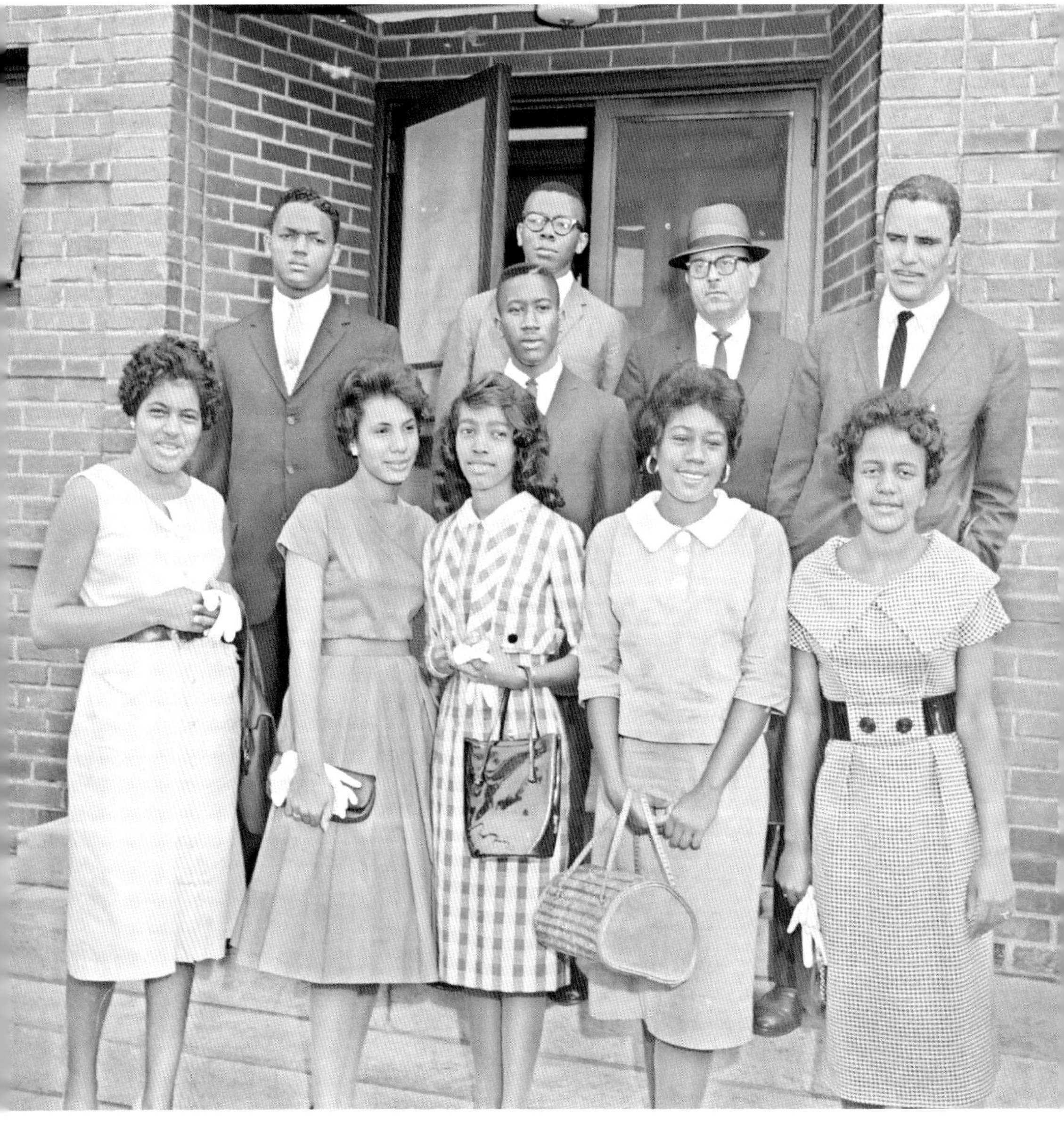

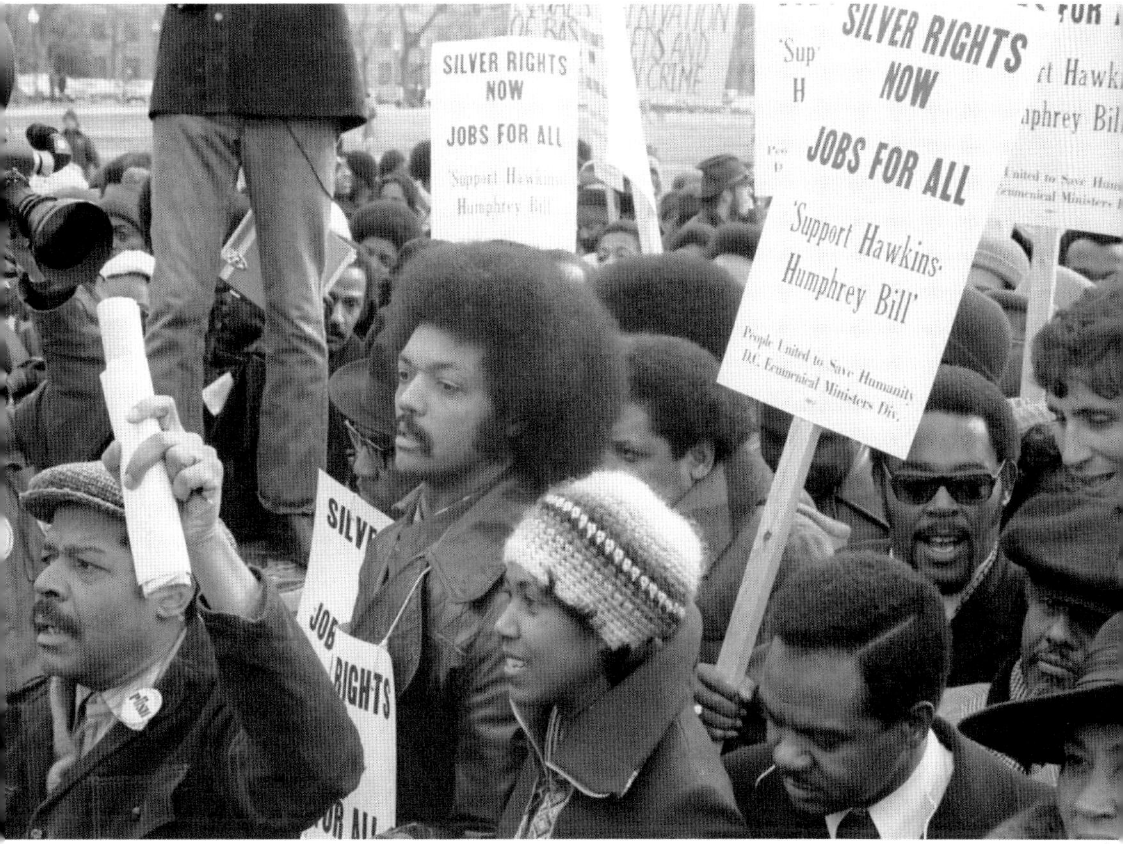

The Reverend Jesse Jackson

Born in Greenville, Rev. Jesse Jackson was class president and a football star at Sterling High School. In 1959, he attended the University of Illinois on a football scholarship. The next year, he transferred to North Carolina Agricultural and Technical College in Greensboro, where he got involved in civil-rights demonstrations. In 1964, he went to Selma, Alabama, to march with Dr. Martin Luther King Jr. He became the director of Operation Breadbasket, the economic arm of King's Southern Christian Leadership Conference. He left the SCLC in 1971, the same year he formed the Rainbow/PUSH Coalition. He ran for the US presidency in 1984, becoming the second African American to do so, and again in 1988. (Courtesy of the Library of Congress, Prints and Photographs Division.)

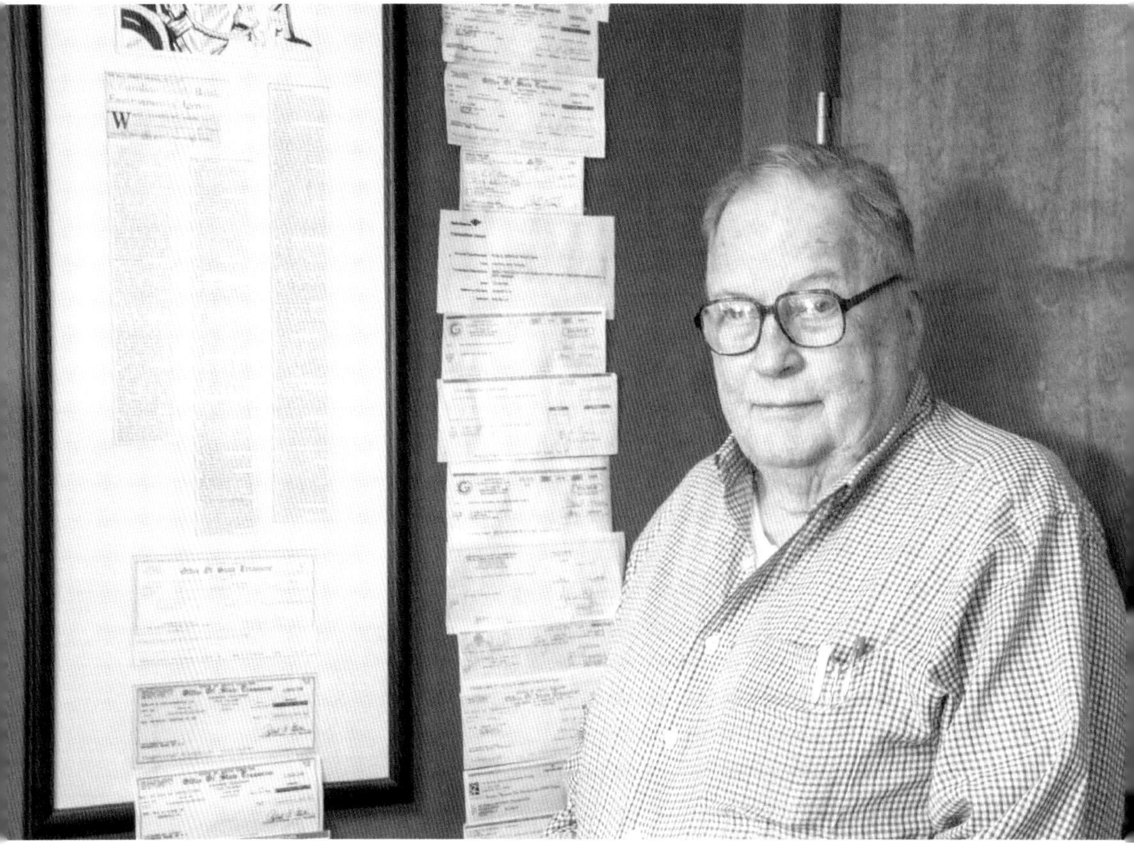

Edward D. "Ned" Sloan Jr.

Edward D. "Ned" Sloan Jr. did not take up a typical retirement hobby. The former paving contractor does not play golf. He does not garden. He sues local and state governmental bodies when he thinks they have violated the law. The self-appointed gadfly has filed dozens of lawsuits, so many he has lost count. He has sued over public records, procurement laws, and financial records. Sloan even formed a nonprofit foundation, South Carolina Public Interest Foundation, in 2005 to help pay for his litigation activities. Sloan does not sue for damages, but when he wins, he seeks reimbursement for legal fees. He is pictured here with copies of some of his checks. (Photograph by Cindy Landrum.)

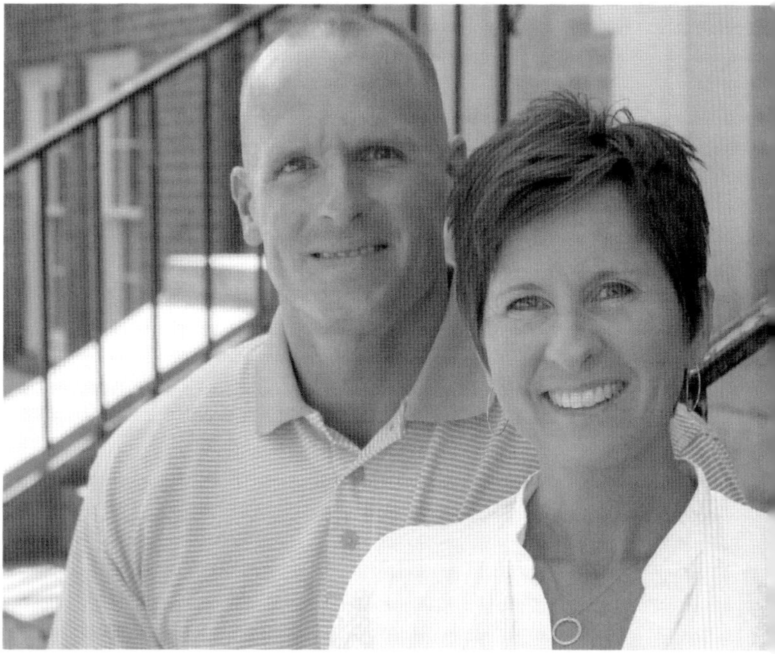

Frazee Dream Center
When Matt Reeves saw an abandoned Baptist church with a gymnasium near downtown Greenville, on the edge of the impoverished Southernside neighborhood, he knew he had found the home of the Frazee Dream Center. He and his wife, Jenny, mortgaged their house to buy it. They sold their successful landscaping business to start the free afterschool program that has four rules for children: work hard, respect authority, love everyone, and forgive quickly. (Courtesy of Frazee Dream Center.)

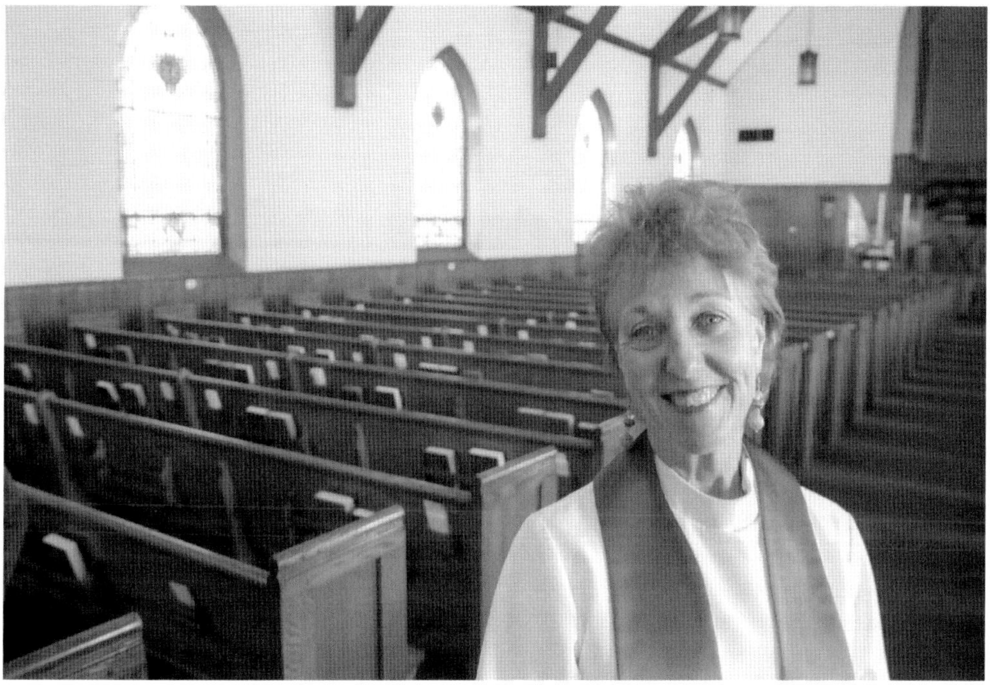

Deb Richardson-Moore
When the managing editor of the *Greenville News* asked Deb Richardson-Moore to take the paper's religion beat, she had no idea it would lead her to her second career. In 2005, she ended a 27-year journalism career to become pastor at Triune Mercy Center, a nondenominational mission church serving the homeless near downtown Greenville. She found her calling where the gospel hit the streets. (Courtesy of the *Upstate Business Journal*.)

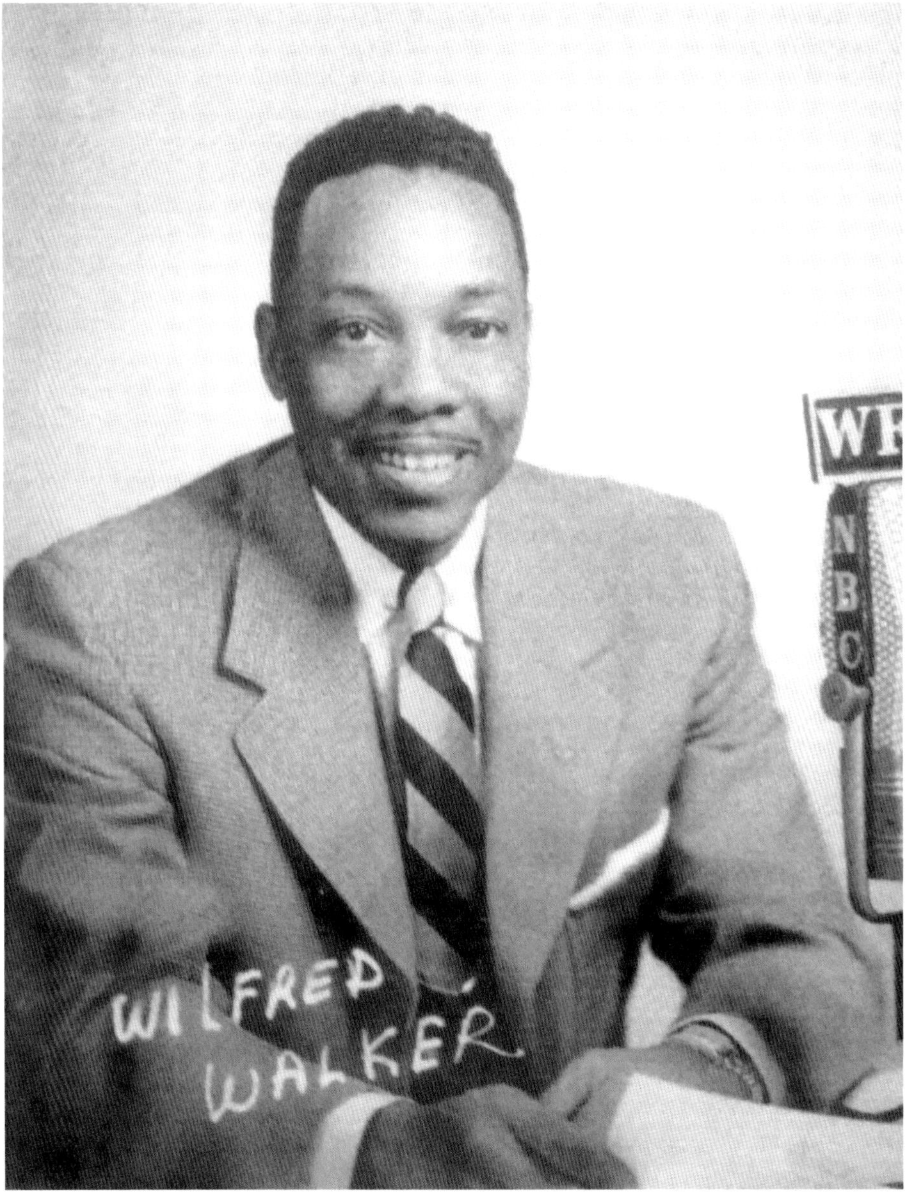

Wilfred Walker

Wilfred Walker was known as the "Ole Sportscaster" after becoming the radio commentator for the Sterling High School Tigers' football games. He became a celebrity through his music show, *Wilfred Walker's Variety Time*. When WESC started broadcasting football games at Sirrine Stadium the fall of 1948, Walker became the first African American sportscaster in South Carolina. Walker used his celebrity stature to support charities. The Red Cross, Community Chest of Greenville, and the March of Dimes all benefited. Walker received the Greenville County Citizenship Award from the Greenville County Council and received the first Special Lifetime Award from Sunbelt Human Resources. Walker, who taught masonry in the Greenville County School District, laid the symbolic last brick in a statue commemorating Sterling High School on Main Street in Greenville. (Courtesy of the Greenville Cultural Exchange Center.)

CHAPTER FIVE

Artists and Athletes

Greenville has had its share of legendary artists and athletes.

They have danced on one of the country's first hit television variety shows. They have starred in the Major League Baseball World Series. They have blazed new trails in music. They have acted on the big screen. They have performed on some of the world's best-known stages. They have had hit records. They are in the sports-history books.

Shoeless Joe Jackson is probably Greenville's most famous athlete. Even though his major-league career ended nearly a century ago, baseball fans across the country know his name. That is what being a part of the sport's biggest scandal can do. His Greenville home is now a museum dedicated to preserving his legacy. It is across the street from Greenville's minor-league baseball stadium, a place where young players start making their diamond dreams come true.

Frank Selvy is still in the record books, too, as the first and only Division I college basketball player to score 100 points in a game. For George Hincapie, fame came on a bicycle as a road-race champion and trusted lieutenant for now-disgraced Tour de France champion Lance Armstrong. The Haases gained famed as Greenville's first family of golf.

In the arts, Greenville residents have found fame on the big screen and little screen, on the stages of the world's most famous performance halls, by soaring to the top of the charts.

Actress Joanne Woodward won an Oscar. Clayton "Peg Leg" Bates managed to overcome a cotton-mill accident that forced the amputation of one of his legs on his mother's kitchen table to dance regularly on the *Ed Sullivan Show.* Renato Moncini was the first illustrator of space.

The accolades keep coming. Players on the city's minor-league baseball team, the Greenville Drive, have made it to the big leagues. Greenville's artistic talent has put the city on the map of best art towns in America.

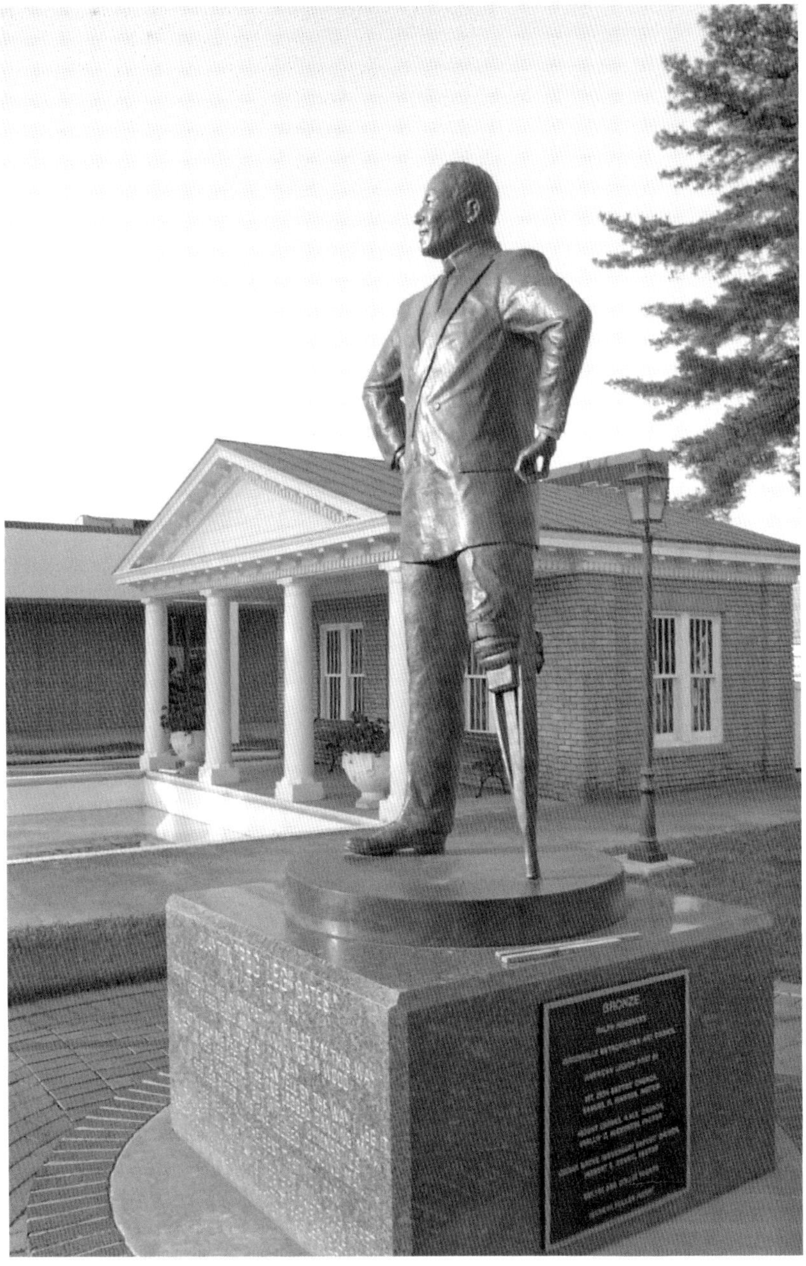

Clayton "Peg Leg" Bates

Clayton "Peg Leg" Bates did not let losing a leg in a cotton-seed gin mill when he was 12 years old stop him from achieving his dream of becoming a dancer. Bates, the son of sharecroppers, started dancing when he was five. After the accident, he danced using two broomsticks under his arms until his uncle made him a wooden leg. After he and his mother had moved to Greenville, he danced at carnivals and county fairs. A New York producer discovered him at the Greenville Black Liberty Theatre in 1927. Bates's flamboyant dancing style made him a regular on the *Ed Sullivan Show* in the 1950s. He appeared on the show more than any other tap dancer. In the 1960s, Bates opened the Peg Leg Bates Country Club in the Catskills in New York. (Courtesy of Jason Tench.)

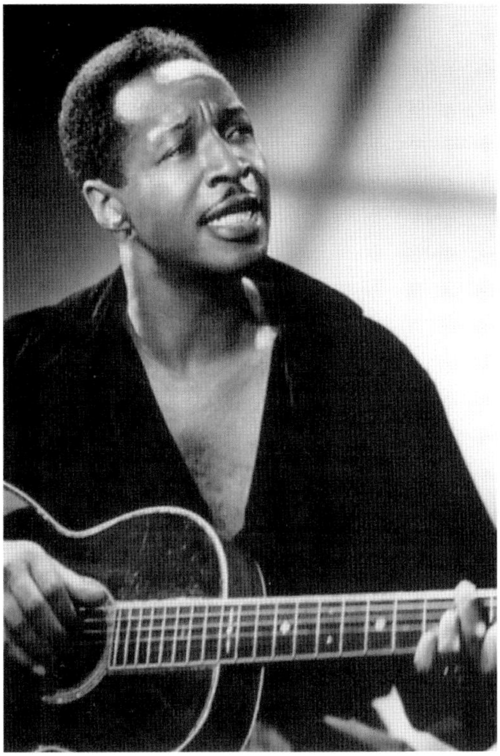

Josh White
Josh White was a music trailblazer who introduced black blues and spiritual music to white America. White's musical career began out of necessity. During the Jim Crow years, White's father was arrested and later institutionalized, for throwing a white bill collector out of his home. White left when he was seven years old to collect coins for a blind singer. He was a popular Piedmont blues and gospel singer in the 1930s, a protest folk star in the 1940s, and a victim of McCarthyism in the 1950s. He volunteered to testify before the House Un-American Activities Committee, a move that alienated both the left wing and conservatives. Biographer Elijah Wald said one of the contradictions of White's life was that politics made him a star and then destroyed him. (Courtesy of the Greenville Cultural Exchange Center.)

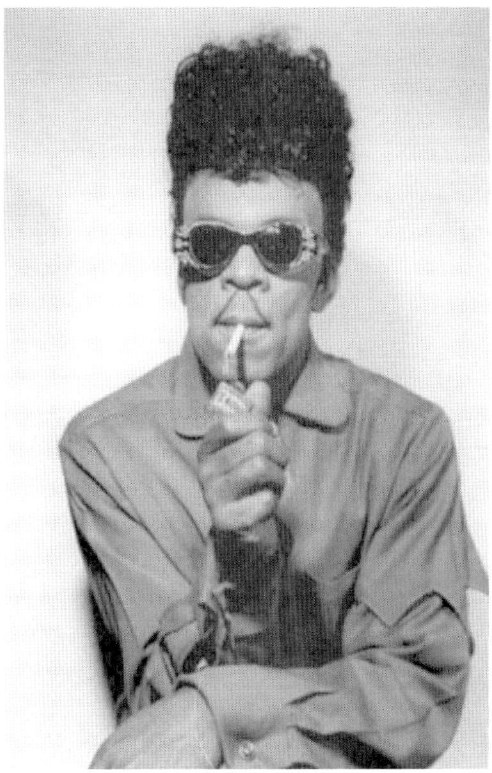

Eskew Reeder
Steven Quincy "Eskew" Reeder Jr. is Greenville's version of Little Richard. Some believe Reeder, who used the stage name Esquerita, originated the rockabilly-soul style for which Little Richard achieved fame. Reeder, who taught Little Richard how to play the piano, never achieved the same notoriety. He died of AIDS in 1986. (Courtesy of the Greenville Cultural Exchange Center.)

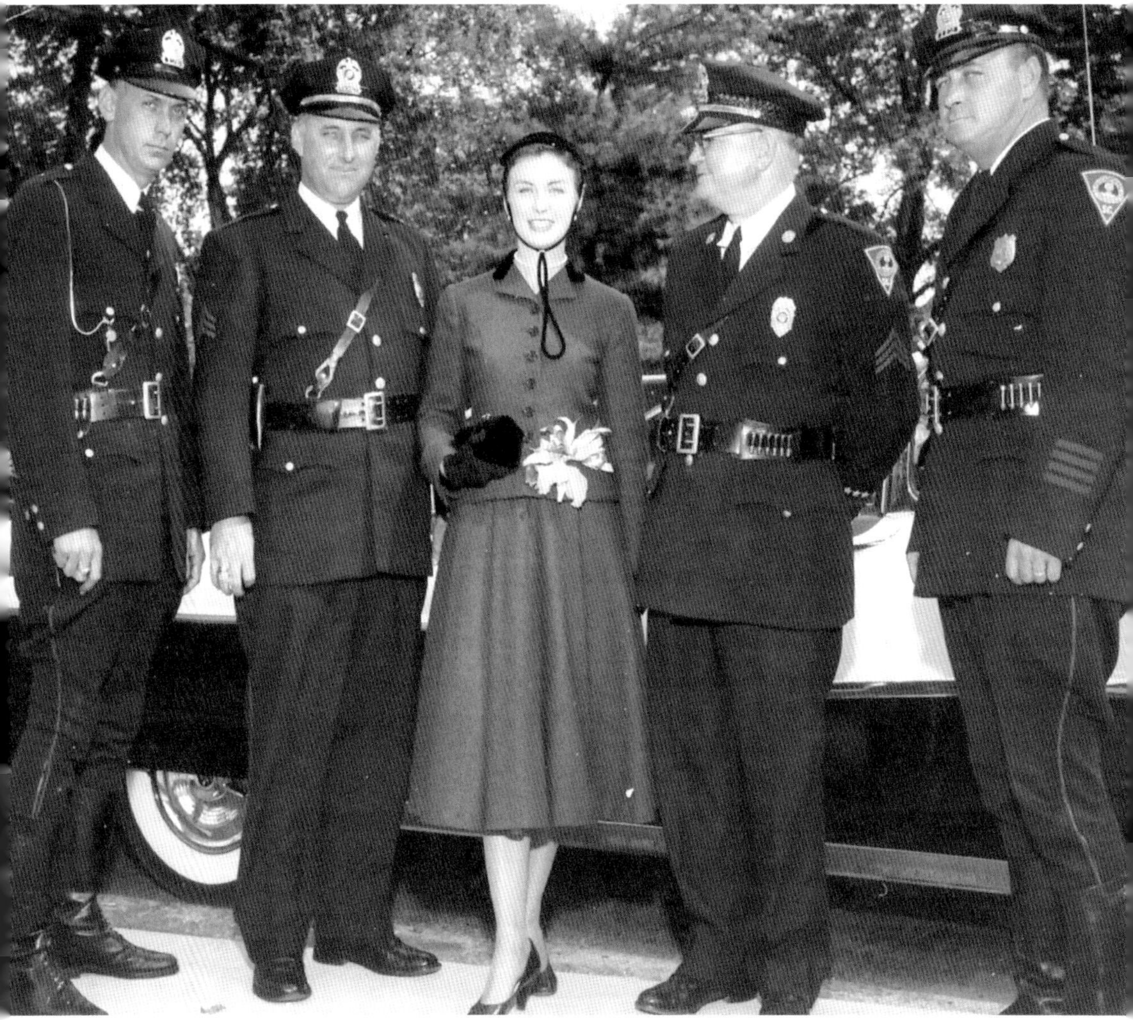

Joanne Woodward

When Joanne Woodward won an award in 1949 for her performance in the Greenville Little Theatre's production of *The Glass Menagerie*, it was a sign of things to come. Woodward won a real Oscar when she won the Academy Award for Best Actress in 1958 for *The Three Faces of Eve*, a movie about a woman with multiple personality disorder. Woodward, a Greenville High School graduate, returned to Greenville in 1976 to star again in *The Glass Menagerie* to honor Robert McLane, her former high school drama teacher and longtime director of the Greenville Little Theatre. Woodward was married to actor Paul Newman for 50 years, until his death from lung cancer in 2008. (Courtesy of the Greenville Little Theatre.)

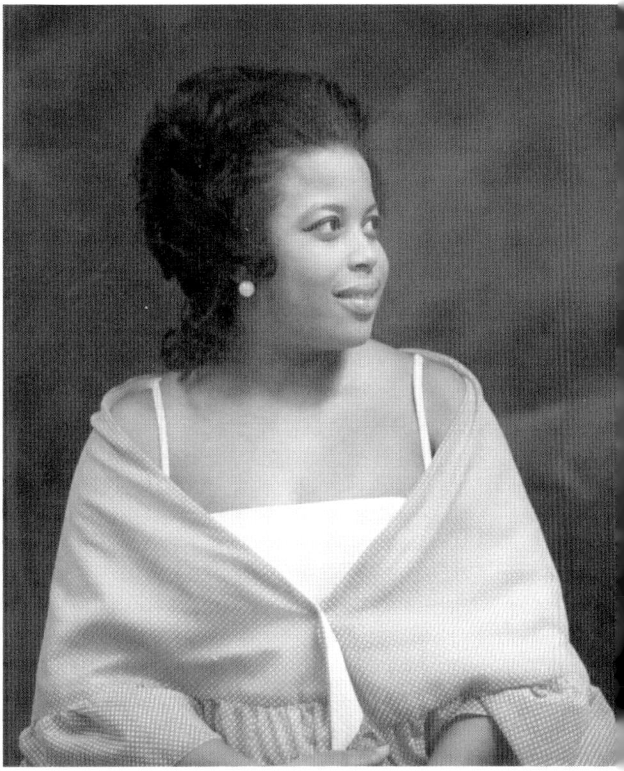

Sarah Reese

Sarah Reese, an internationally renowned opera singer, knows the power of teachers. Linda Gamble, the choir teacher at the all-black Bryson High School in Fountain Inn, first noticed when Reese was in the eighth grade the voice that would carry her student to Carnegie Hall. Reese, shown on right in her 1971 yearbook photograph and below at a Furman integration commemoration in 2014, was one of the first two African American women to graduate from Furman. She returned to Greenville as a guest artist at the opening gala of the Peace Center for the Performing Arts. Reese was playing Clara in *Porgy and Bess*, and the producers would not let her miss a performance. A jet was sent to pick her up, take her to Greenville to perform and return her to New York for that night's show. She now teaches at Pendleton High School. (Both, courtesy of Furman University.)

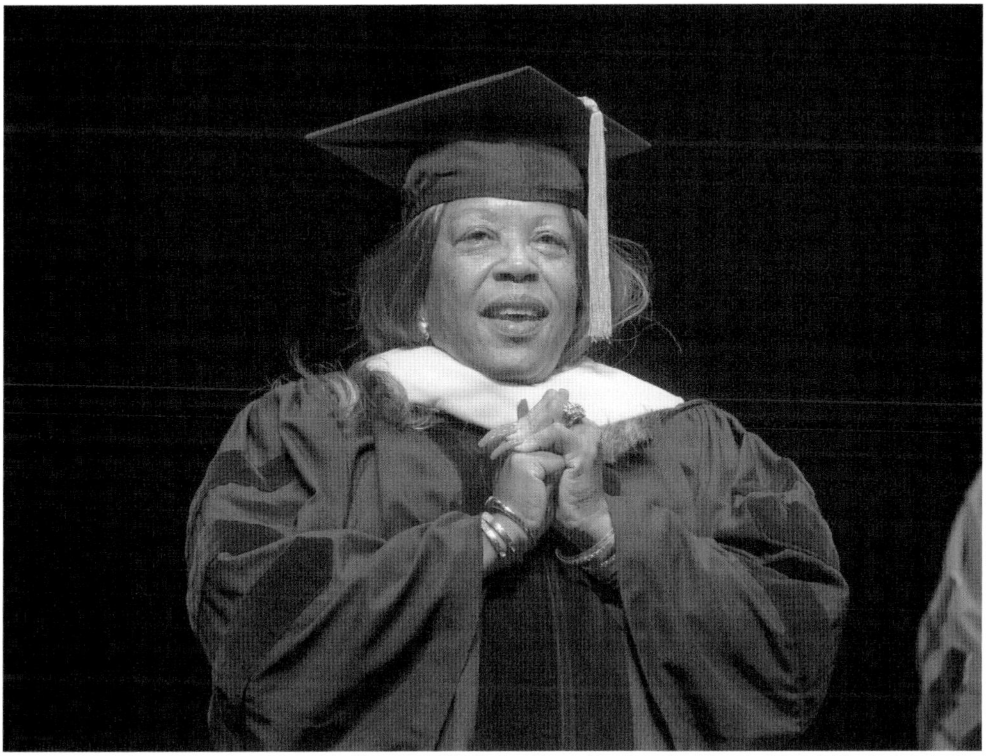

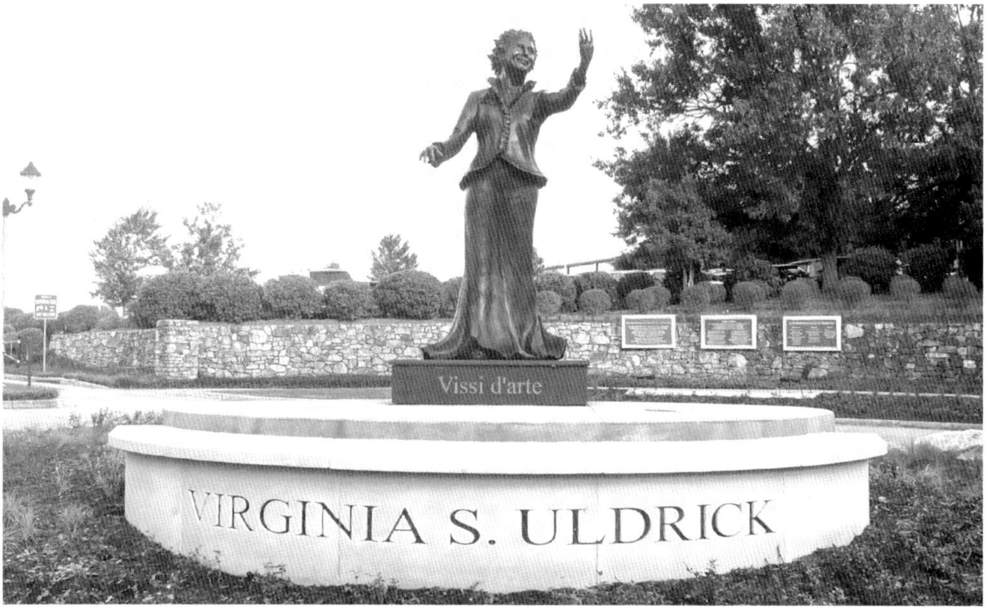

Virginia Uldrick

Virginia Uldrick dreamed of a career as an entertainer. Instead, she spent a career creating opportunities in the arts for generations of students. Uldrick wanted to sing and act on New York stages but gave up that dream when her husband got a job in Greenwood. She started teaching and knew she found her true calling.

She directed Greenville's Singing Christmas Tree and helped establish the Greenville County School District's Fine Arts Center, South Carolina's first specialized arts school, which opened in 1974. She founded the county's first arts magnet school. But opening the South Carolina Governor's School for the Arts and Humanities as a full-time residential high school for the artistically talented was her crowning achievement. She was its president for four years. (Both, courtesy of the *Greenville Journal*.)

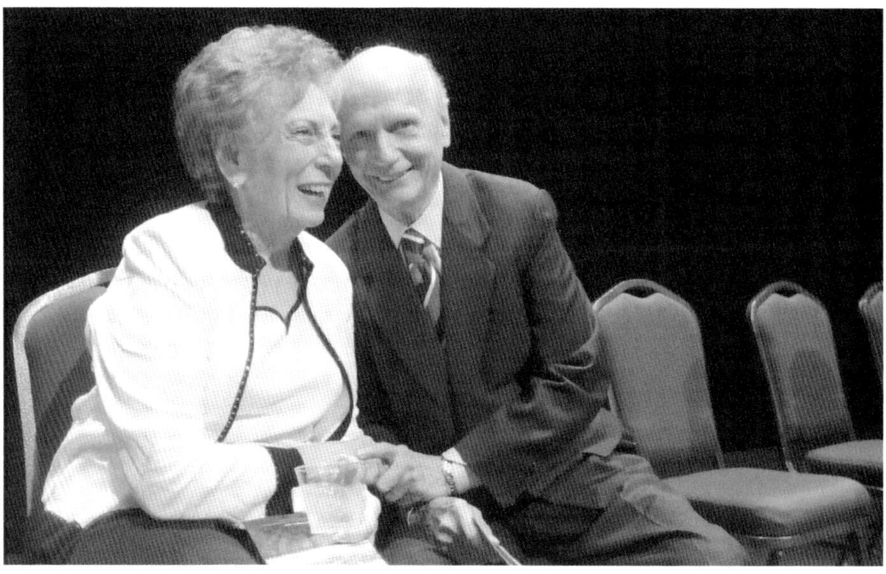

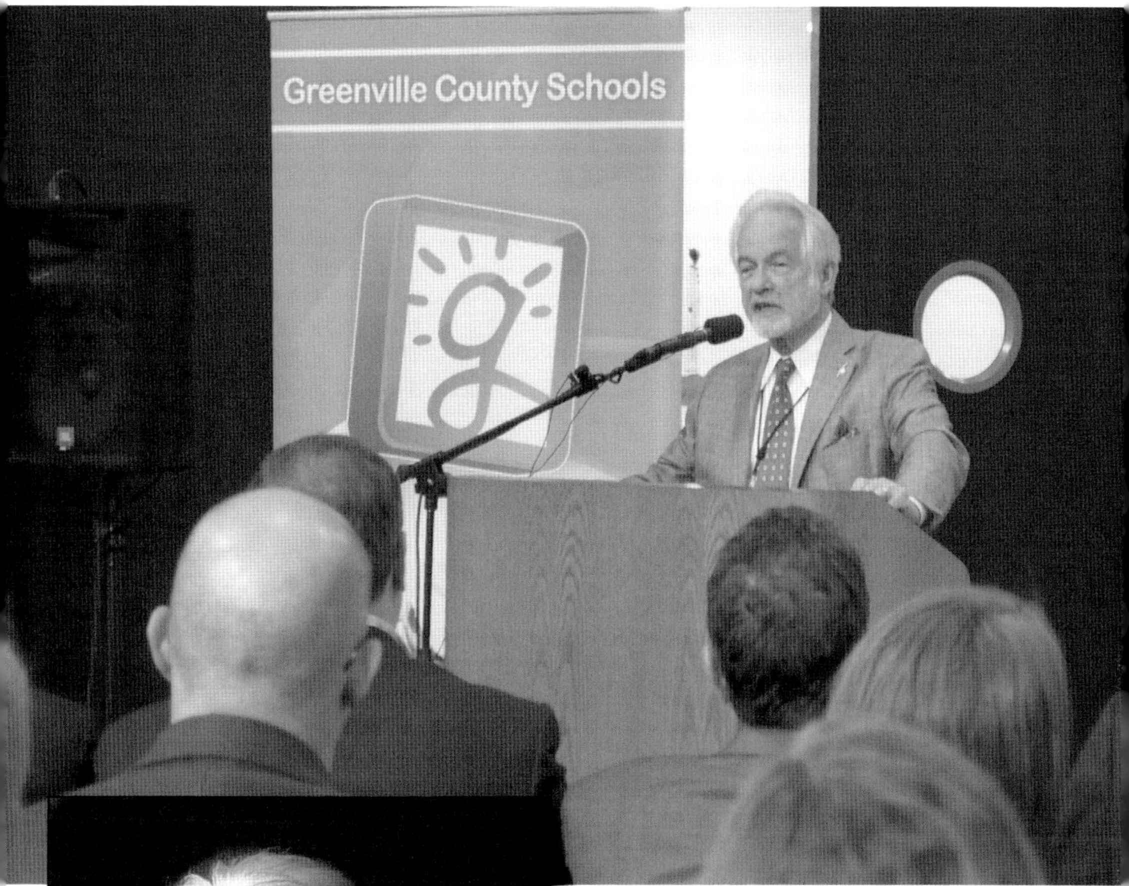

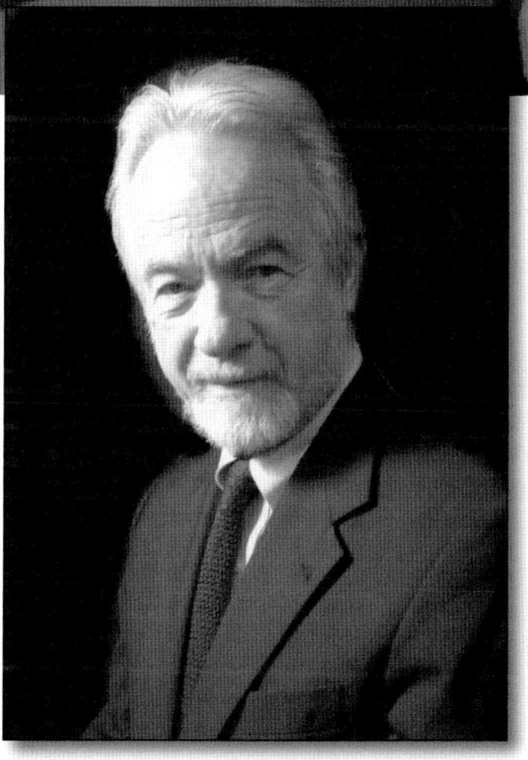

Roy Fluhrer

Roy Fluhrer has spent a lifetime in theater. When he was a baby, he slept in a trunk while his parents performed with the Hallie Flannagan Federal Theater Project. He studied theater at Northwestern University, auditioned for a role at the Toledo Repertoire Theatre, and got it. When the theater's artistic director resigned, he took the job. He worked as chairman of the theater department at the University of Idaho and vice chancellor at North Carolina School of the Arts. In 1989, he came to Greenville as director of the school district's Fine Arts Center. At least three times during his 25 years at the helm, Fluhrer had to fight for the school's right to exist. Fluhrer is pictured here at a press conference announcing a Fine Arts Center partnership with Clemson University. (Above, courtesy of Clemson University; left, courtesy of Roy Fluhrer.)

Edvard Tchivzhel

Edvard Tchivzhel's journey to Greenville sounds like a real-life spy novel. The Soviet-born Tchivzhel, whose grandfather was executed by Stalin as a Latvian spy, came to Greenville with the USSR State Symphony in 1991 as part of a month-long US tour.

While at Chuck E. Cheese's on Haywood Road, Tchivzhel whispered in Russian to translator Lena Forster, then general manager of the Greenville Ballet, that he wanted to defect. That kicked off a series of events reminiscent of a spy novel. While Tchivzhel completed the tour with the USSR Orchestra, Greenville attorney Larry Estridge worked on preparing the papers Tchivzhel, his wife, Luba, and their four-year-old son, Arvid, needed for political asylum. The work required secret late-night conversations, and Tchivzhel, an avid runner, carried dimes in his pocket when he ran each night so he could call Forster and Estridge without the KGB knowing.

When the symphony's plane landed in Washington, DC, the tour's last stop, six FBI agents were waiting to escort the Tchivzhels to their new life in the United States in a three-car caravan. Stationed throughout the terminal were armed INS and FBI agents. Tchivzhel stepped onto the bus, even though he knew that the KGB had plants on board, to say good-bye to the musicians before his escape.

Soviet Embassy officials chased the FBI caravan all the way to the immigration office in Baltimore, Maryland. Soviet officials left after an FBI agent ordered them to get off official government property. After filing paperwork, the Tchivzhels flew to Greenville, the city the maestro considers his American cradle.

He became the Greenville Symphony Orchestra's music director and conductor in 1999, the same year he and his wife became US citizens. Tchivzhel was music director of the Fort Wayne Philharmonic from 1993 until 2008. He returned to Russia for the first time since his defection in April 2003 to conduct the St. Petersburg Philharmonic Orchestra in a performance of Mahler's Fifth Symphony. (Courtesy of the Greenville Symphony Orchestra.)

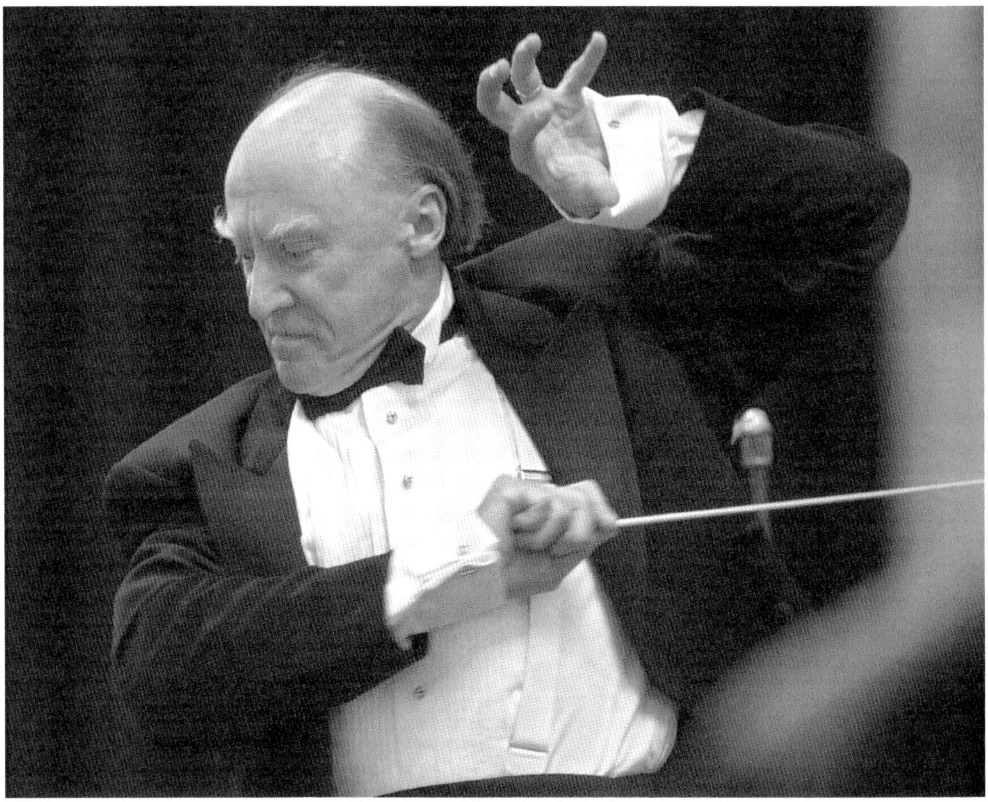

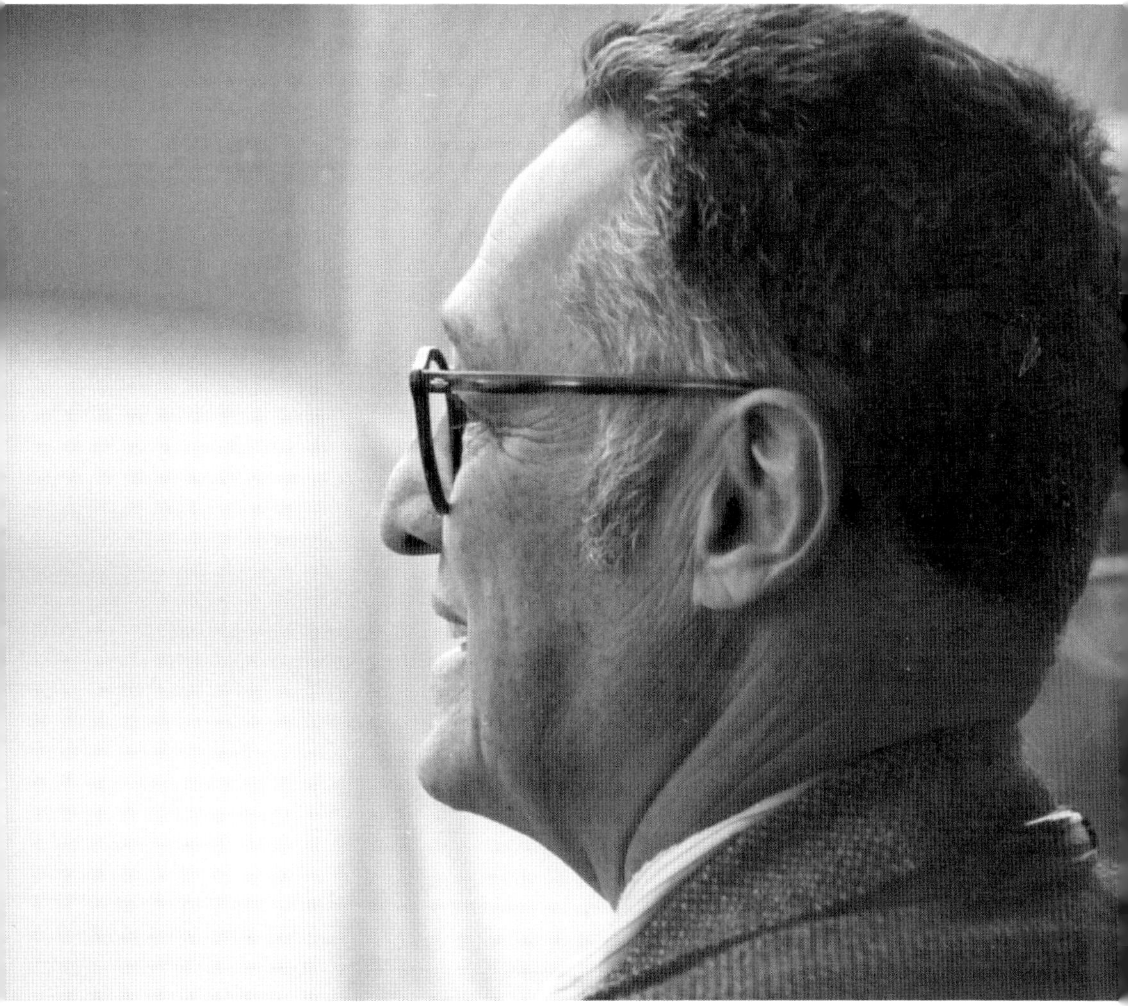

Arthur Francis Magill

Arthur Francis Magill shocked the art world when in 1979 he bought 26 oil paintings by Andrew Wyeth, then a relative unknown, and loaned them to the Greenville County Museum of Art. The Metropolitan Museum of Art and the Museum of Fine Arts in Boston had wanted the paintings, but Magill was the only one who would promise permanent display. He bought the works, which became the cornerstone of the Greenville County Museum of Art's collection, for an estimated $4.5 million. Magill, who made millions from the children's clothing business Her Majesty Industries, which he inherited from his father, had donated half the construction cost of the museum. In 1990, Magill sold the paintings to a Japanese firm for $42 million, giving $6 million to the museum. Magill died in 1995 at the age of 88. (Courtesy of the Greenville County Library System.)

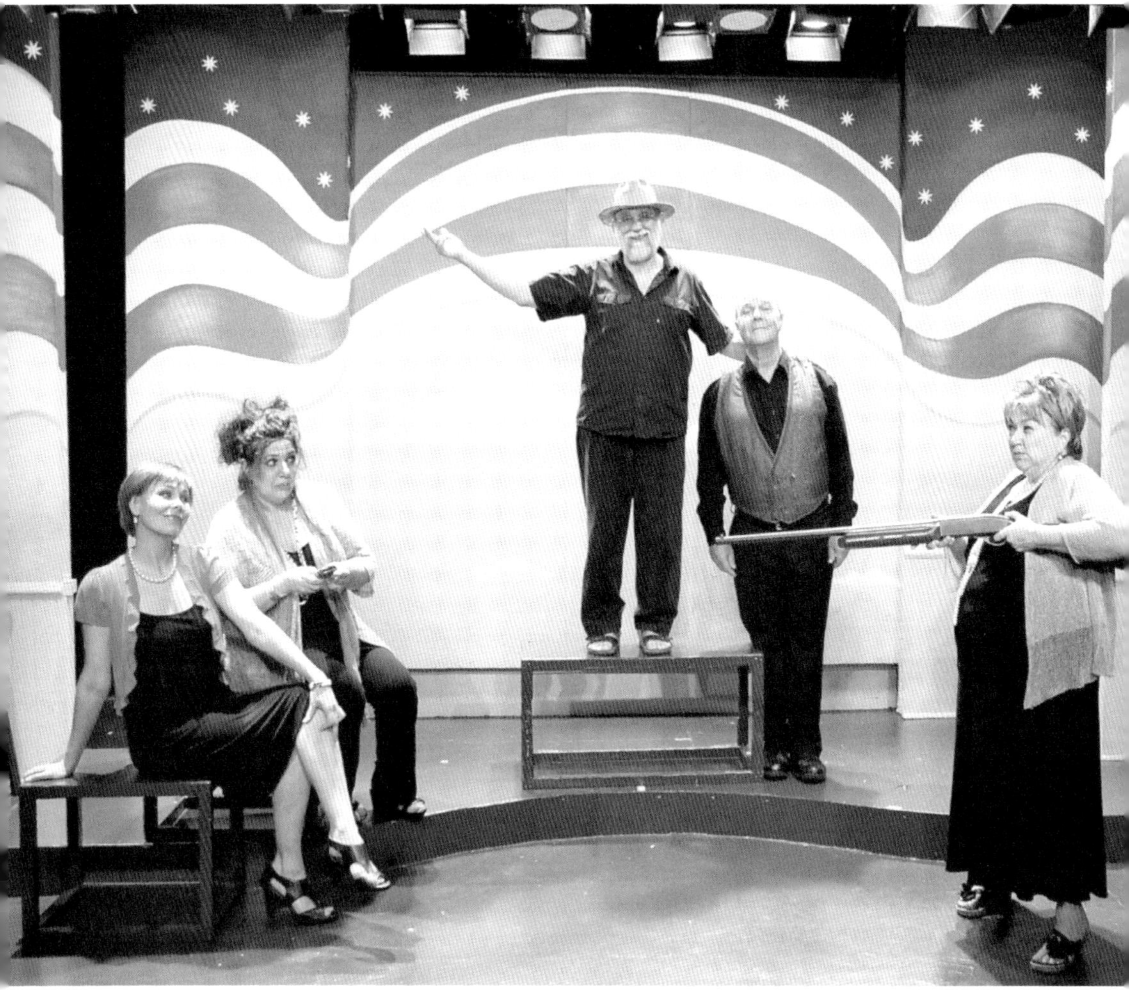

Café and Then Some

The comics at Café and Then Some, Greenville's dinner theater and comedy club, believe in equal opportunity humor. They will make fun of anybody. Susan Smith, her husband, Bill Smith, Ted Bruce, Maureen Abdalla, Traysie Amick, Jim Wilkins, and Yvonne Mason comprise the Café Players. They have spoofed politicians and made fun of Greenville's bluebloods and Southern life in original musical comedies for more than 30 years. Ron Whisenant writes and directs the comedies. Bill and Susan Smith both graduated from Wade Hampton High School but did not meet until the late 1970s when Susan, a social worker by day, was performing at the Warehouse Theatre. They formed a sketch-comedy troupe in 1979, and they opened their restaurant and venue in 1983. (Courtesy of Café and Then Some.)

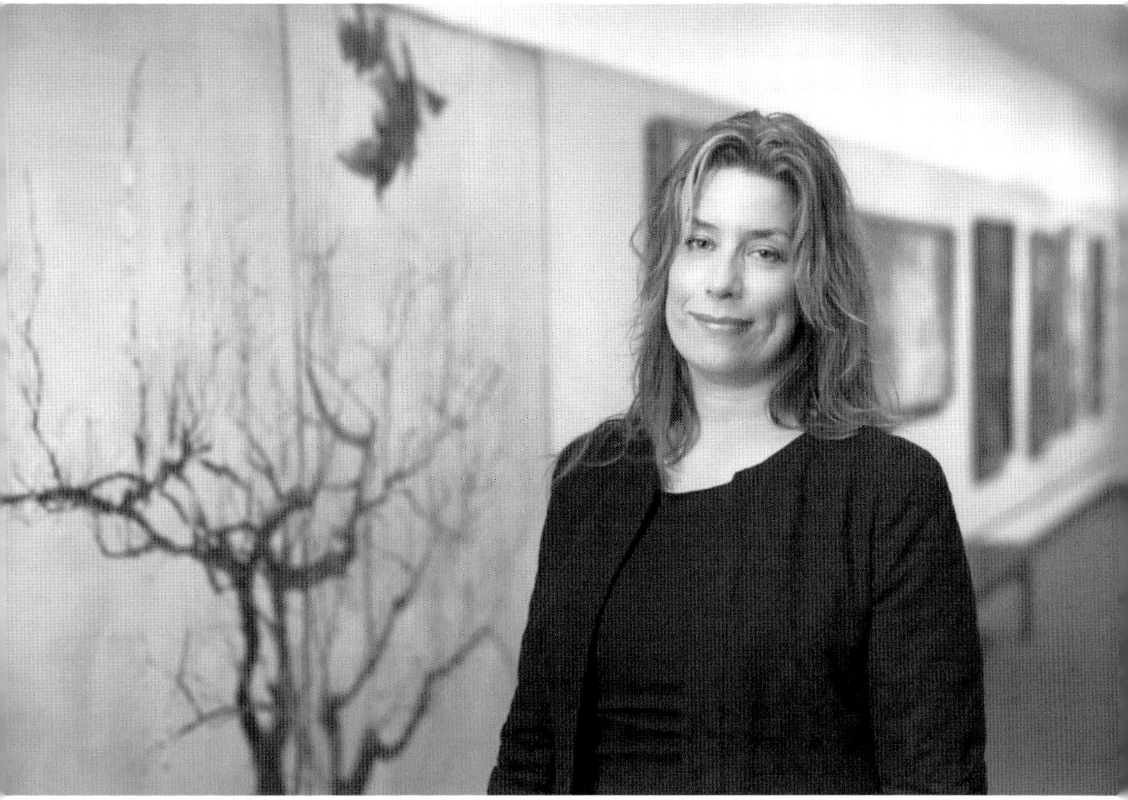

Diane Kilgore Condon
After Diane Kilgore Condon had visited the famed Torpedo Factory, an old manufacturing facility in Virginia converted into artist studio space, she knew she wanted to do the same in Greenville. While driving down Pendleton Street in West Greenville, she saw the old building that had served as the general store for the Brandon Mill village that was being used as a motorcycle repair shop. Condon formed a nonprofit organization, ArtBomb, in 2000. The artist collective sparked the transformation of the once-forgotten part of the city into an arts district. In 2014, dozens of artists called the village of West Greenville home. (Courtesy of Bob Jones University.)

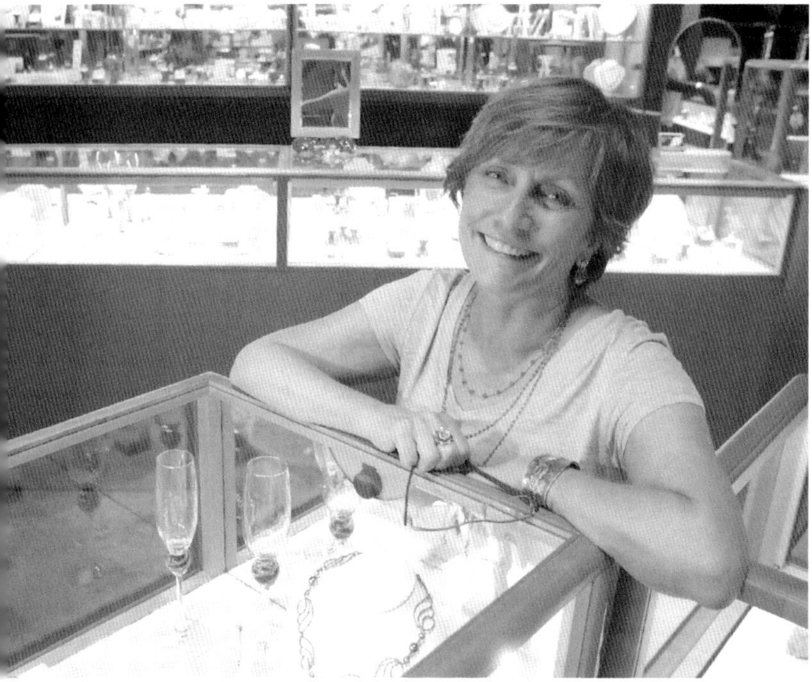

Llyn Strong

Strong is a fitting name for jewelry designer and manufacturer Llyn Strong. She started llyn strong jewelers (she prefers lowercased letters) in 1989, the worst year of her life. Her father died that year, her mother had major surgery, her sister moved away, and her husband moved out. Her store has been a mainstay on Main Street since 1991. (Courtesy of the *Greenville Journal.*)

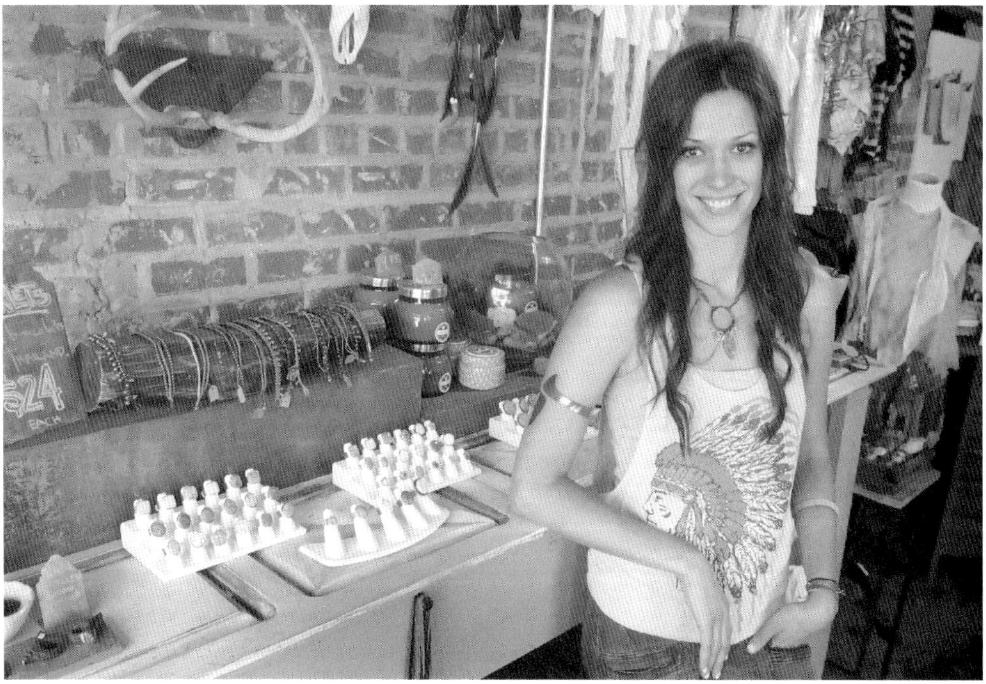

Lily Wikoff

Lily Wikoff did not plan to become a jeweler. It just happened. She expected to be a potter in New York City. But after she made some hand-stamped and fired-clay jewelry for her mother, somebody saw the pieces on Facebook, and they wanted some, too. After a couple of home shows sold out in 2007, Wikoff had the start of a business, Lily Pottery. (Courtesy of the *Upstate Business Journal.*)

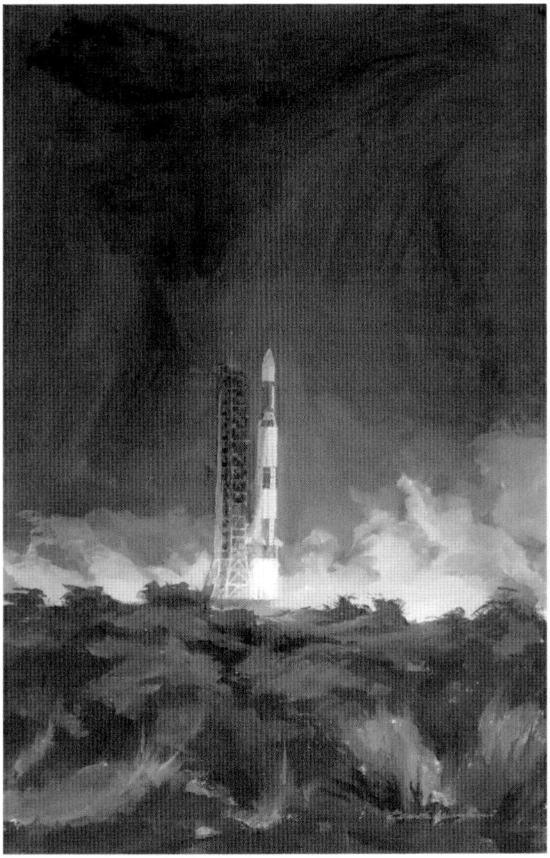

Renato Moncini
Greenville is home to the first artist of space, Renato Moncini. An Italian immigrant who worked for NASA from 1962 to 1974, Moncini's job was to create images to promote the space program to politicians and the American public. He drew technical renderings for NASA projects and conceptual art for the Apollo space missions. Nobody knew what the moon's surface was like, Moncini said. Nobody knew if the landing gear would sink. "Fortunately, we guessed right," Moncini said in a 2014 interview. While he was NASA's payroll, Moncini attended each launch at Cape Canaveral and painted what he saw. He later worked as creative director and lead illustrator at Fluor Daniel in Greenville. (Courtesy of Renato Moncini and TL Norris Gallery.)

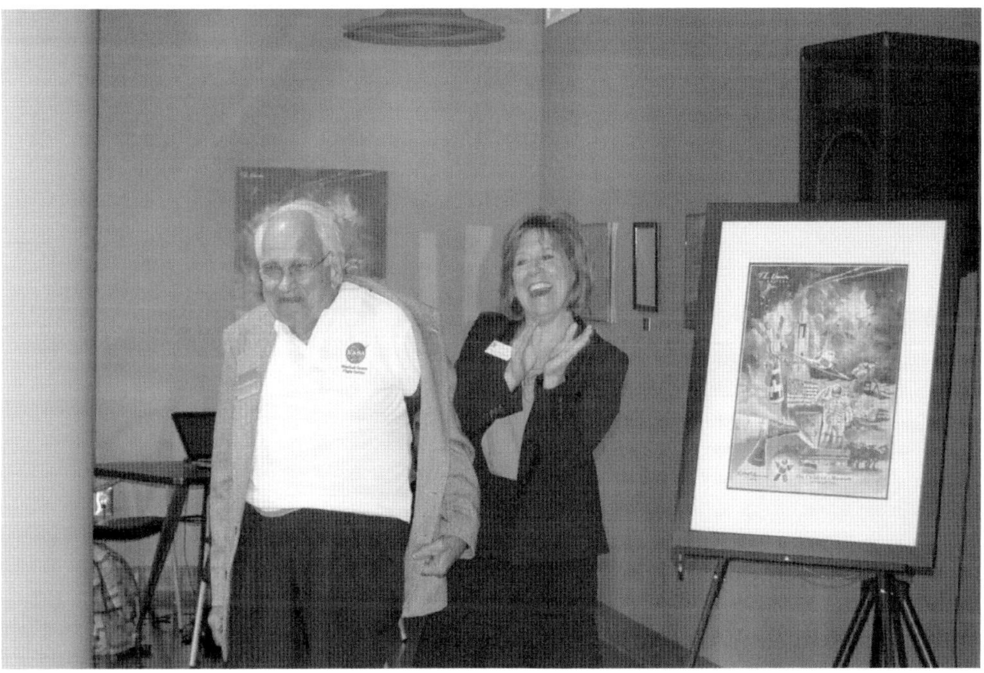

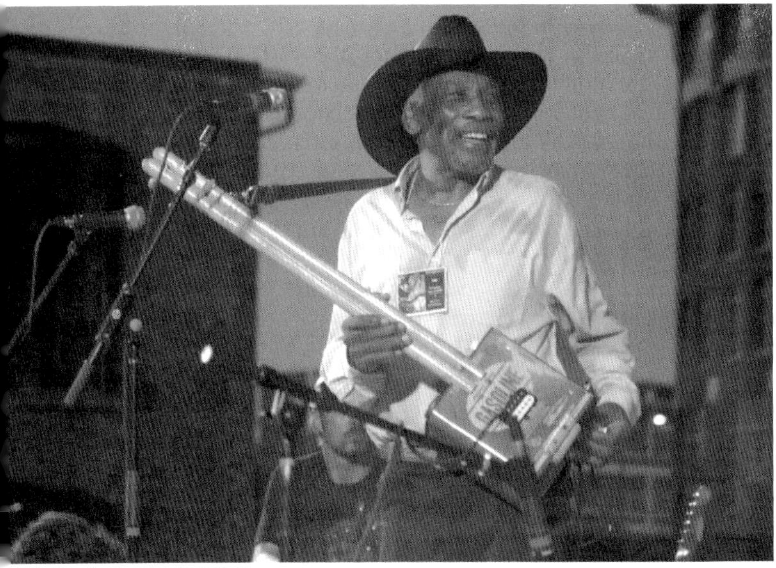

Mac Arnold

Mac Arnold played the blues with Muddy Waters, B.B. King, Jimmy Reed, and Buddy Guy. He played on Soul Train and the television soundtrack for *Sanford and Sons*. But he gave it all up in the 1980s to return to his roots in southern Greenville County. He started another band in the 1990s, thanks to a chance encounter with another musician at a UPS office. (Courtesy of Brian Kelley Photography.)

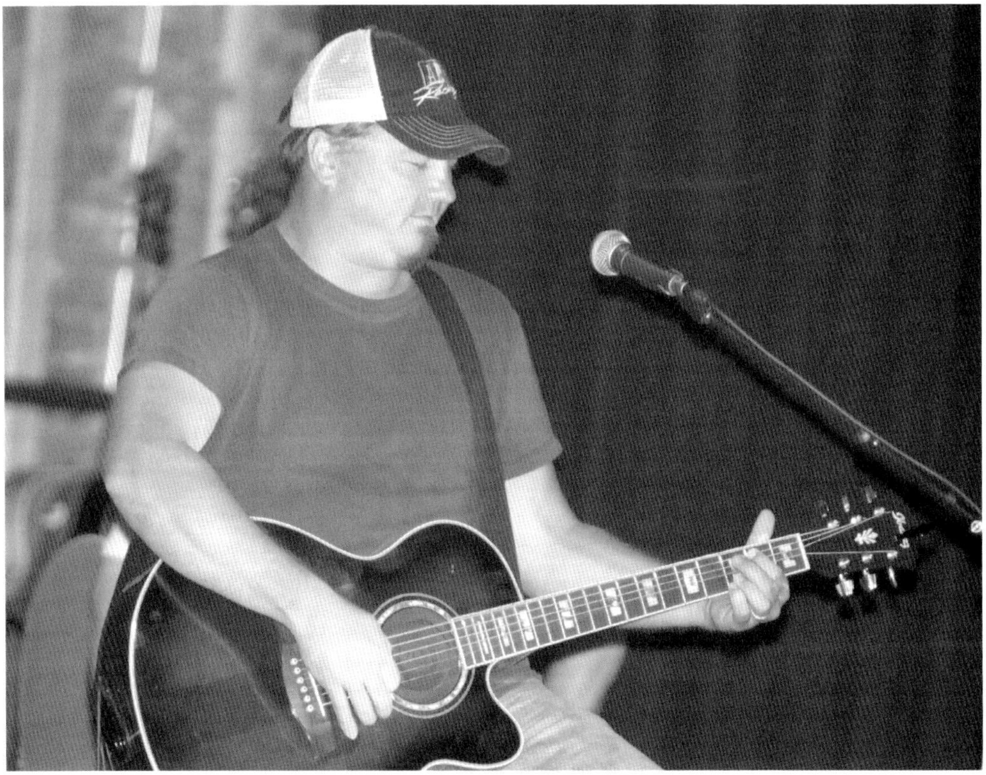

Edwin McCain

Edwin McCain found large audiences in the 1990s with his hit songs "I'll Be," a Top 5 song that has become a wedding favorite, and "Could Not Ask for More." But the Greenville singer-songwriter decided that superstardom was not for him and asked for release from his record deal with Atlantic Records. He releases new music independently and tours with his four-man band. (Courtesy of admedia/Shutterstock.com.)

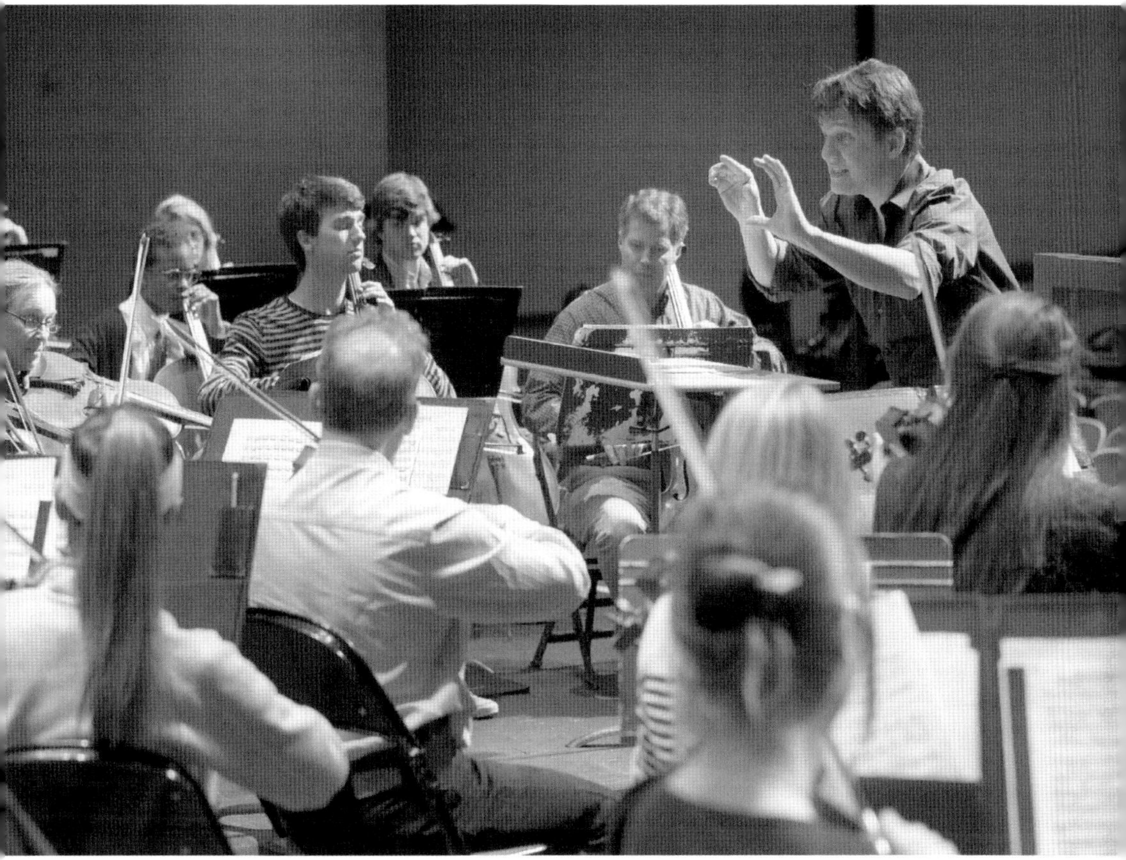

Keith Lockhart

When Keith Lockhart was a student at Furman University, he earned extra money playing the piano for an Elvis impersonator. Lockhart was named Boston Pops Orchestra musical director in 1995, becoming only the third man to lead the famous group since 1930, succeeding Arthur Fielder and composer-conductor John Williams. During his time as conductor, "America's Orchestra" performed the national anthem at major sporting events and dozens of television shows. Lockhart led the Utah Symphony from 1998 to 2009. While there, the symphony performed at the 2002 Olympics and on a European tour, the group's first in two decades. (Courtesy of Furman University.)

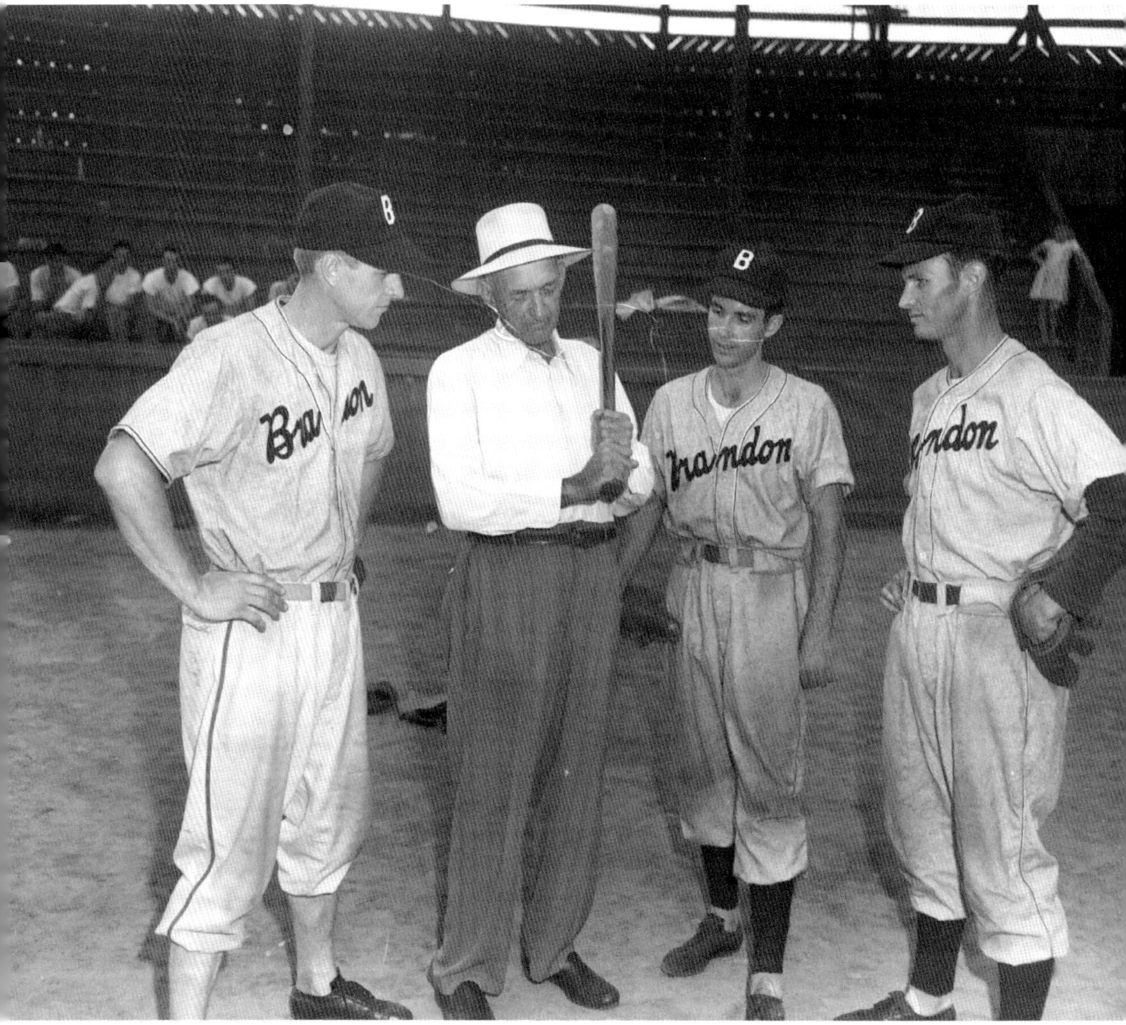
Brandon
Brandon

Shoeless Joe Jackson (OPPOSITE PAGE AND BELOW)
"Shoeless" Joe Jackson is considered by many, including Babe Ruth, as one of the greatest natural hitters to play major-league baseball. He has the third-highest major-league lifetime batting average at .356. But Jackson is best known for his role in the Black Sox scandal.

Although heavy favorites to win the 1919 World Series, the Chicago White Sox lost to the Cincinnati Reds. Afterward, Jackson and seven other White Sox players were accused of conspiring to throw the World Series. Jackson hit .375 during the series with 12 hits, six runs batted in, and one home run. Although acquitted at trial, judge Kenesaw Mountain Landis, baseball's first commissioner, banned them from the game for life.

In 1999, the US House of Representatives passed a resolution encouraging Major League Baseball to rescind the ban, a move that would make Jackson eligible for the National Baseball Hall of Fame.

Jackson started working as a "linthead" in a mill when he was six years old, and he never went to school because he was working 12-hour shifts. Jackson never learned to read or write; however, he could play baseball. He started playing for Brandon Mill in 1900 at age 13.

In 1908, he signed with the Greenville Spinners, the city's new semiprofessional team, for $75 a month. He earned his nickname that season after playing a game in his stocking feet after a pair of new baseball spikes gave him blisters. It was the only game he played without shoes. Philadelphia Athletics manager Connie Mack bought his contract in August 1908, and Jackson singled in his first major league at-bat. He was traded to Cleveland in 1910, and the next season, he hit .408 and set team records for hits, average and outfield assists. He was traded to the White Sox in 1915.

After his banishment from the majors, Jackson played and managed semiprofessional ball in Georgia and South Carolina. He moved back to Greenville in 1933 and operated a liquor store with his wife, Katie, until his death in 1951. (Opposite page, courtesy of Upcountry History Museum–Furman University; right, courtesy of Greenville County Historical Society.)

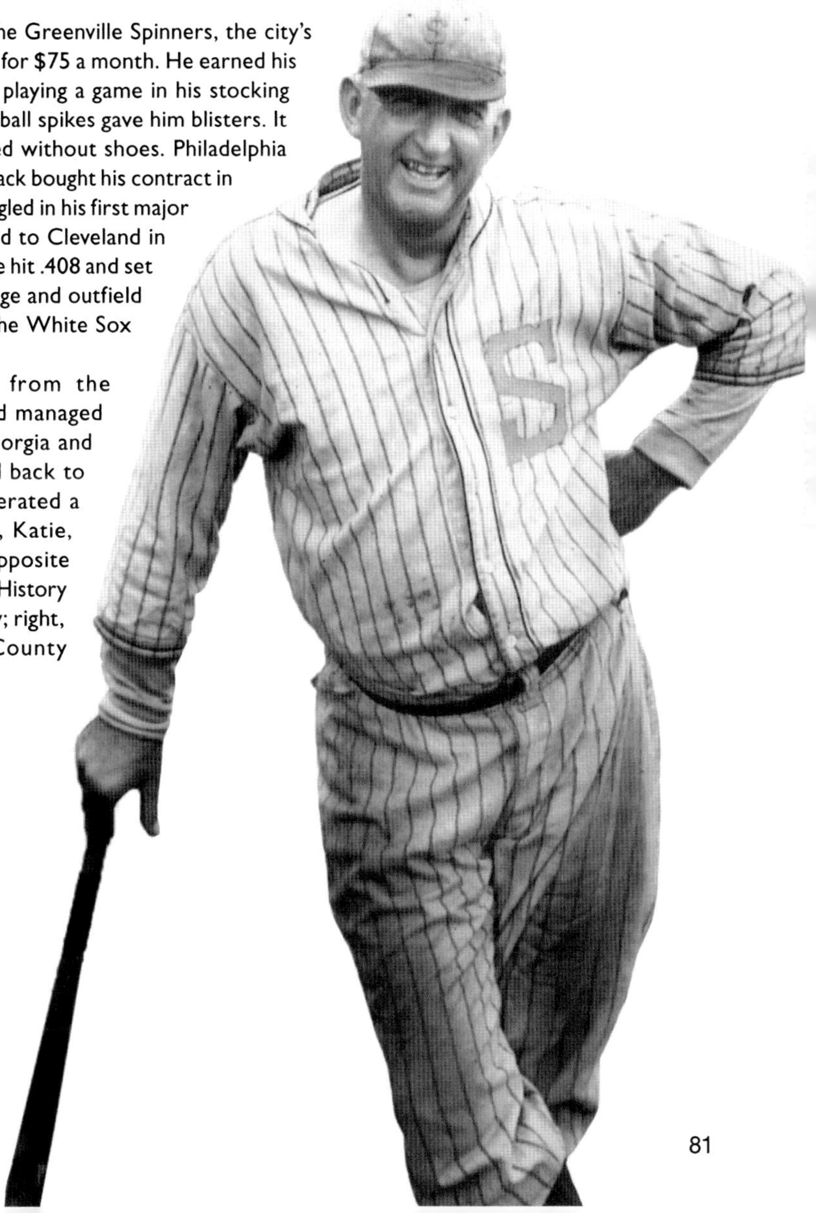

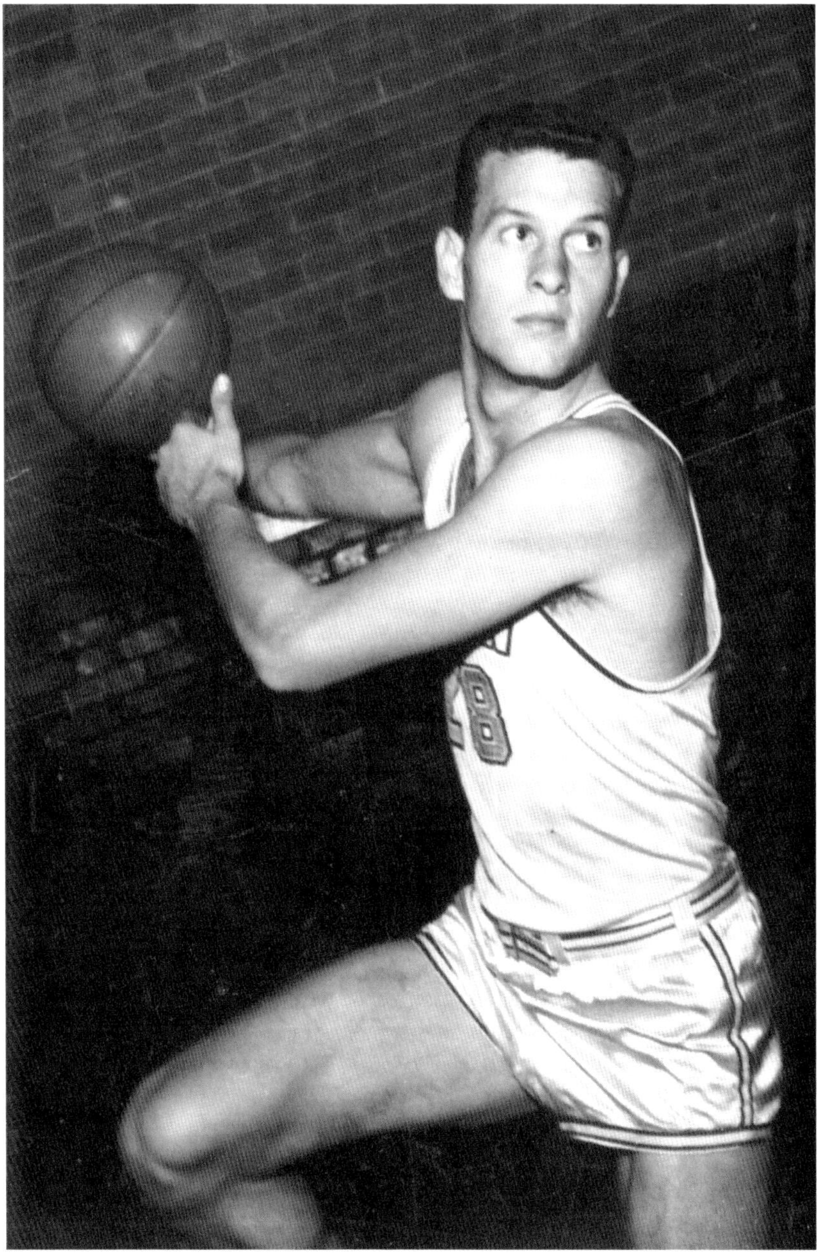

Frank Selvy

Frank Selvy took a lot of shots in his basketball career, but two stand out. The first one, a 40-foot shot in Furman's 1954 game against Newberry, went in and made him the first Division I college basketball player to score 100 points in a game. He missed the second shot. If the 18-foot baseline jumper in Game 7 of the 1962 National Basketball Association Finals against the Boston Celtics had gone in, it would have given the Los Angeles Lakers their first championship. Instead, the Celtics won in overtime. As a senior at Furman, Selvy averaged 41.7 points per game, the nation's best. He scored 1,209 points that season. His 100 points came on Frank Selvy Night. (Courtesy of Special Collections and Archives, Furman University.)

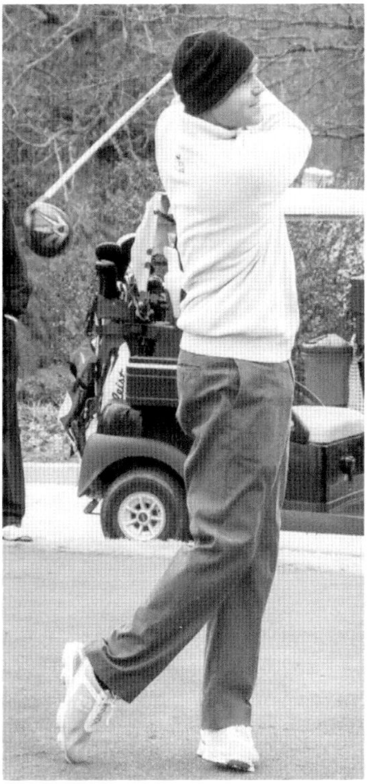

William "Bill" Haas

William Harland "Bill" Haas (top left) comes from Greenville's first family of golf. He is the son of former PGA Tour player Jay Haas, and his great-uncle Bob Goalby won the 1968 Masters. His brother and uncle are also former PGA Tour players. As of January 2015, Haas had won six PGA Tour tournaments. He also won the Ben Hogan Award, college golf's player of the year. (Photographs by Cindy Landrum.)

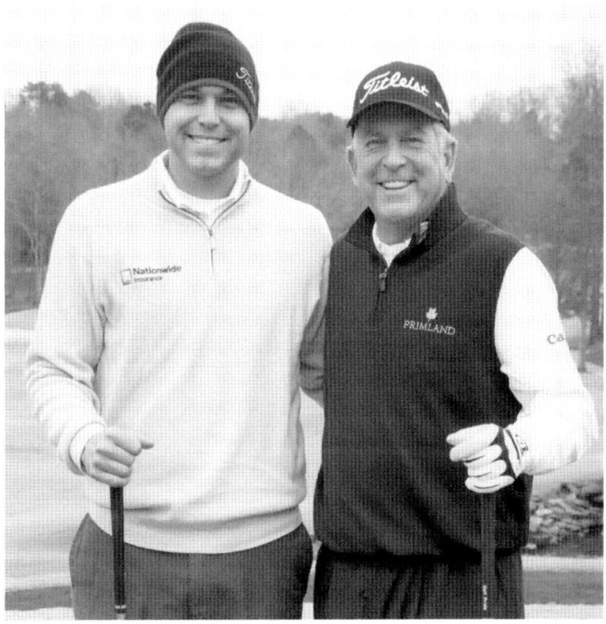

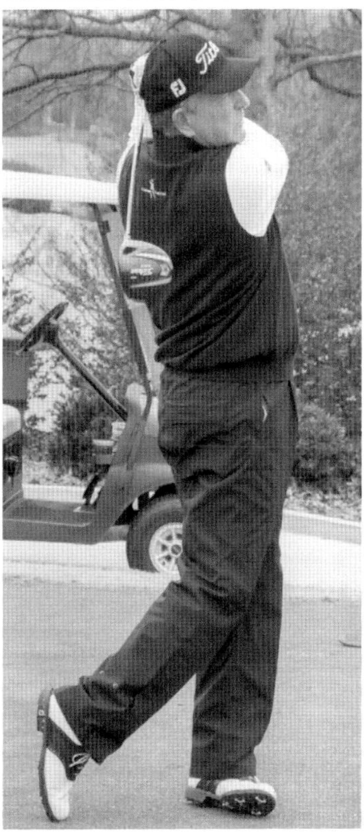

Jay Haas

During the 2014 Champions Tour, professional golfer Jay Haas (bottom left) shot over par in only two of the 64 rounds he played, the fewest ever by a player in a full season. In 2005, Haas and his son Bill became the first father-son duo to compete in the same US Open, twice. The PGA Tour selected him to be captain of the 2015 US Presidents Cup team. (Photographs by Cindy Landrum.)

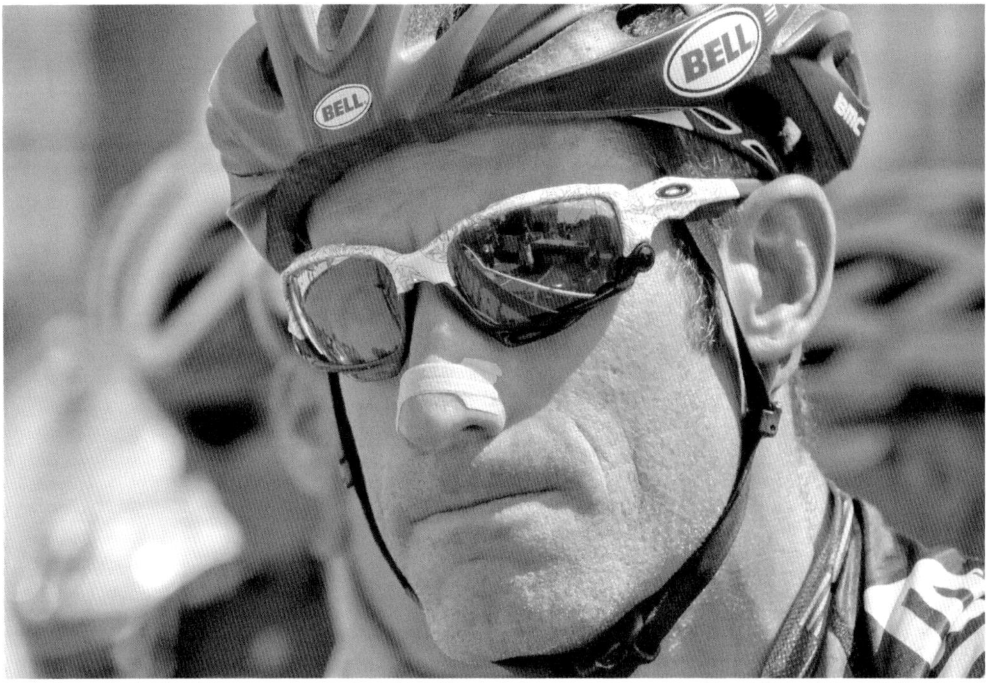

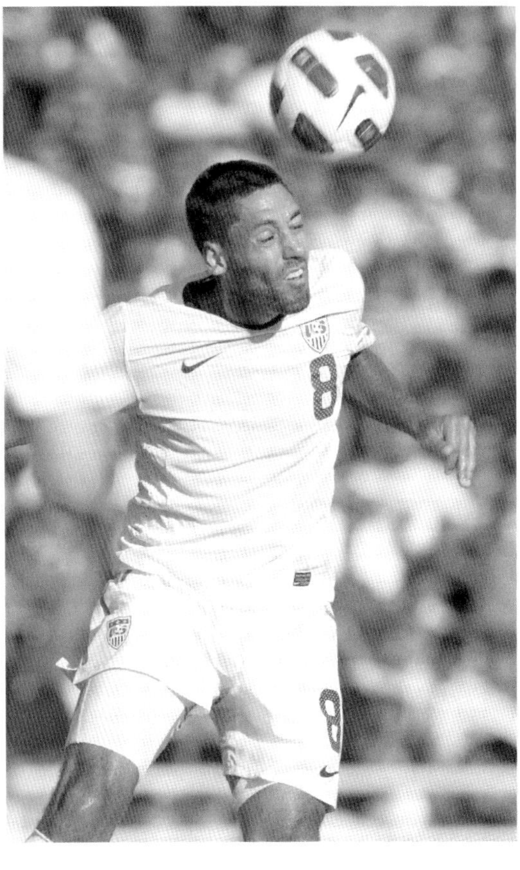

George Hincapie

Cyclist George Hincapie is a five-time Olympian, a three-time national road race champion, and the co-owner of a successful cycling apparel company and a mountain bed-and-breakfast. But he is best known as the *domestique* (assisting teammate) for Lance Armstrong during the former cycling champion's seven Tour de France victories. Armstrong's titles were stripped when he received a lifetime ban from cycling. Hincapie retired in 2012 and later admitted in a statement on his website that he used banned substances during part of his career. (Courtesy of Daniel Huerlimann-Beelde.)

Clint Dempsey

Clint Dempsey has had to prove himself his entire soccer career. He came to Furman University to play in one of the best collegiate soccer programs in the country despite not getting a full scholarship. Dempsey captained the 2014 United States World Cup team, and when he scored a goal against Ghana, he became the first American to score in three consecutive World Cups. (Courtesy of Photo Works.)

CHAPTER SIX

Educators

Greenville has long been a place of education innovation.

It started with Furman University's relocation from rural Winnsboro to downtown Greenville in 1851. Richard Furman, a clergyman many consider the most prominent Baptist leader before the Civil War, originally founded the school as a men's academy and theological institute in 1826.

Furman formed a close relationship with the Greenville Baptist Female College when it was established by the South Carolina Baptist Convention three years later. Eventually, Mary Camilla Judson, a discrete feminist, took over as principal of the female college. She started the college's Judson Literary Society, which was Greenville's first women's club. She introduced calisthenics and elocution.

Alberta Tucker Grimes fought for educational opportunities for preschool children of poor families.

Lawrence Peter Hollis, considered one of the greatest educators in South Carolina history, was beloved by mill workers and students and respected by community leaders. His years as superintendent of the Parker School District made him a Greenville hero. He made Parker School District and its high school a model program. He organized the state's first student government and Greenville's first science fair.

But Greenville's list of education heroes does not stop there. A.J. Whittenberg fought for equal education when he sued the Greenville County School District for denying his daughter the opportunity to attend the all-white school in his neighborhood.

Education pioneers included Joseph Allen Vaughn, handpicked to become Furman's first African American undergraduate student. Furman president John E. Johns led the school in its controversial split from the Southern Baptist Convention.

Margaret Ann Moon worked tirelessly to found a Catholic high school that many thought would never get built. Tom Barton opened a technical college on an old garbage dump. William Brown founded a charter school that strives to send students to college in a neighborhood where many do not earn high school diplomas.

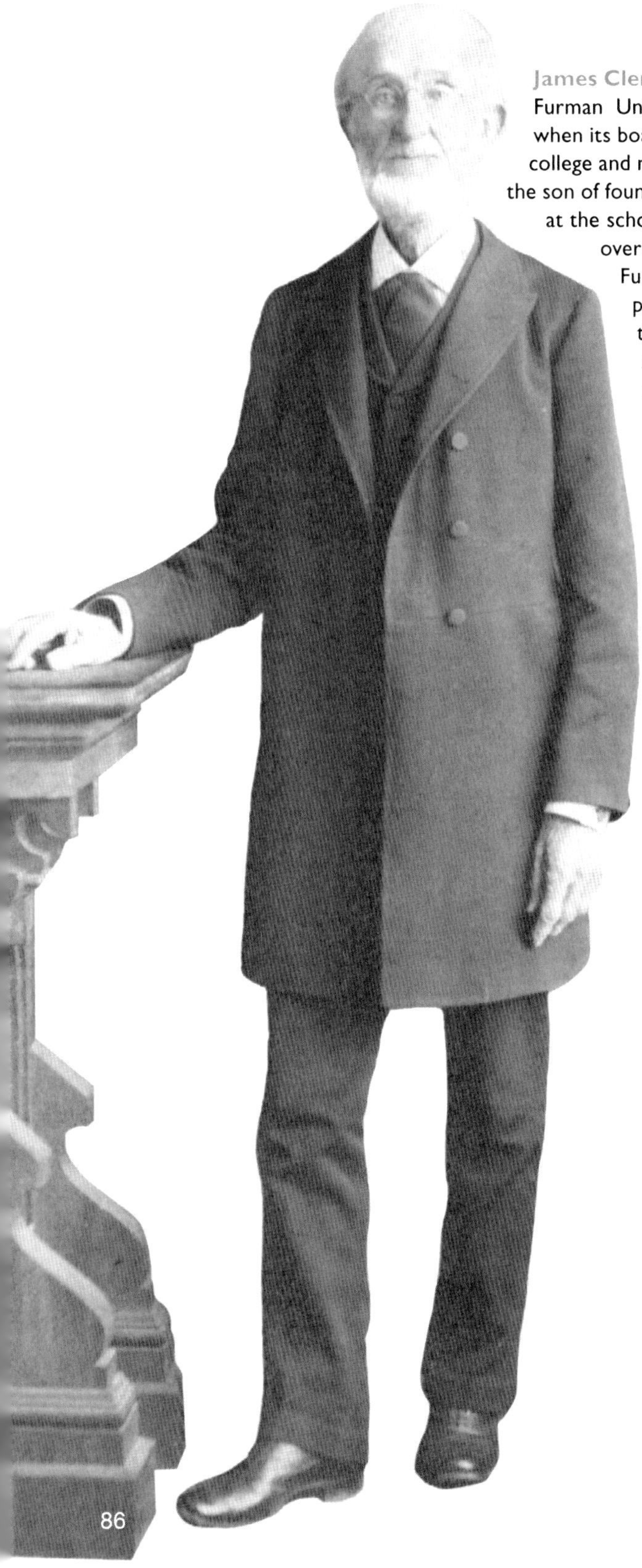

James Clement Furman

Furman University was a school to train ministers when its board of trustees decided to add a liberal-arts college and move it from Winnsboro. James C. Furman, the son of founder Richard Furman and a senior professor at the school, found land in 1850 for the new campus overlooking the Reedy River in Greenville. Furman served as the university's first president and preached for secession from the pulpits of Greenville's Baptist churches. After South Carolina had seceded, Furman returned to teaching, even though most of his students left to join the Confederate army. When the school reopened in 1866, the school had little money and was unable to collect bonds it issued before the Civil War. There was talk of closing the school, but Furman refused. (Courtesy of Special Collections and Archives, Furman University.)

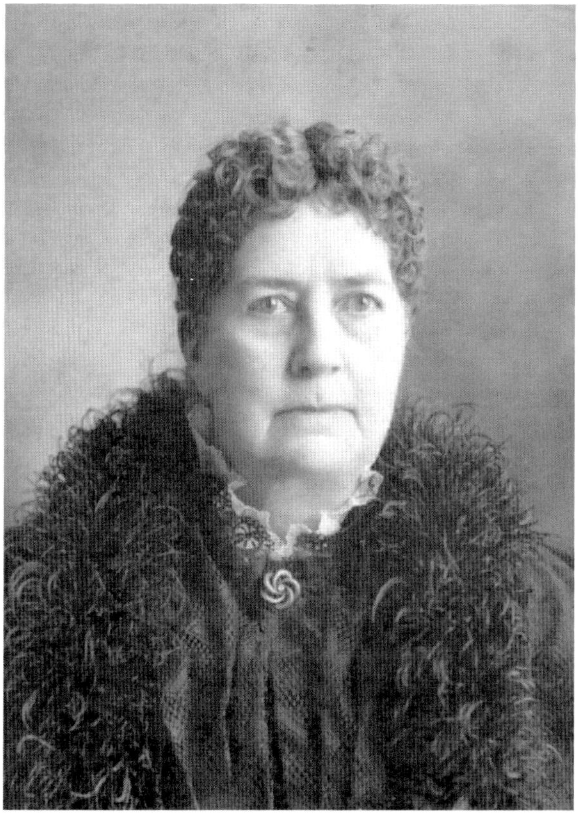

Mary Camilla Judson

Mary Camilla Judson served as principal of Greenville Female College even though she had not officially attended college.

Judson, born in 1828, had fulfilled all of the educational requirements of her local school in Connecticut by the age of 14. When a private institution run by a Yale University graduate opened nearby, she enrolled. She attended until 1845 when her family moved to New Haven, Connecticut. Although she was not allowed to enroll at Yale University, she attended many lectures and had access to the school's library.

She first came to Greenville to visit her brother Charles Judson, a mathematics professor at Furman University. She stayed in Greenville until 1860, when she left to teach at schools across the North. Her brother, then president of Greenville Female College, asked her to return to Greenville in 1874 to help run the school.

Judson organized the school's first club, the Judson Literary Society, and started a school library funded by assessing literary-society members 25¢ per term. Judson later said the library had a "choice collection of high-toned literary works." She implemented a calisthenics class and started a class in elocution so the women would develop public-speaking skills. Additionally, she taught English, French, drawing, logic, astronomy, and botany.

"No matter what she taught, no student in her classes left G.F.C. in those years without carrying away in her mind the lasting impression of a great teacher," a later president was quoted as saying in *Greenville: Woven From The Past.*

In 1894, when the college's president resigned and started a new private school next door, Judson loaned the school her life savings of $30,000. She eventually turned the loan into a gift. Mary Camilla Judson retired but continued to live on campus until her death on December 29, 1920. (Courtesy of Special Collections and Archives, Furman University.)

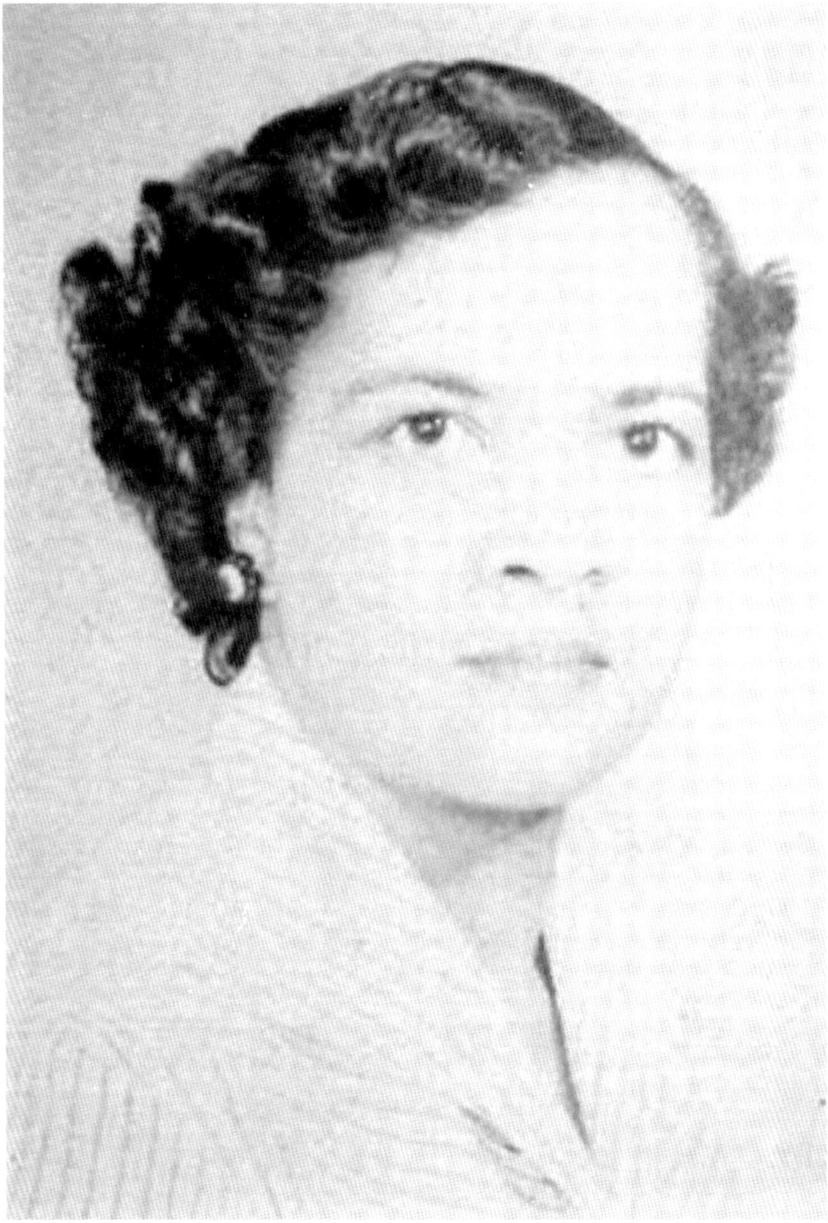

Alberta Tucker Grimes

When school counselor Alberta Tucker Grimes heard about the creation of a Head Start project as part of Pres. Lyndon Johnson's Great Society program, she wanted to find out more. She made a trip to Washington, DC, at her expense to get the information. As a result, the first Head Start program funded in South Carolina started in Greenville, a grant paid to educate 450 preschool children from disadvantaged homes. Grimes considered it her most significant achievement. "The need for preschool education was so urgent," she was quoted in her biography for the South Carolina African-American History Calendar. "I always resented discrimination; all children should have the same opportunities." Grimes's application was used by 15 other South Carolina counties to establish their own Head Start programs. (Courtesy of the Greenville Cultural Exchange Center.)

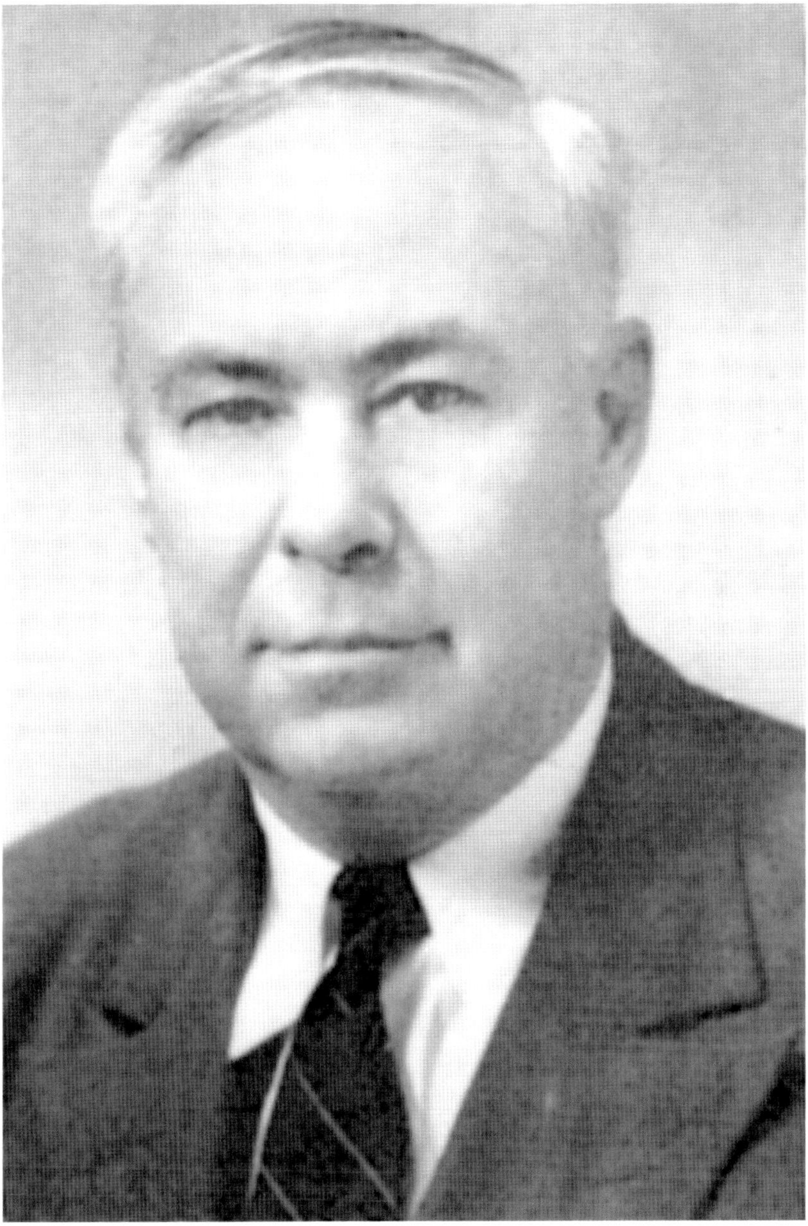

Lawrence Peter "Dr. Pete" Hollis

Lawrence Peter "Dr. Pete" Hollis is considered one of the greatest educators in South Carolina history. Hollis was the first superintendent of the Parker School District, formed to educate the children of Monaghan Mill textile workers. In 1949, *Look* magazine called Hollis one of the 100 finest educators in America. Hollis introduced vocational education to Parker, and he founded the county's first adult-education center. But educator is not Hollis's only title. He established the state's first Boy Scout troop, organized the Greenville Senior Citizens' Center, and started the Singing Christmas Tree. He was crucial in establishing the Greenville County Library. When he met Dr. James Naismith, the inventor of basketball, he brought the sport to Greenville and organized the first basketball game in South Carolina. (Courtesy of the Greenville County Historical Society.)

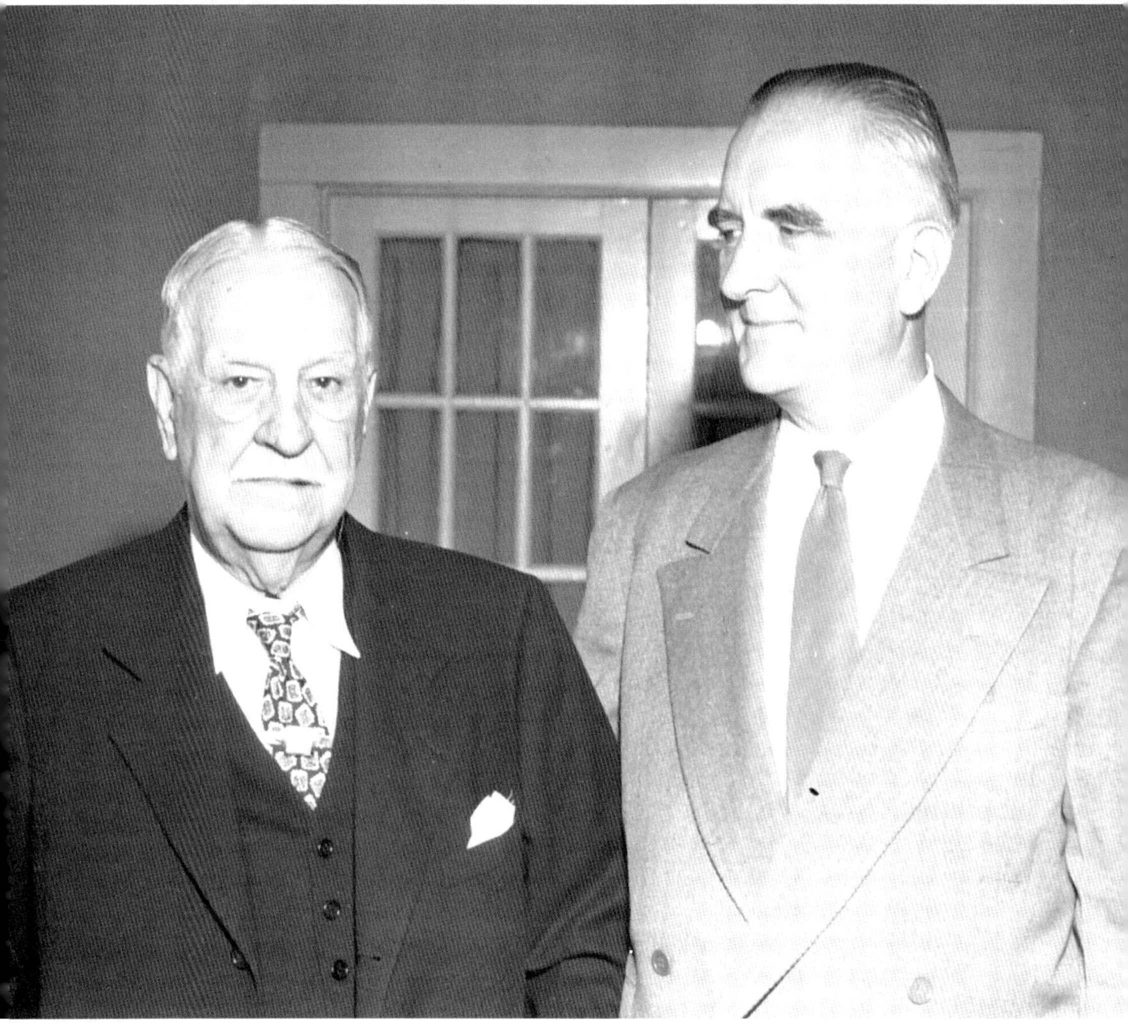

John Laney Plyler

First as dean of Furman's short-lived law school and then as the university's president, John Laney Plyler proved he could handle challenging situations. After the school failed its first accreditation examination for inadequate law library and classroom facilities, Plyler, a former judge, corrected the problems. But the school's accreditation coincided with the Great Depression, and enrollment plummeted. The law school could not meet changing rules. The problems threatened the university's accreditation, so the law school closed. As president, he was able to attract military training programs to the campus during World War II when male enrollment dropped. Plyler is the school's longest-serving president, holding the position from 1939 to 1964. The school moved from downtown Greenville to its campus on Poinsett Highway during that time. He is pictured on the right with businessman Alester Garden Furman. (Courtesy of Special Collections and Archives, Furman University.)

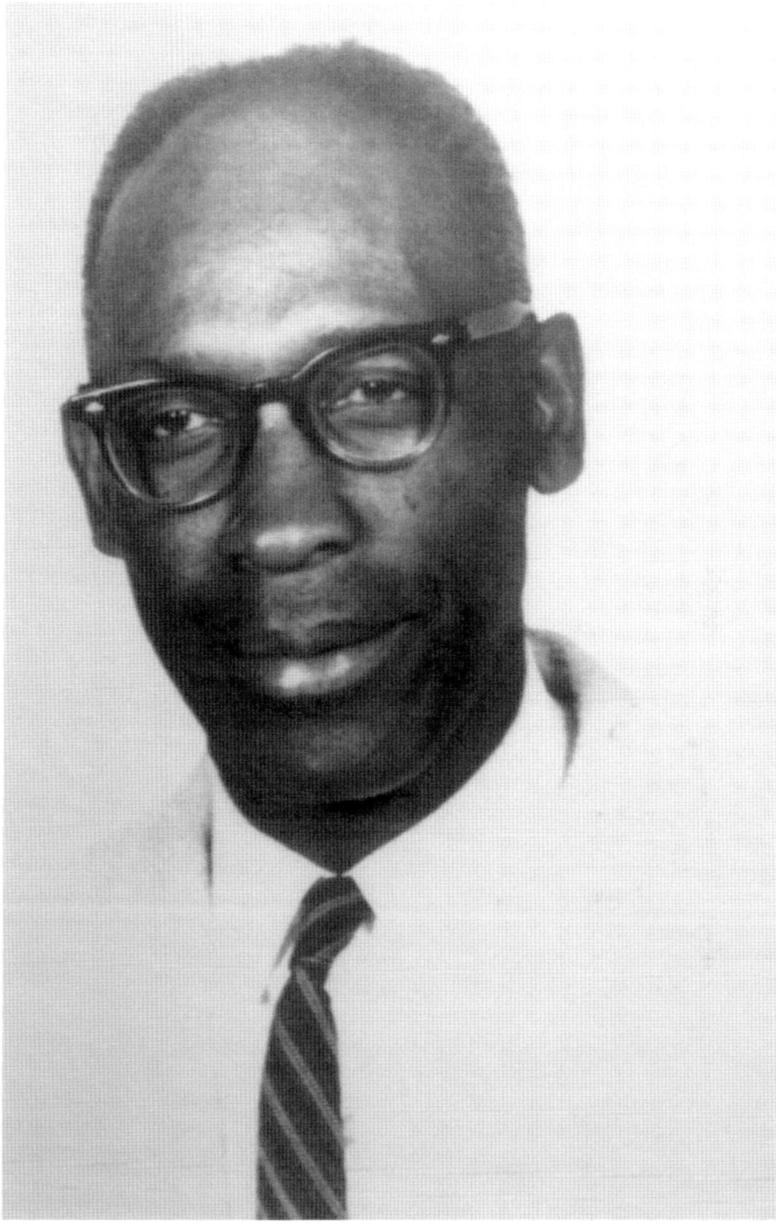

A.J. Whittenberg

When A.J. Whittenberg attended a Democratic Party meeting at the whites-only Anderson Road Elementary School, he noticed the current and unmarred textbooks. His daughter's all-black school had well-worn hand-me-downs. Whittenberg and five other parents sued the Greenville County School District in 1963 after it denied a request for their children to attend a white school. People stopped trading with his service station, and two white men offered him a Chevrolet truck and $2,500 to drop his lawsuit. He refused. Playing an important role in desegregating Greenville County public schools was not Whittenberg's first foray into fighting for civil rights. He championed voting rights and participated in a boycott of white taxicab companies after the lynching of black cabbie Willie Earle. (Courtesy of the Greenville Cultural Exchange Center.)

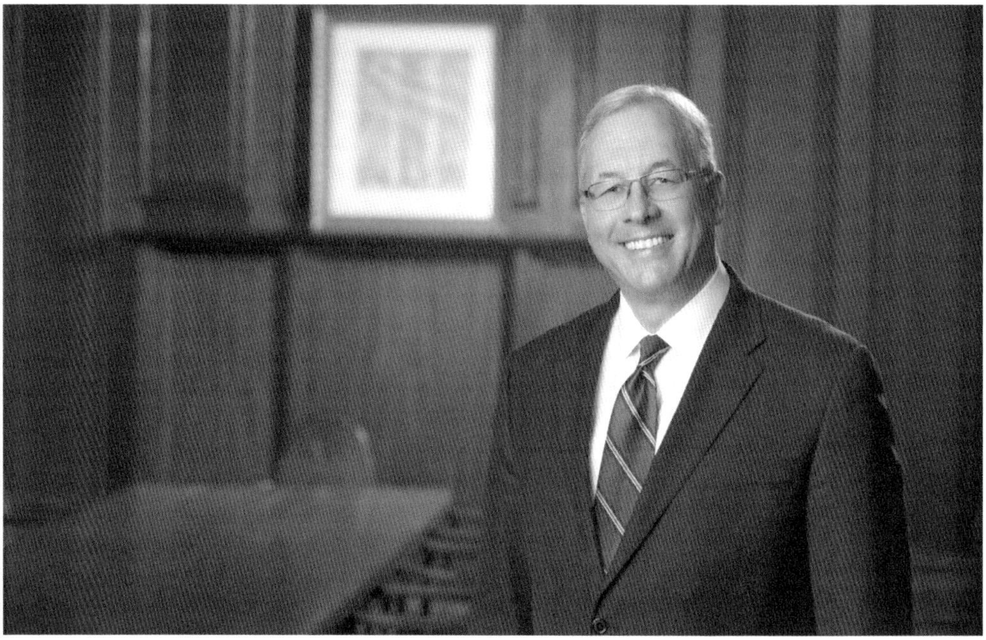

Stephen D. Pettit
When he was named president of Bob Jones University in May 2014, Stephen D. Pettit Sr. became the university's fifth president since its founding in 1927 and the first without the last name of Jones. His mother's maiden name is Jones, however. Pettit, who traveled the world evangelizing, had served on the school's board of trustees prior to his presidential appointment. (Courtesy of Bob Jones University.)

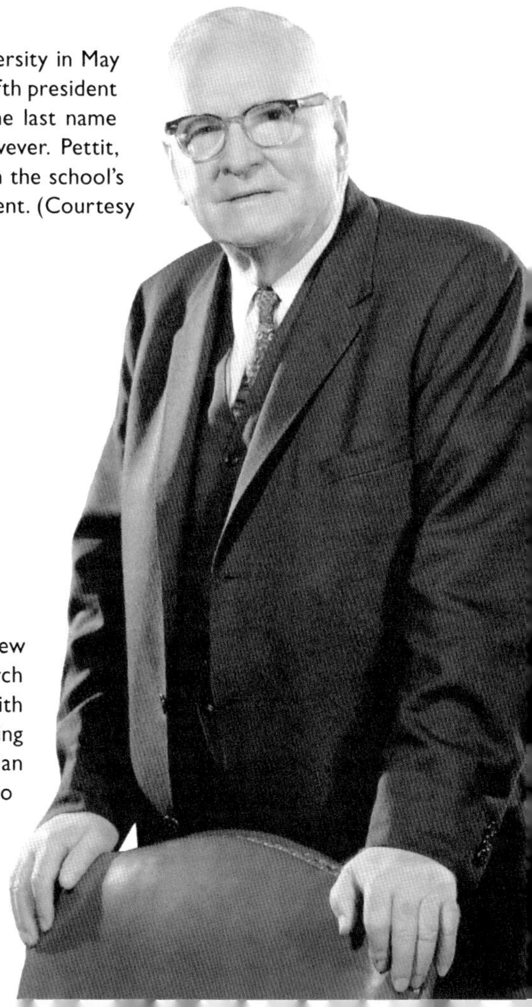

Bob Jones Sr.
During the 1920s, evangelist Bob Jones Sr. grew increasingly concerned about children of church members going off to college and rejecting the faith of their parents. In 1925, he told his wife he was going to start a conservative nondenominational Christian college. It opened in 1927 in Florida and moved to Tennessee in 1933. Bob Jones Jr. became president in 1947, just before the institution moved to Greenville. (Courtesy of Bob Jones University.)

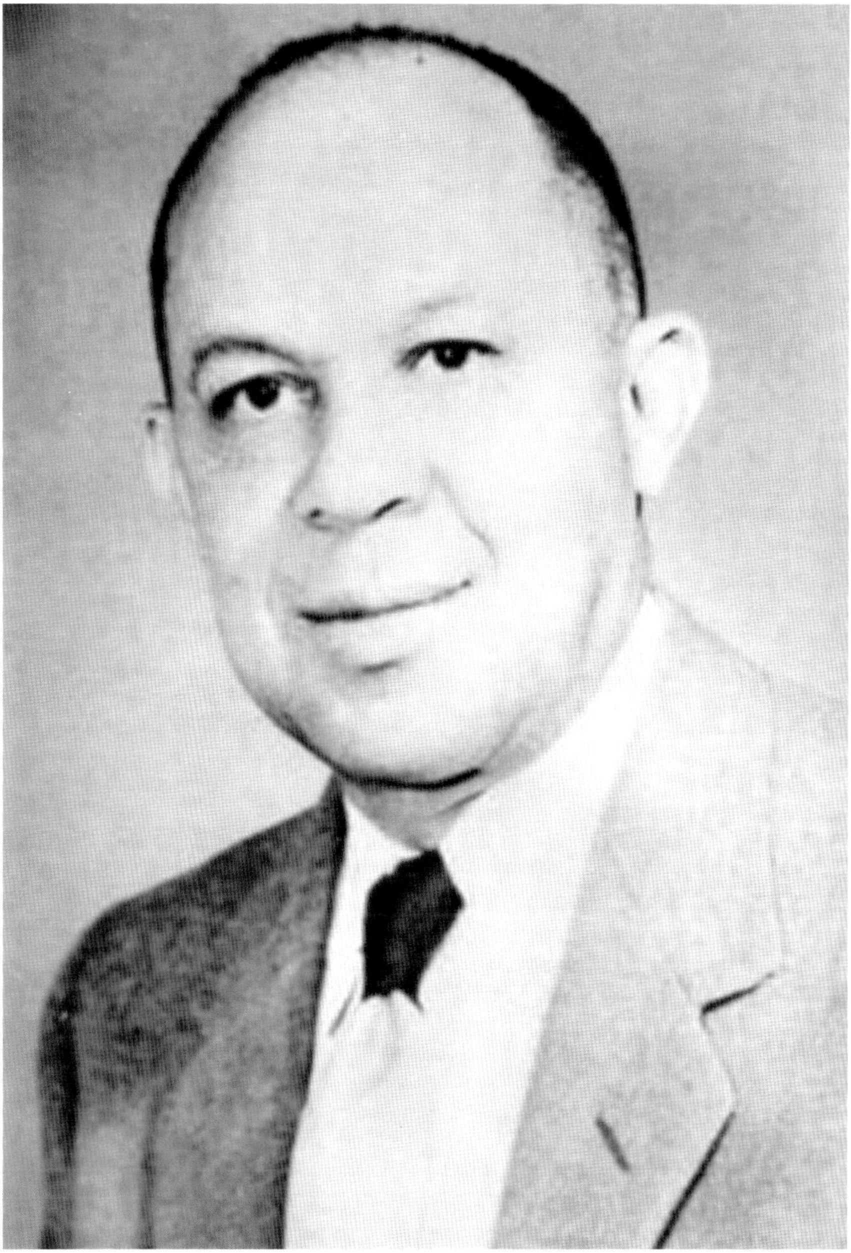

Dr. Joseph E. Beck

Dr. Joseph E. Beck served as principal of Sterling High School for two decades. During his reign, Sterling added a 12th grade. The beloved educator broadened the curriculum, giving students the opportunity to take trade courses and study science. In 1953, the school received accreditation from the Southern Association of Colleges and Schools. Beck retired in 1960 after working more than 30 years in the school district. Four years later, the school board decided to name a new school, built to relieve overcrowding at Sterling High, Joseph E. Beck High School. It opened in August 1965, and the school operated as a high school for only four years. It is now a middle school. (Courtesy of the Greenville Cultural Exchange Center.)

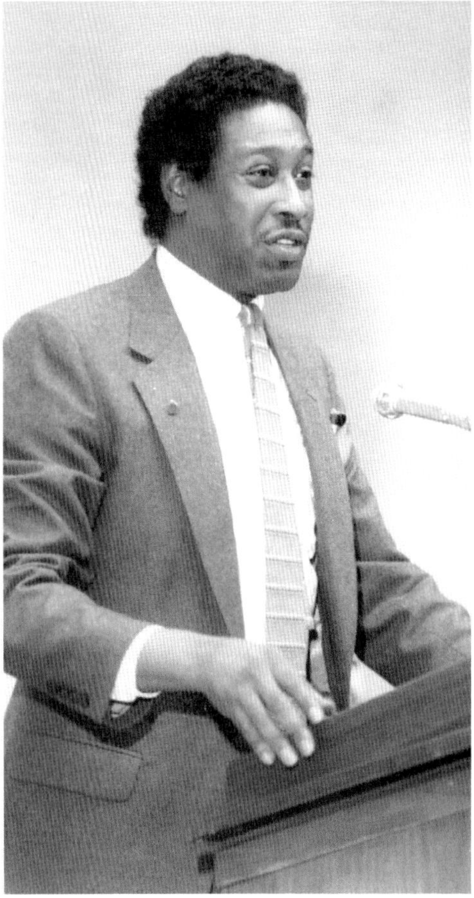

Joseph Allen Vaughn

When Joseph Allen Vaughn walked into a Furman University classroom on February 2, 1965, to become the first African American undergraduate student at the school, he was not trying to be a trailblazer. He was just trying to get the best education possible.

In October 1963, the Furman trustees voted to consider applications from "all qualified applicants," and a school representative started looking for the right African American student. The student needed a strong academic and leadership record and a personality that could handle the pressures of desegregation.

That was Vaughn, a Sterling High School student who graduated third in his class. He was also president of the student body, vice president of the National Honor Society, president of the school's French and Physics Clubs, and a member of the student newspaper and yearbook staffs. He also was president of the Greenville and Southeastern NAACP youth chapters.

Furman trustees voted to delay desegregation, so Vaughn attended the all-black Johnson C. Smith University in Charlotte, North Carolina, for one semester. In December 1964, the trustees reaffirmed the school's nondiscriminatory admission policy.

In an April 1986 talk on "Racial Integration at Furman: 21 Years Later," Vaughn said he could remember nothing he would consider a negative racial incident, but he admitted there were students who probably wished he was not there.

"I readily realized that this was going to be new experience not only for Joe Vaughn, but also for the some-2,000 white students, most of whom had never gone to school with a black student," Vaughn said in the speech.

Vaughn majored in English and minored in French. He joined the Pershing Rifles and the Baptist Student Union, served as chairman of a committee that organized forums to discuss race relations, and acted in at least two plays. He was a cheerleader his senior year.

Vaughn, born into a poor single-parent family, graduated cum laude in 1968.

He worked as an English teacher in the Greenville County School District from 1969 to 1982. He was English department chairman at Hughes Middle School and served as president of the Greenville County Association of Teachers. In 1981, he served as president of the South Carolina Education Association.

Vaughn retired from teaching in 1982, and he died in 1991. (Courtesy of Special Collections and Archives, Furman University.)

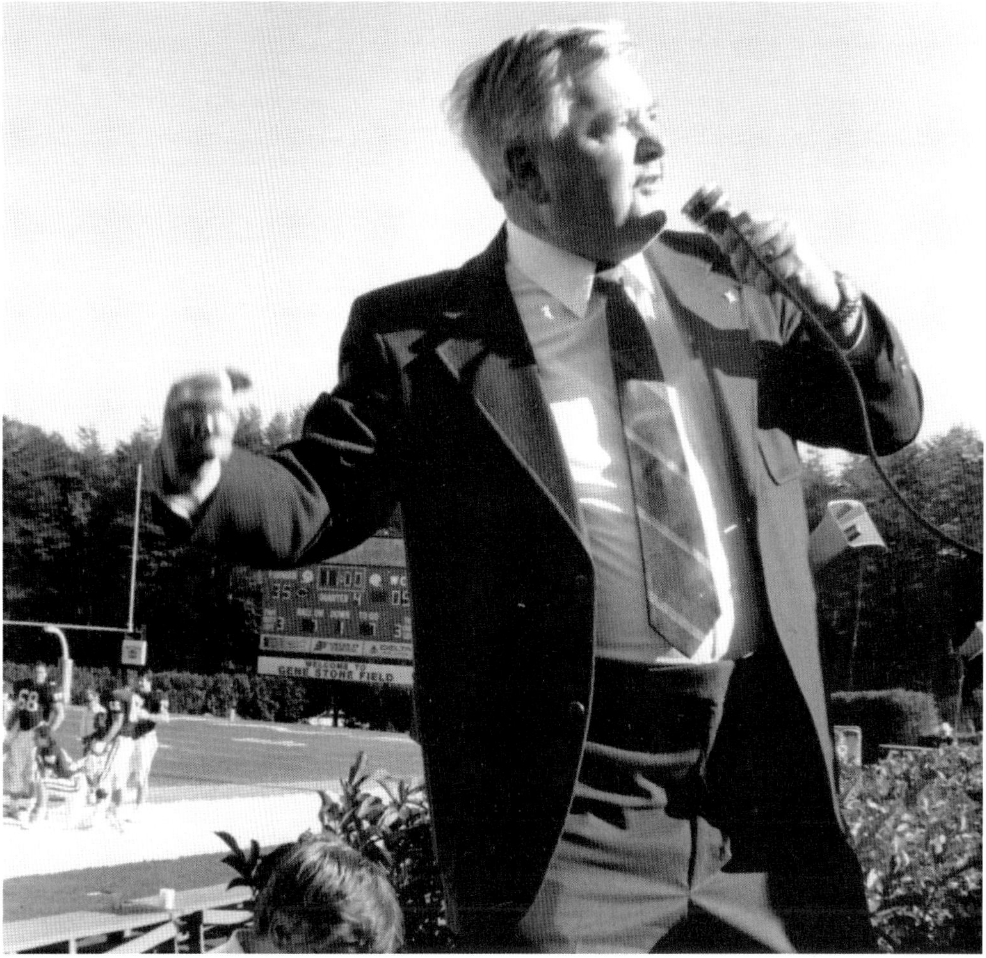

Dr. John E. Johns

During his 18 years as Furman University president, Dr. John E. Johns was known as an irreverent but dynamic leader.

Johns led the school from 1976 to 1994 and was president during its tumultuous split with the South Carolina Baptist Convention as a result of trustees fearing fundamentalists would gain a majority on the board and threaten the school's academic freedom. The *Greenville News* quoted Johns in a story about Furman's 175th anniversary as saying, "The separation was best for Furman and best for the South Carolina Baptist Convention."

He led the school through two capital campaigns that raised more than $115 million.

But it he was his approachability that endeared him to students. When a group of students showed up at the front door of White Oaks, Furman's president's house, at midnight, he answered the door in his pajamas and a bomber jacket. When he learned they were there to wish him a happy birthday, he invited them in for cake.

Johns was famous for leaving his presidential box during football games to lead a cheer. "FU one time, FU two times, FU three times, FU all the time," he would shout with a Southern drawl into a megaphone to the delight of the crowd.

Johns, who died in 2007, was a World War II bombardier who flew 35 combat missions in the European theater aboard B-17s. He received the Distinguished Flying Cross and the Air Medal with three oak leaf clusters. (Courtesy of Special Collections and Archives, Furman University.)

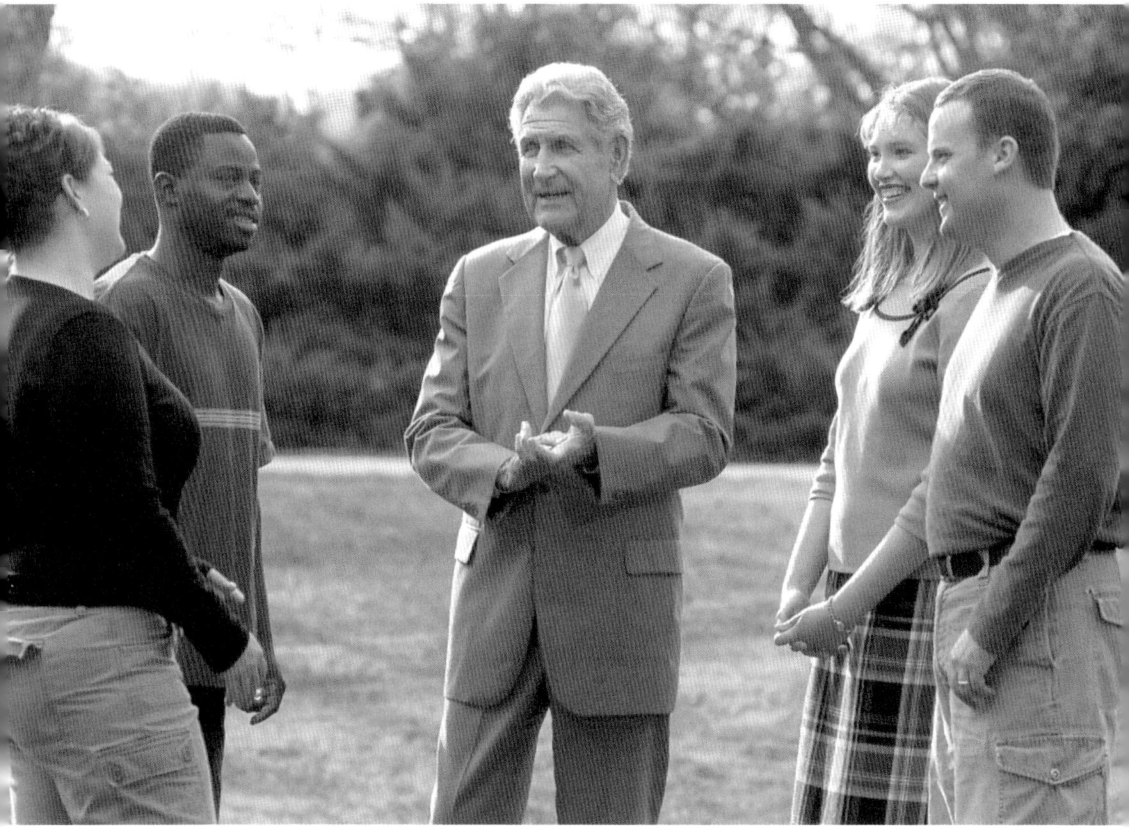

Dr. Thomas E. Barton Jr.

When Dr. Thomas E. Barton Jr. was an All-American defensive lineman on the Clemson University football team, he earned the nickname "Black Cat." During his long career in education, some called him "Mr. Greenville Tech."

The Pittsburgh Steelers drafted Barton in the sixth round of the NFL draft, but his professional career was over before it started when he injured his knee in a college all-star game at Chicago's Soldier Field. Bobby Dodd, the Georgia Tech coach who was coaching the all-star game, helped him get a teaching and football coaching job in Atlanta.

Barton returned to South Carolina a few years later and worked as a teacher, coach, and superintendent. Then-governor Fritz Hollings was his playing partner in a charity golf tournament and told him he was thinking about starting a technical college system. The man who was hired to run Greenville Technical College resigned for personal reasons before the school opened. Barton, who was in Greenville for training so he could open a technical college in Charleston, got the job. "I guess it was destiny, something that was just meant to be," Barton told the *Greenville Journal* in a 2007 interview.

Greenville Tech rose from an abandoned city landfill on Pleasantburg Drive, and it opened in 1962 with one building, 12 full-time instructors, and 800 students. By the time Barton retired as president, it had four campuses, more than 15,000 students, and was the third-largest institution of higher education in South Carolina.

Barton was the longest-serving college president in the country when he retired in 2008 at age 79. (Courtesy of Fred Rollison Photography.)

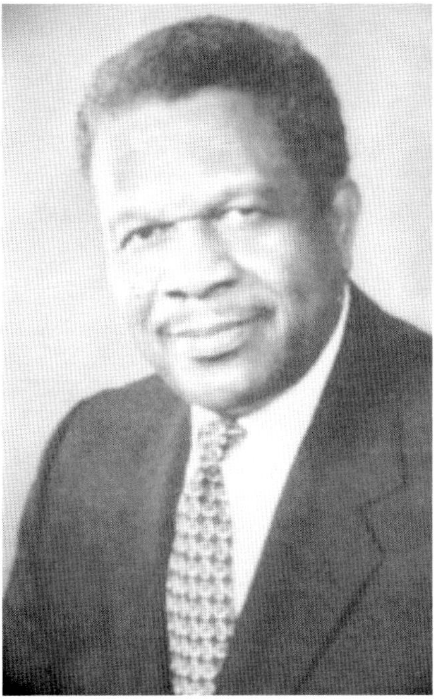

Dr. Thomas Elliott Kerns

When Dr. Thomas Elliott Kerns attended the all-black Sterling High School, he never imagined he would eventually lead an integrated Greenville County School District. Kerns became his hometown's first African American school superintendent in 1989. He returned to his alma mater to teach social studies and French before advancing in the administrative ranks. (Courtesy of the Greenville Cultural Exchange Center.)

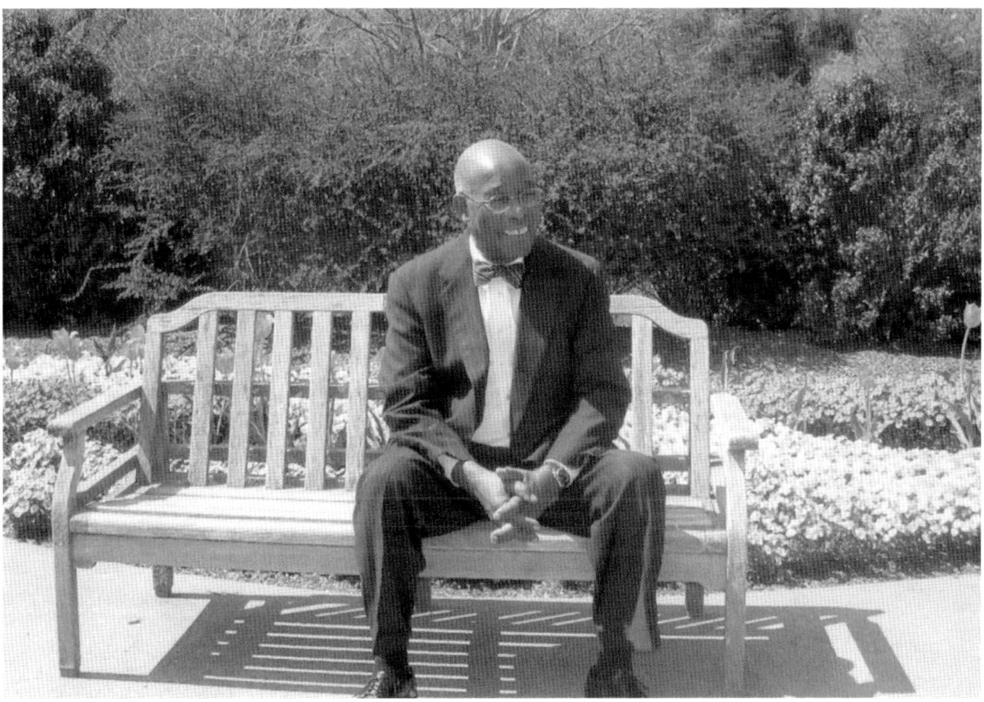

Dr. Rudolph Gordon

Dr. Rudolph Gordon took teaching classes as a backup in case he could not find an engineering job. He started as a math teacher in 1959. "Teaching, done right, is perhaps the most difficult job there is," he told the *Greenville News*. He retired as Greenville County School District superintendent, and he led the creation of the district's education plan and a makeover of its schools. (Courtesy of Melanie Gordon.)

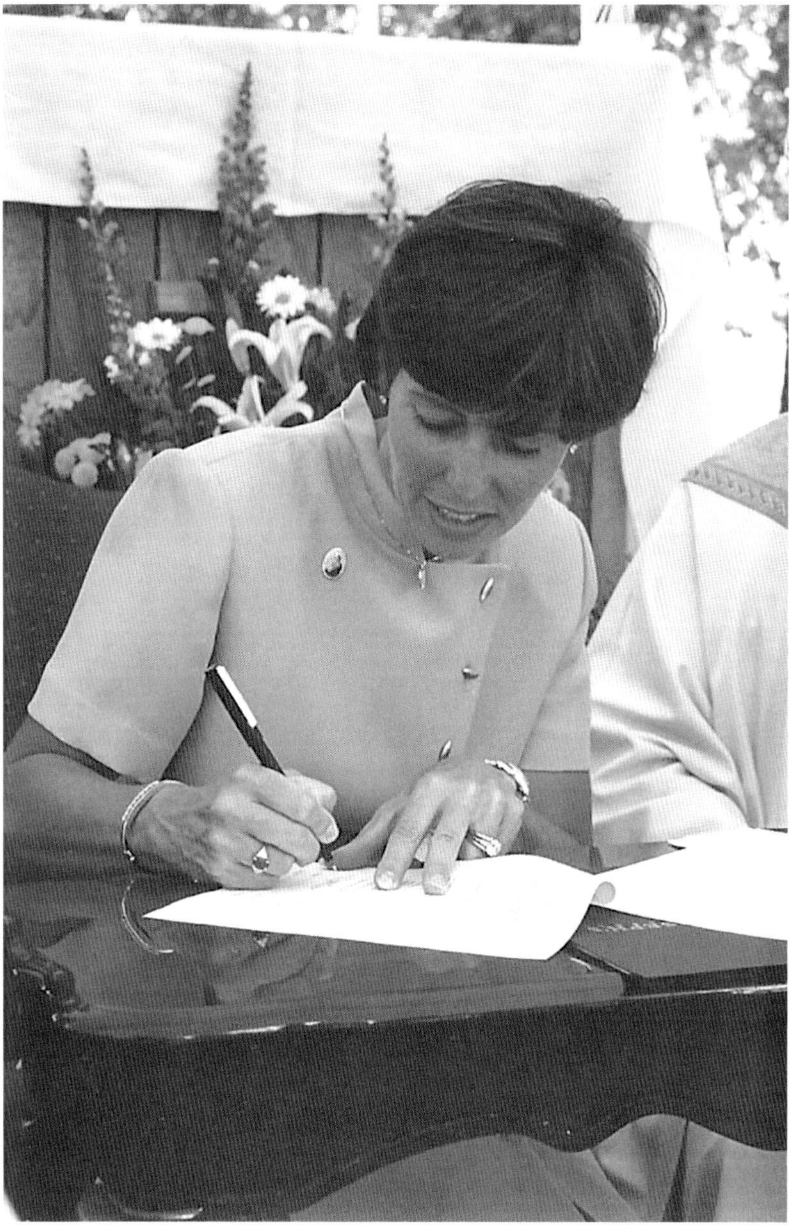

Margaret Ann Moon
At times, the dream of starting a Catholic high school in Greenville seemed impossible to St. Joseph's Catholic School's nine original founders. But Margaret Ann Moon did not let that stop her. As founding board chair, Moon took the lead as the founders faced one hurdle after another. They started with an $800 donation from her mother, $200 of which was used to produce a newsletter. In a video made by the school in 2012, Moon said one night in prayer she asked God what he wanted from her. "A Catholic high school. I heard it in my ear, and I heard it in my heart," Moon said. The school opened in 1993 in a small house leased from St. Michael's Lutheran Church, and it had 13 students. The school now has a 36-acre campus on Interstate 85. In January 2015, the school dedicated a chapel that sits in its center, another one of Moon's visions. (Courtesy of St. Joseph's Catholic School.)

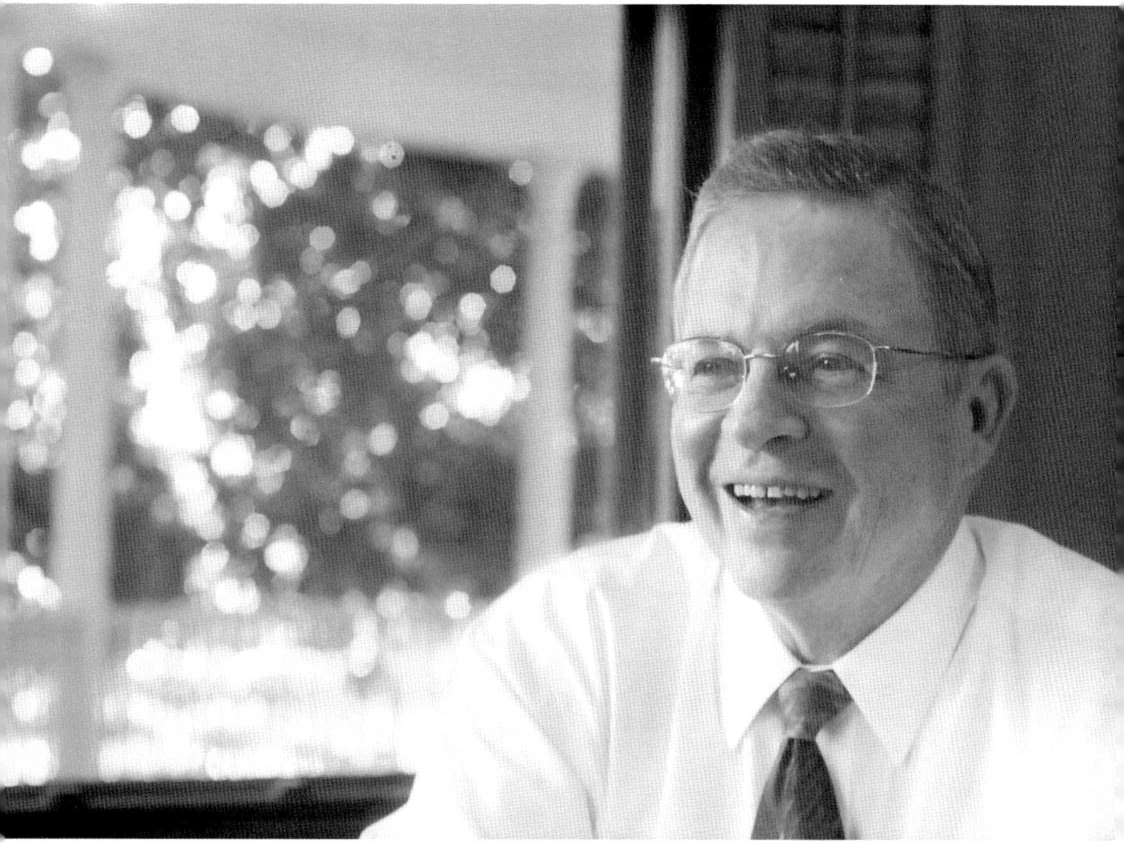

William Brown
William Brown does not think the zip code in which a child grows up should determine his or her future success. In 2010, Brown decided to found a charter school that has high academic standards, a college focus for each student starting in kindergarten, and daily physical education. Part of the school's financial support comes from Campbell Young Leaders, a foundation created by Brown's mentor, the late Bob Campbell, vice president of Vulcan Materials. Campbell talked about leveling the playing field. Brown, who is from Gaffney, wanted to be a doctor until he spent 1968 in Vietnam. After he came home, he enrolled in the Citadel and graduated in 1971 with a degree in accounting. (Courtesy of the *Greenville Journal*.)

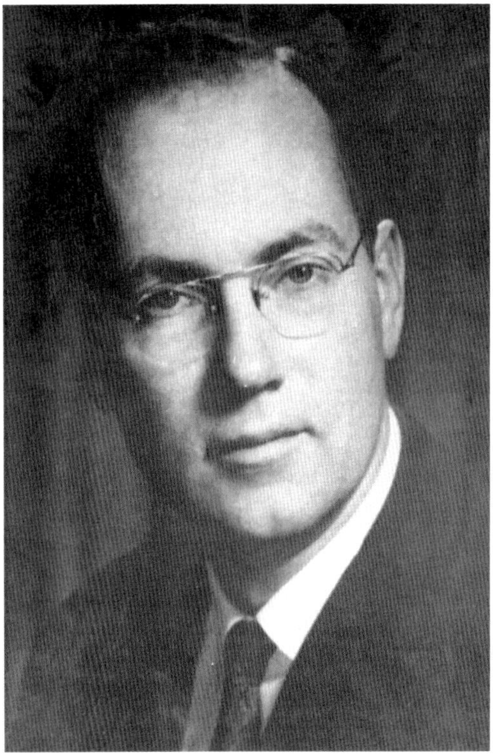

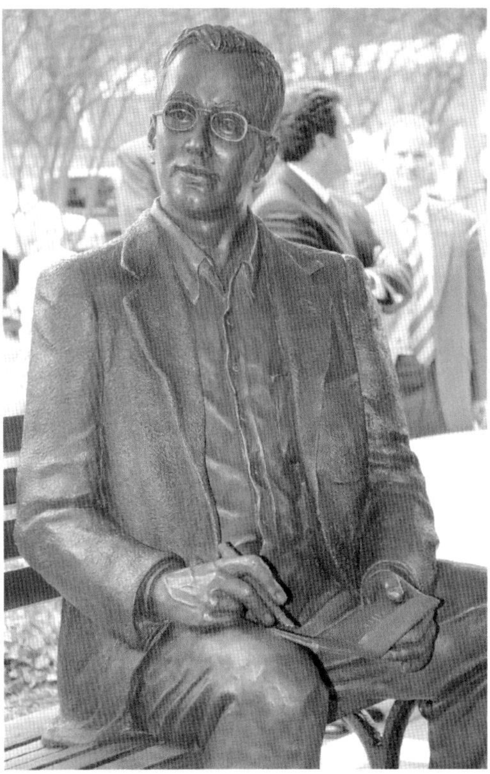

Dr. Charles H. Townes

When Dr. Charles H. Townes scribbled on a piece of scrap paper the theory that would lead to the laser, he transformed everyday life. It was 1951, and scientists were trying to figure out how to create a pure beam of short-wavelength, high-frequency light. Townes, a 1935 Furman University graduate, built the first microwave amplifier—the maser—and shared the 1964 Nobel Prize in Physics with two Russians for the invention of the laser. Dr. Townes developed radar bombing systems during World War II, advised presidents and government commissions on lunar landings, and helped discover the black hole at the center of the Milky Way. In 2005, he won the Templeton Prize for contributions to spiritual understanding. Townes died in January 2015 at the age of 99. (Above, courtesy of Special Collections and Archives, Furman University; below, courtesy of the *Greenville Journal*.)

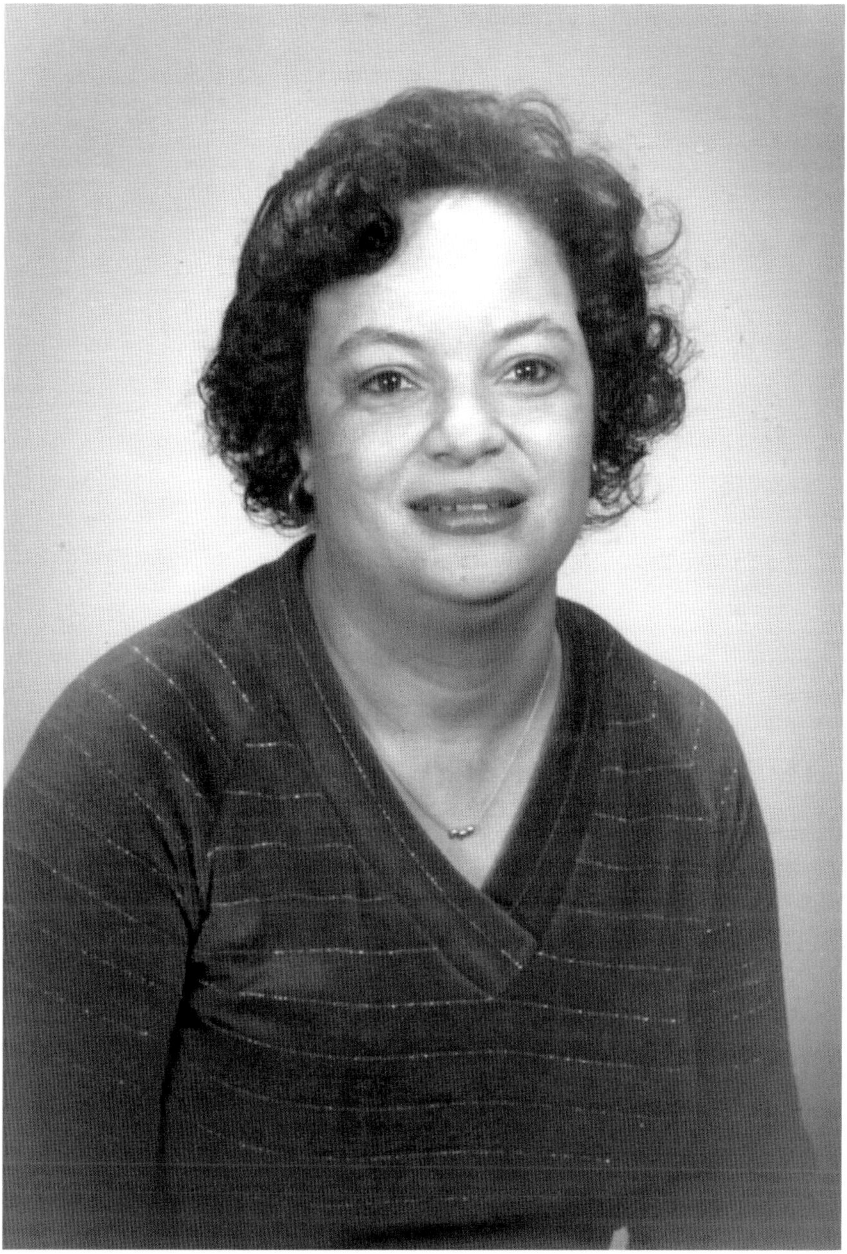

Ruth Ann Butler

Ruth Ann Butler *taught* history for 18 years in Greenville County schools, but her true purpose is to *preserve* history. Butler founded the Greenville Cultural Exchange Center, Greenville's only museum dedicated to black history, in 1987. The idea came from Butler's sister, who invited her to visit the Beck Cultural Center in Tennessee. Like the people whose history it preserves, the center's journey has not been easy. The city condemned its building in 2001, giving Butler one hour to get out. It took two years to raise the money needed for repairs and to reopen. Today, funding remains tight, but overcoming challenges is nothing new for Butler, the ninth of 10 children, and born with cerebral spastic infantile paralysis. (Courtesy of the Greenville Cultural Exchange Center.)

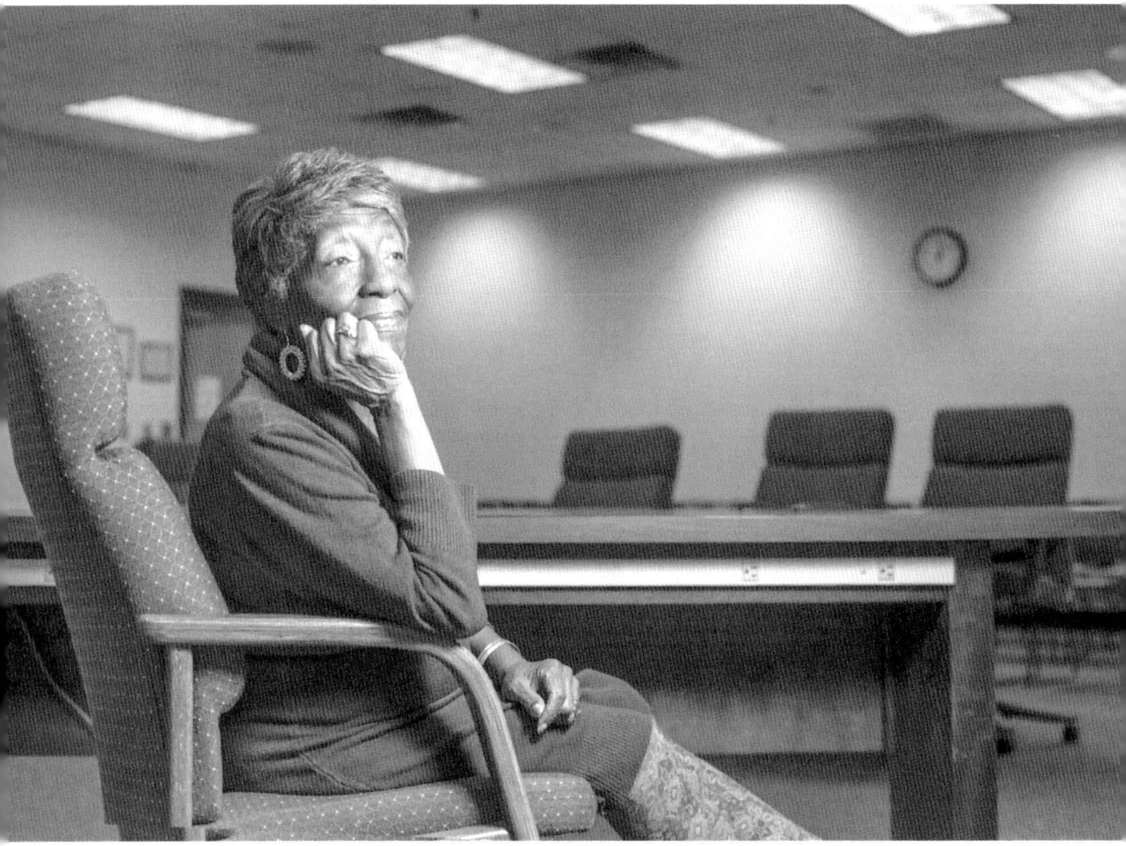

Xanthene Norris

Education and public service have been hallmarks of Xanthene Norris's life. She graduated from Sterling High School as valedictorian and returned to her alma mater after graduating from Clark College in Atlanta to teach a World War II veterans training program. She went on to teach geography, world history, and French at Sterling, which became known as one of the best schools in South Carolina. After desegregation, Norris worked as head guidance counselor at Greenville High School until 1984. Norris, who holds a master's degree from Furman, taught and counseled thousands of students during her career in education. She has held a seat on the Greenville County Council since 1997 and played an instrumental role in getting Greenville County to ratify a Dr. Martin Luther King Jr. holiday. (Courtesy of *TOWN Magazine*.)

CHAPTER SEVEN

Business Leaders and Entrepreneurs

Greenville has demonstrated a unique ability to transform itself, and its business leaders and entrepreneurs are a primary reason.

The city's earliest settlers took advantage of the city's earliest days as a vacation town for Lowcountry aristocrats and a center of commerce for travelers making their way to and from the Blue Ridge Mountains.

They set up sawmills, gristmills, and trading posts near the Reedy River, and starting in the 1890s, Greenville became a cotton-mill town. Thomas Fleming Parker, the Woodside Brothers, Francis Poe, and others began building textile mills near the Reedy River. It set the foundation for Greenville's eventual proclamation as the "Textile Capital of the World."

The 1915 Textile World Record, Volume 50, said cotton mills, with a payroll of $3 million per annum, enabled Greenville to "weather the financial storm of the past year with perfect comfort and absolute security."

Entrepreneurs such as Herman Lay, William R. Timmons Sr., and W. Frank Hip sold potato chips and insurance policies and built businesses that would turn into multimillion-dollar ventures.

After World War II, Charles Ezra Daniel became a force in reshaping Greenville and creating the industrial New South. Manufacturing came in.

Robert Earle "Red" Hughes built shopping centers and subdivisions, including the crown jewel, Chanticleer. Frank Halter developed McAlister Square, the state's first enclosed shopping mall.

The transformation continued with the arrival of international companies such as Michelin and BMW, which located in nearby Greer. The automotive industry is big. So are advanced materials and bioscience. Greenville is targeting distribution and logistics operations as well as data centers and corporate headquarters. It is home to 40 Fortune 500 companies.

Alongside them are a new set of entrepreneurs waiting for their turn to transform Greenville, such as artist and retailer Lily Wyckoff and Peter Barth, a man who is trying to shape Greenville into a tech hothouse.

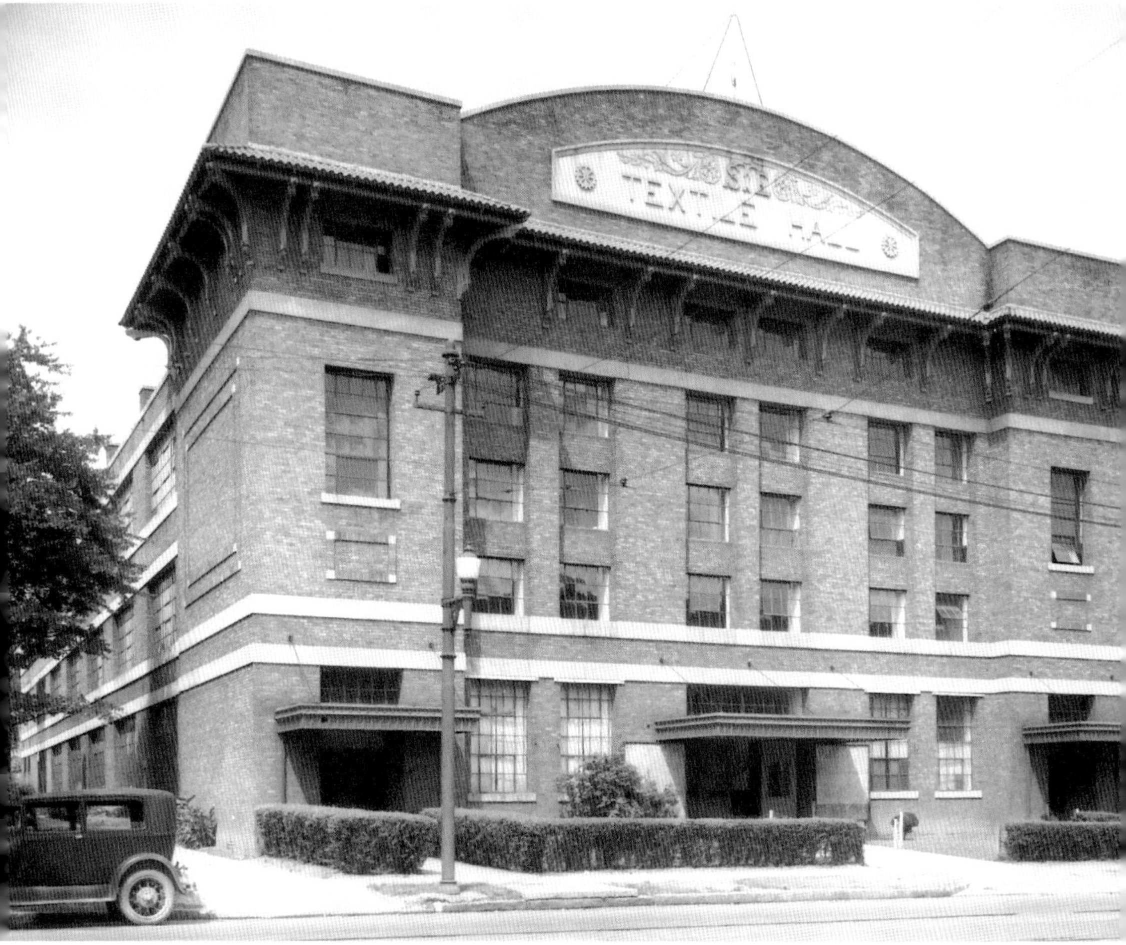

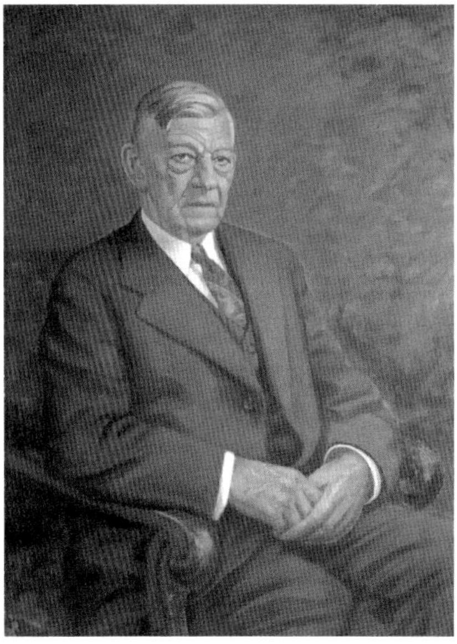

Joseph Emory Sirrine

Joseph Emory Sirrine literally and figuratively built Greenville. The New England engineering firm of Lockwood, Greene & Company hired Sirrine when it planned its first mill in Greenville. He was named the company's Southern manager during the textile boom. In 1902, Sirrine started his own business but did not limit his work to textile-mill construction in the South. The company's engineers and architects worked on Greenville's city hall, high schools, the Poinsett Hotel, and Textile Hall, built to house the Southern Textile Machinery Exposition. He was such an influential business and civic leader that the day he died, Furman University's bell tolled all day, and WFBC broadcast his funeral. His influence is felt today through the Sirrine Scholarship Fund, which helps Greenville students attend college. (Both, courtesy of the Greenville County Historical Society.)

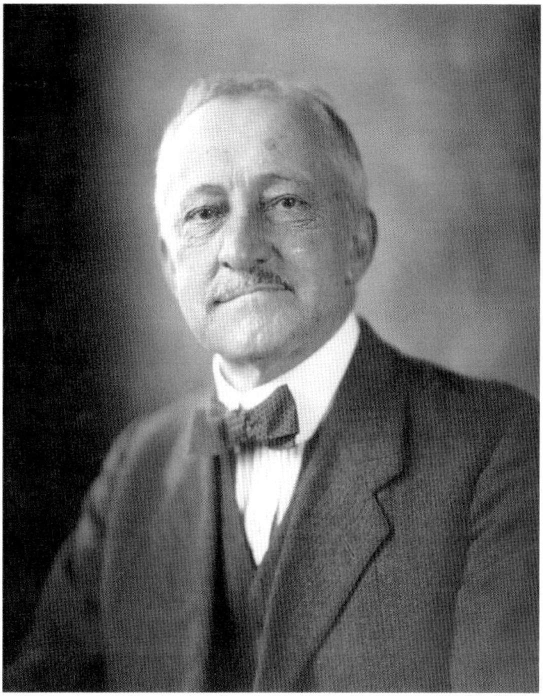

Thomas Fleming Parker

Growth of Greenville's textile industry created a market for labor in the early 20th century, and workers flooded into the city. Thomas Fleming Parker, president of Monaghan Mill, strove to make the mill a model of paternalistic management. He started a community medical clinic and hired Dr. Fletcher Jordan, one of the area's most beloved doctors, to run it. He built an elementary school, a playground, and the first industrial YMCA in the South. It became the center of community life and offered residents of the mill village a chance to take adult-education classes, see moving pictures, and play sports. Parker saw the social improvements as a way to avoid unionization and keep underpaid workers content. Parker also helped Hattie Logan Duckett establish the Phillis Wheatley Center. (Both, courtesy of the Greenville County Library System.)

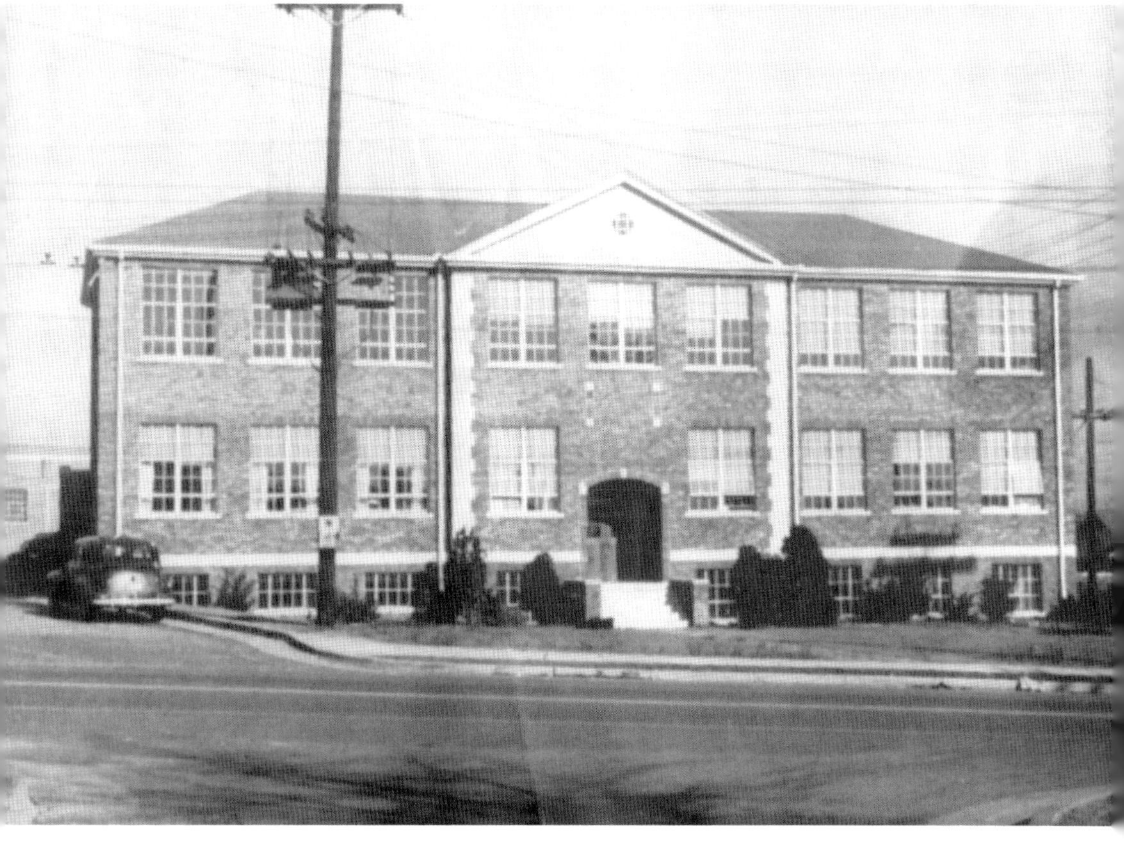

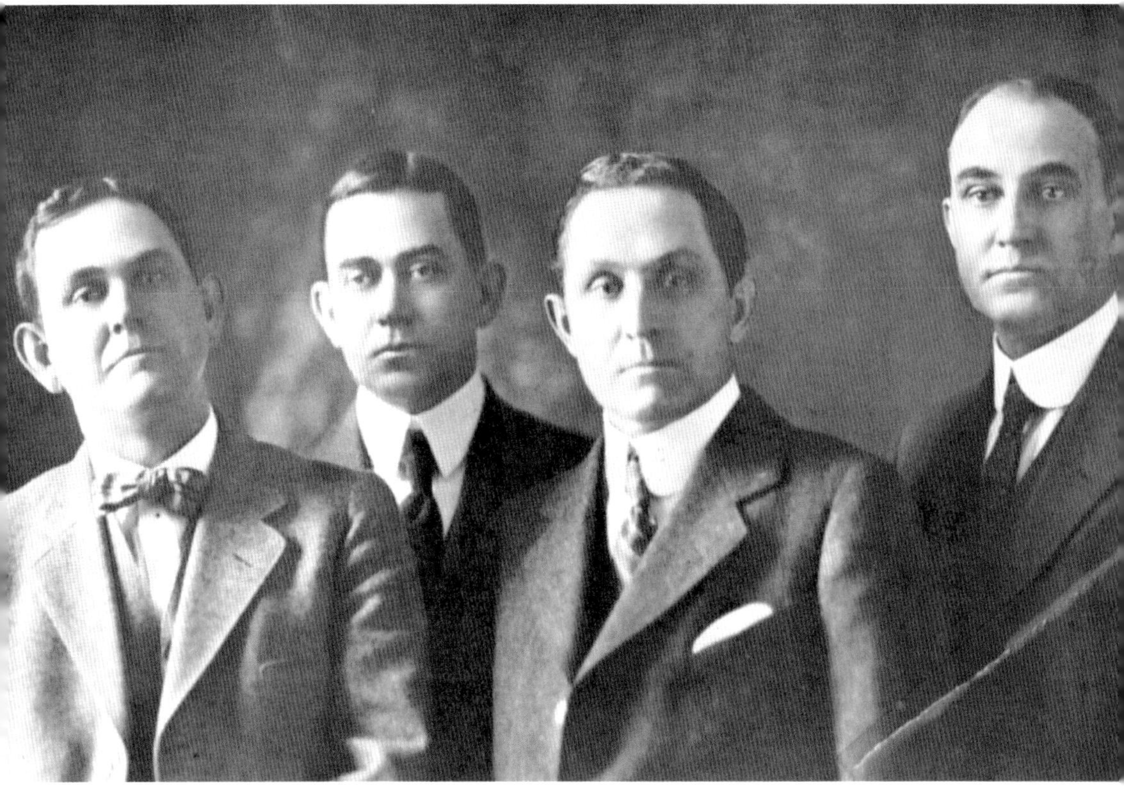

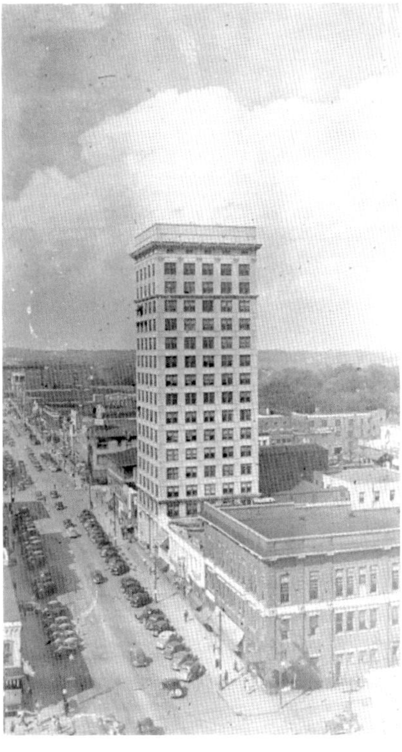

The Woodside Brothers

John T. Woodside once referred to himself and his three brothers as "the big four." In early-20th-century Greenville, they were. The brothers, from left to right, Edward F., Robert I., J. David, and John T. Woodside, undertook projects that others would not. Eldest brother John T. said, "We have always stepped in where the other fellow was holding back." They had complementary talents: John T. was a businessman, Robert a banker, and Edward and David textile manufacturers. In 1902, they built the Woodside Mill, eventually the largest textile plant under one roof in the world. John Woodside declared himself the richest man in Greenville County before World War I, and they financed the Poinsett Hotel and built a big office building downtown. But their holdings were wiped out by the Great Depression. (Both, courtesy of the Greenville County Historical Society.)

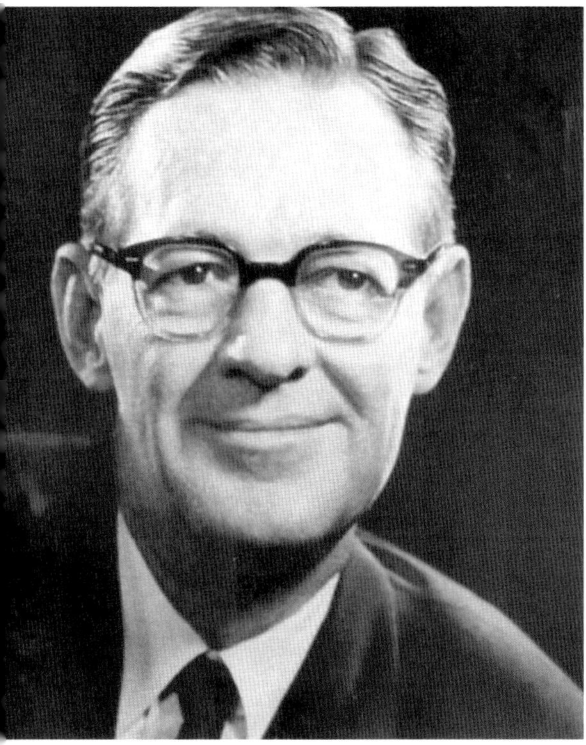

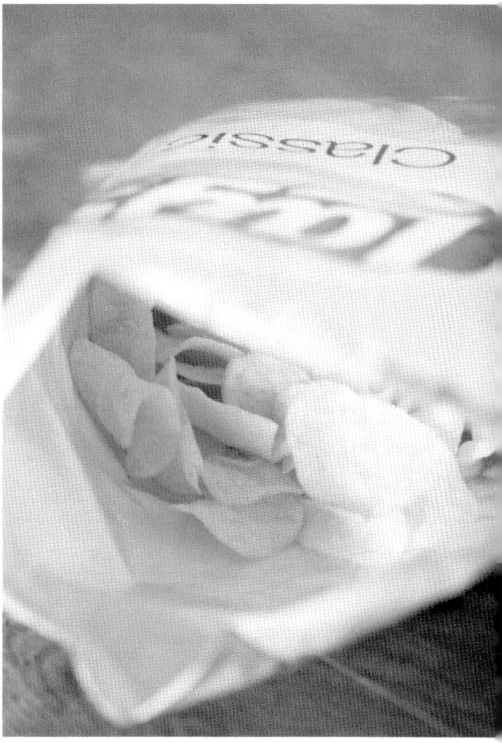

Herman Warden Lay

Herman Warden Lay first sold Pepsi-Colas from a makeshift stand in the front yard of his family's home when he was 11 years old. The city baseball park was across the street and charged 10¢ a bottle. He charged 5¢.

Lay was still selling Pepsi 45 years later, but by that time he was chairman of the multibillion-dollar conglomerate PepsiCo., Inc.

Lay lettered in baseball, basketball, and track at Greenville High School, and he received an athletic scholarship to Furman. He left school after two years to hitchhike to Houston, Texas, for the Democratic National Convention, where he planned to sell ice cream along the parade route. But the route changed at the last minute, and his investment melted.

After writing 200 application letters, Lay landed an interview for a job as a snack-food salesman for Barrett Food Company, distributor of Gardner's Potato Chips. They offered him the job, but he turned it down, thinking there "wasn't a future in potato chips." He reconsidered and took a job with the company.

Lay bought Barrett's plants in Atlanta and Memphis in 1938 and started H.W. Lay Co., and the company merged with Pepsi-Cola in 1965. (Left, courtesy of Special Collections and Archives, Furman University; right, photograph by Cindy Landrum.)

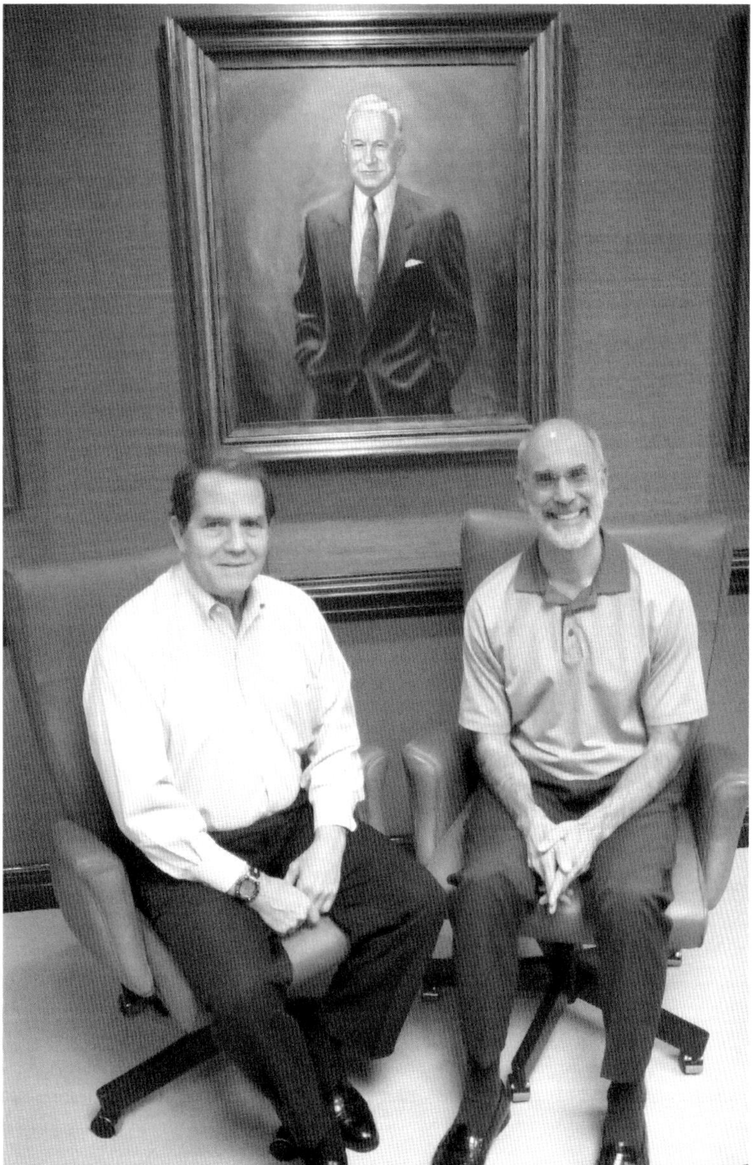

William R. Timmons Sr.

Like many of Greenville's successful businessmen, William R. Timmons Sr. seized opportunity when he saw it. In the 1930s and 1940s, Southern states began passing legislation requiring long-haul truckers to have insurance. Timmons had started his own real-estate and insurance company. He was selling policies from other insurance companies and became frustrated when some went broke and left him scrambling to find underwriters. Seeking a stable truck insurer, Timmons acquired Canal Insurance Co. in December 1942 from the National Bank of Columbia for $17,500, the surplus at the time. Timmons served as CEO of the Greenville Chamber of Commerce in the 1920s, and he led efforts to construct a chamber building on Main Street in 1925. Today, the third generation of Timmons are among the company's top leaders. Shown sitting in front of a portrait of founder William R. Timmons Sr. are William "Rick" Timmons III (left) and David Firstenberg. (Courtesy of the *Greenville Journal*.)

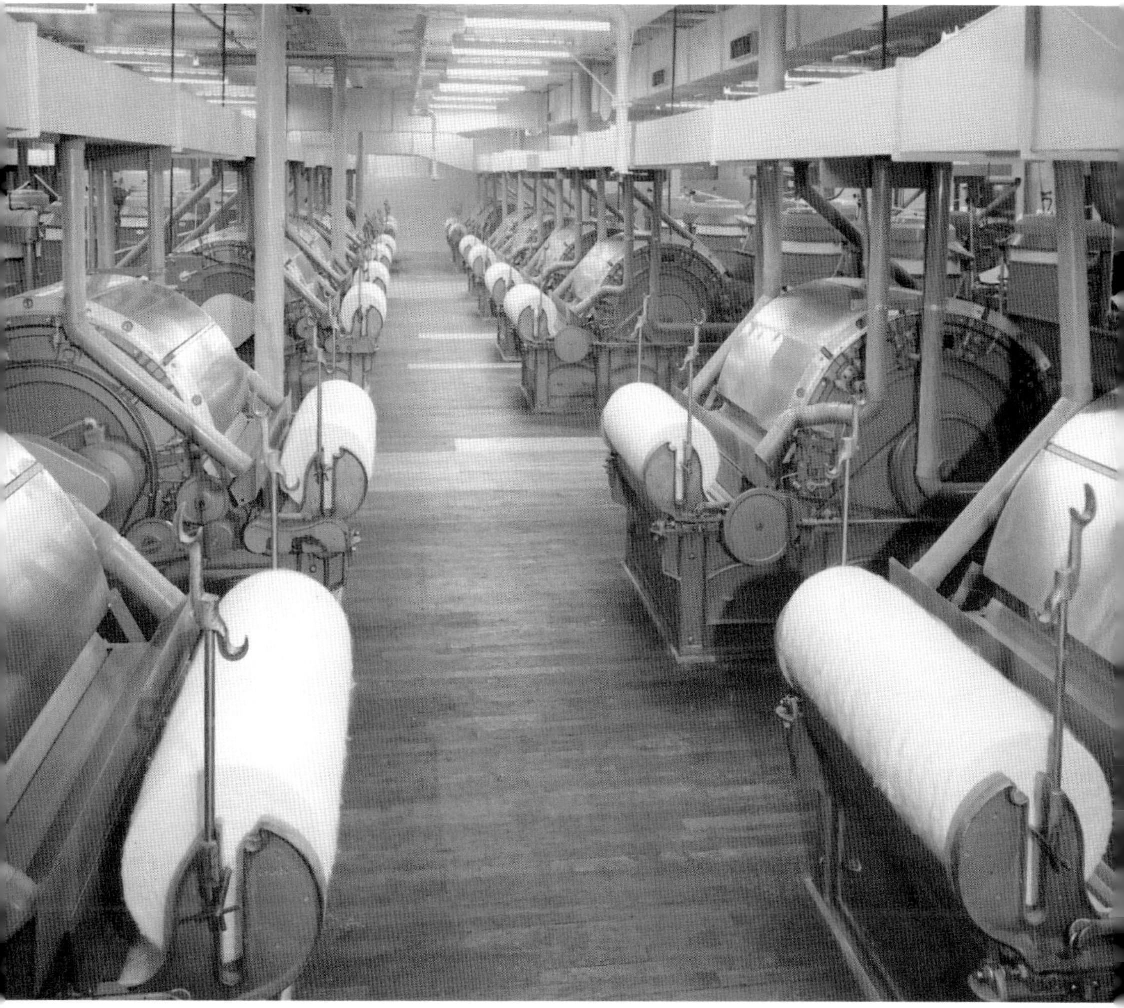

John D. Hollingsworth Jr.

John D. Hollingsworth Jr. was an eccentric, reclusive textile magnate who made the small textile machinery company his grandfather founded into an international conglomerate. Hollingsworth's father bought a truck and ran John D. Hollingsworth on Wheels out of the garage of his Greenville home, and Hollingsworth Jr. started to tag along when he was 10 to help fix machinery. Despite building a fortune that put him among the 400 wealthiest Americans, he lived in an Airstream trailer in the woods behind his plant. In 1976, he established Hollingsworth Funds, Inc., a charitable foundation, 24 years before his death. Furman University gets 45 percent of the yearly distribution, and the local YMCA gets 10 percent. The rest goes to local charities. (Courtesy of the Greenville County Historical Society.)

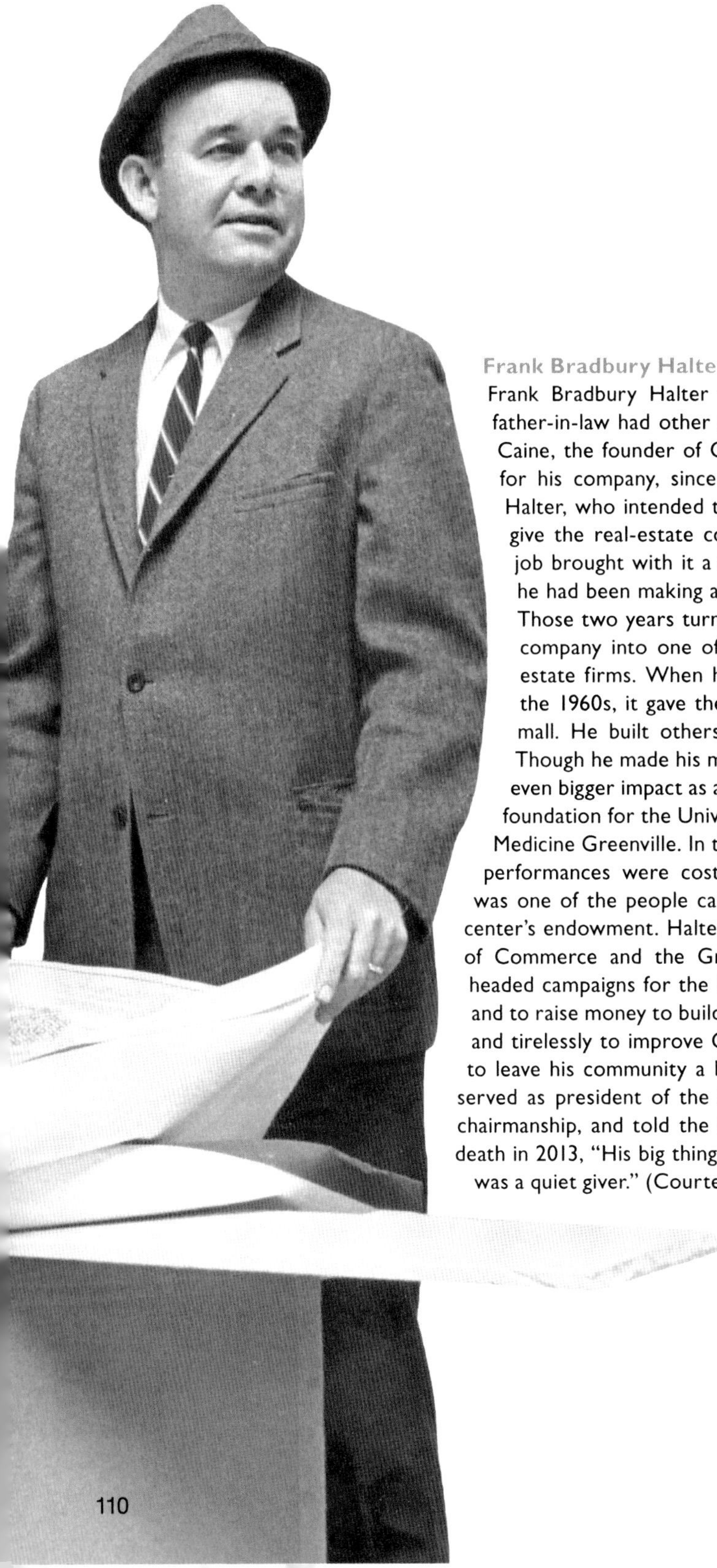

Frank Bradbury Halter

Frank Bradbury Halter wanted to be a lawyer, but his father-in-law had other ideas. Robert "Bubber" Monteith Caine, the founder of Caine Co., insisted he come work for his company, since he was marrying his only child. Halter, who intended to be a lawyer, told him he would give the real-estate company a try for two years. The job brought with it a $100 a month pay cut from what he had been making as an Air Force intelligence officer. Those two years turned into 60, and he developed the company into one of the state's most successful real-estate firms. When he developed McAlister Square in the 1960s, it gave the state its first enclosed shopping mall. He built others in Columbia and Myrtle Beach. Though he made his mark as a businessman, he made an even bigger impact as a civic leader. Halter helped lay the foundation for the University of South Carolina School of Medicine Greenville. In the early days of the Peace Center, performances were costing more than expected; Halter was one of the people called to raise more money for the center's endowment. Halter chaired the Greenville Chamber of Commerce and the Greenville Hospital Board, and he headed campaigns for the United Way of Greenville County and to raise money to build a new YMCA. He worked quietly and tirelessly to improve Greenville, believing he had a duty to leave his community a better place. His son Brad Halter served as president of the family business under his father's chairmanship, and told the *Greenville Journal* after his father's death in 2013, "His big thing was being a giver, not a taker. He was a quiet giver." (Courtesy of Brad Halter.)

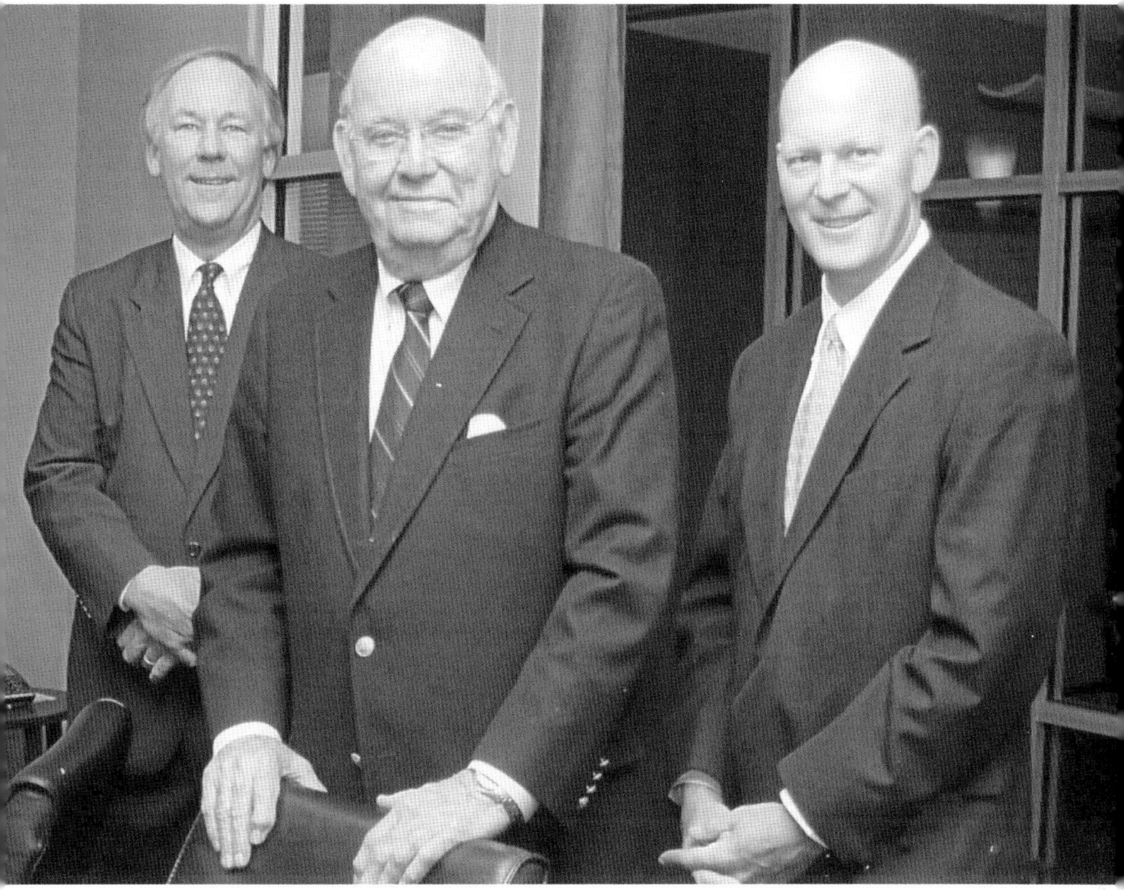

Robert Caine Halter

As a child, Robert Caine Halter swam in the Cleveland Street YMCA pool and played in its gym and on its sports fields. As an adult and the president of Coldwell Banker, Caine helped raise $8 million for its renovation. The facility now bears his name. "The Y is the thread of the community," Halter told the *Greenville News* in 2003. "It stands for people helping people." Helping people was something that came naturally to Halter, known for his generous spirit and incredibly positive attitude. Halter, a lifetime nonsmoker, maintained that positivity all the way up to his death in 2007 from lung cancer. In business, he had a role in nurturing and steering Greenville's development, especially downtown. When it made more sense to look elsewhere for development opportunities, he looked downtown, and Greenville is now reaping the benefits. Pictured here from left to right are Brad Halter, Frank Halter, and Caine Halter. (Courtesy of Brad Halter.)

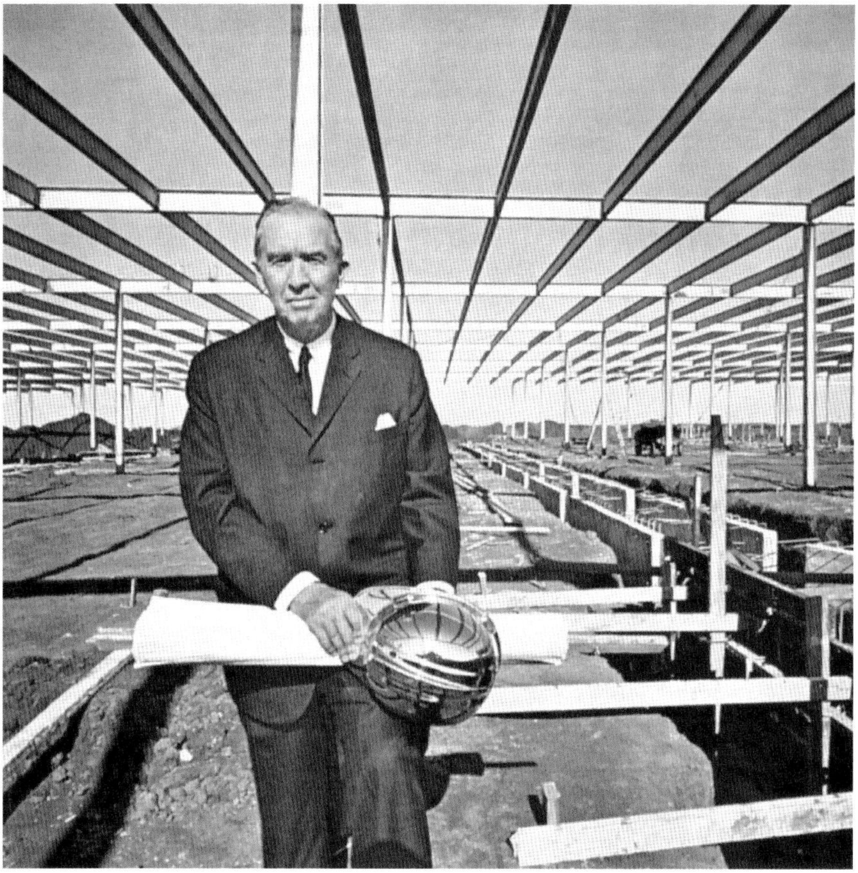

Charles Ezra Daniel (OPPOSITE PAGE AND ABOVE)
After World War II, Charles Ezra Daniel became a leading force in the shaping of Greenville and the industrialization of the South. Part of it was self-preservation.

In 1935, he started Daniel Construction Company, which would later become the largest construction company in the world.

With the arrival of World War II, Daniel won the contract to build at Donaldson Air Force Base. Despite weather challenges, he met the 90-day completion deadline. After the war, he became concerned about the lack of work. He started calling on potential industrial customers in New York, the North, and the Midwest—and then persuaded them to locate plants down South. A 1954 *Fortune* magazine article said, "If the customer permits himself to be lured into Daniel's hometown, he is a gone goose."

He was a heavyweight in the recruitment of companies to the region, prompting business leaders to give him the moniker of "Industrial Ambassador of the South." Through his efforts, the "Textile Capital of the World" was transformed. Manufacturing ballooned as more than $650 million in new industrial investment came to Greenville County, much of it outside the textile industry.

In 1964, ground was broken for the 25-story Daniel Building in downtown Greenville. When it opened in 1967, three years after Daniel's death, it was the tallest building in South Carolina.

He also spent a short time in politics. In September 1954, Daniel was appointed by Gov. James F. Byrnes to the US Senate to fill the seat left vacant by the death of Burnet R. Maybank. Daniel served for three months and did not seek reelection.

Daniel was a life trustee of Clemson College, and he was inducted into the South Carolina Business Hall of Fame in 1985. On the opposite page, Daniel (left) is pictured with then-governor Strom Thurmond. (Both, courtesy of Fluor Corp.).

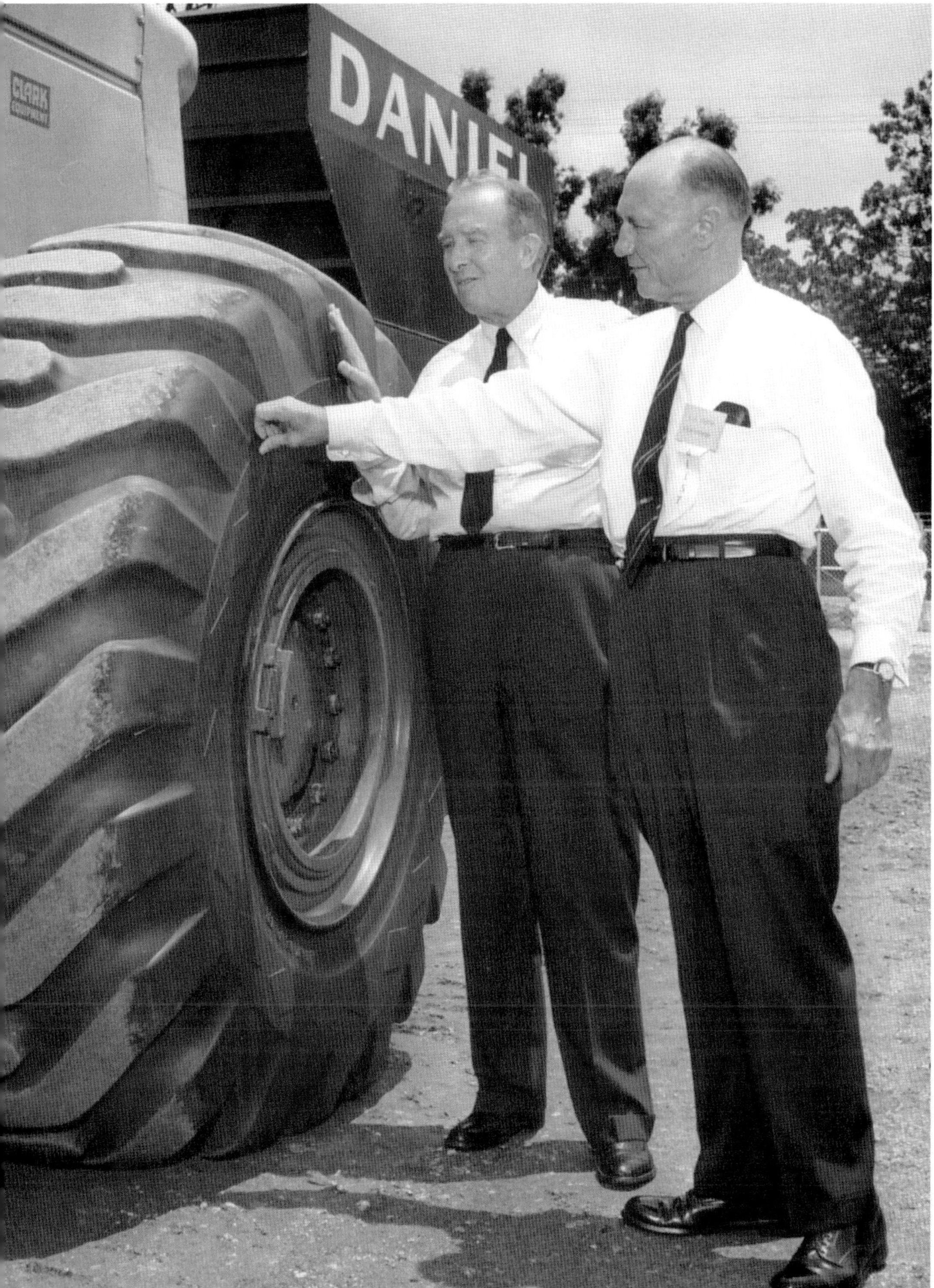
CLARK
DANIEL

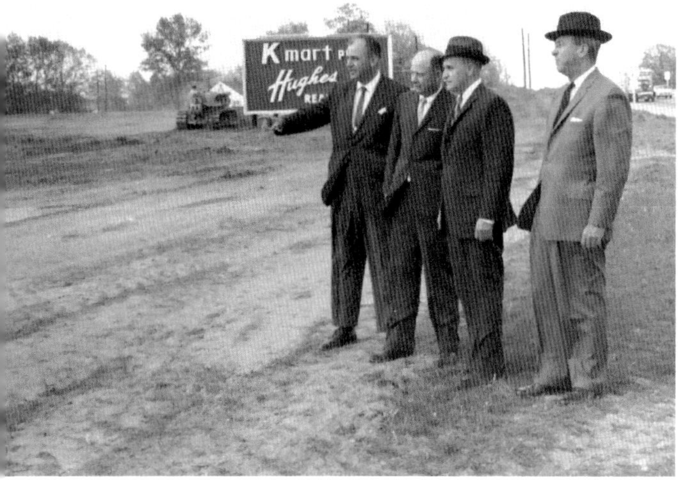

Robert Earle "Red" Hughes

Robert Earle "Red" Hughes personified the building boom in Greenville in the 1960s. He built the Kmart on Church Street Extension, the first outside of the company's Michigan home base. Hughes got into the real-estate business because his mother did not want her son to be a grease monkey. He had landed a part-time job at a service station to help cover the cost of attending Furman University. His mother did not like seeing grease underneath his fingernails, and she told him to apply for a help-wanted advertisement selling lots on Augusta Road. (Courtesy of Bob Hughes.)

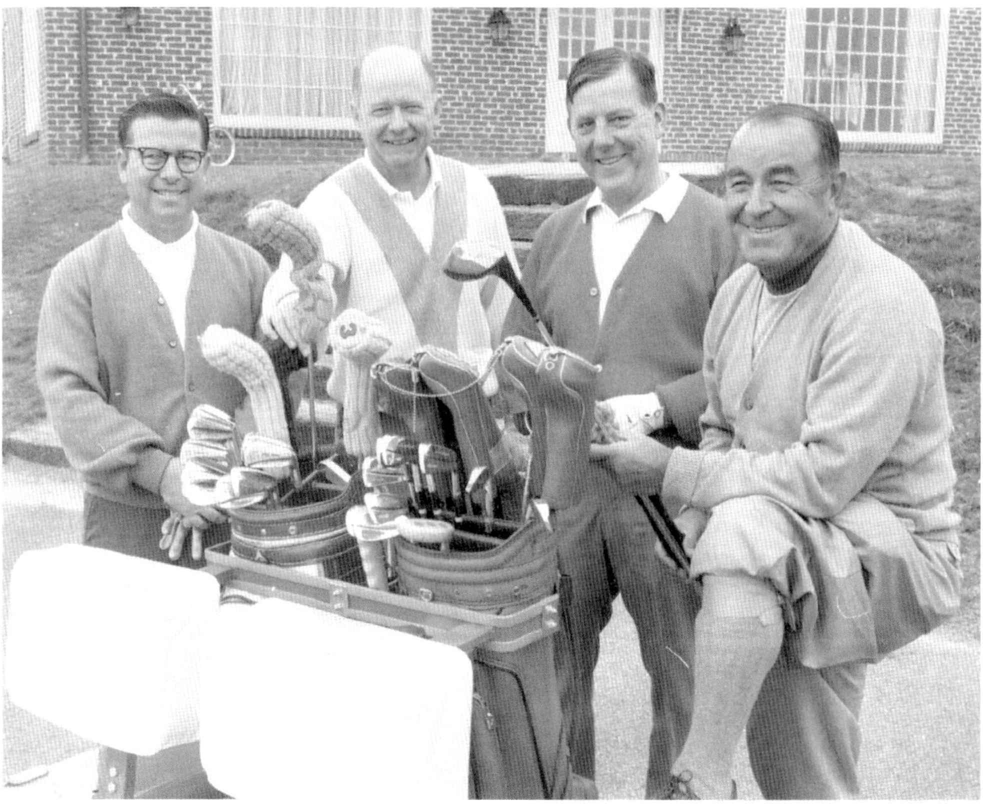

Chanticleer

Red Hughes turned a wooded area near the Greenville Hospital into Chanticleer, a large upscale subdivision with a nationally ranked golf course. The first homes were constructed in the early 1960s. Shown at the opening of the Chanticleer course are, from left to right, unidentified, Red Hughes, Charles Ballenger, and professional golfer Gene Sarazen. (Courtesy of Bob Hughes.)

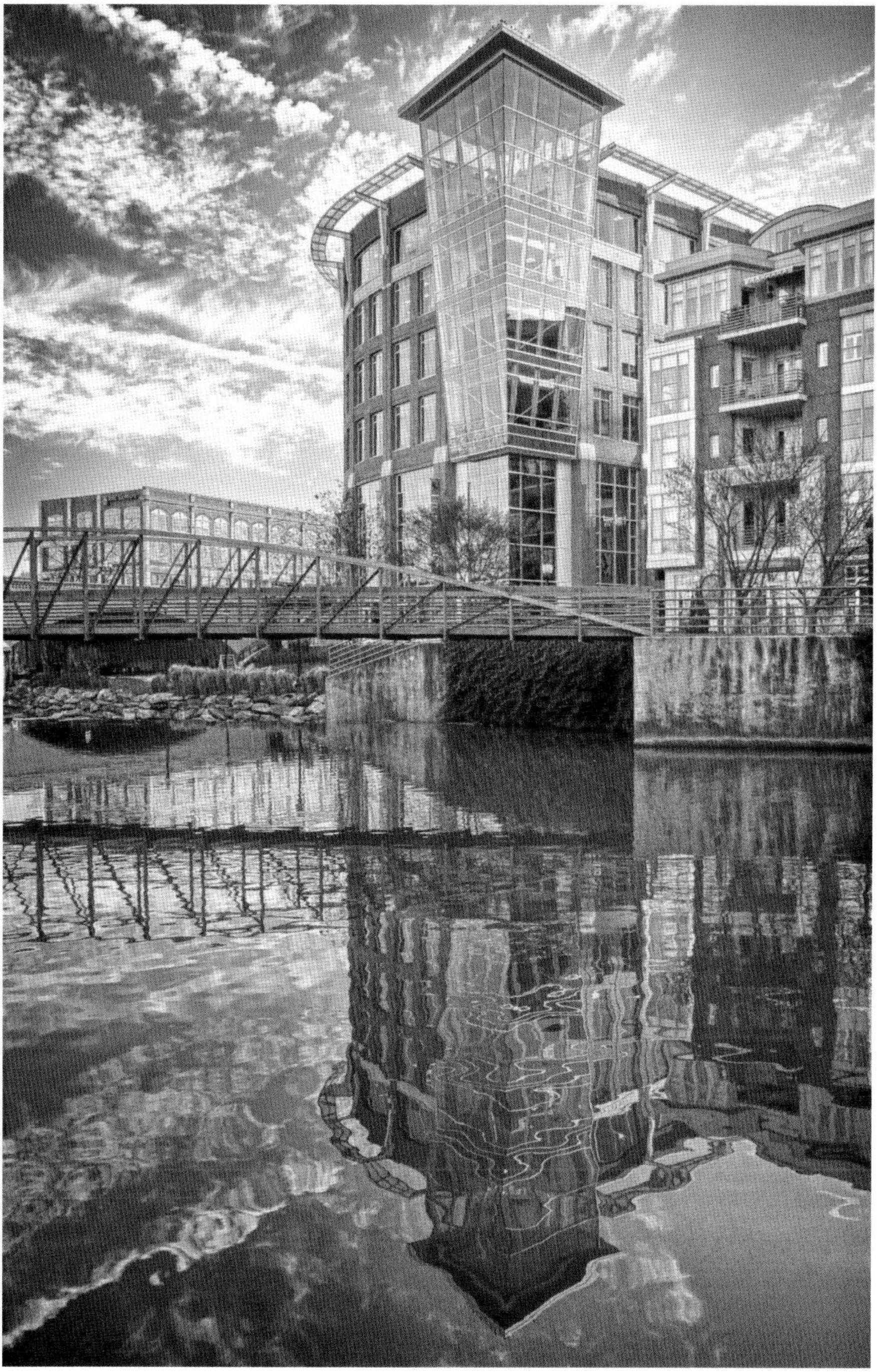

Riverplace

Together, Bob and Phil Hughes developed Poinsett Plaza and RiverPlace (pictured above), key parts of downtown redevelopment. Along with Falls Park and the Peace Center for the Performing Arts, RiverPlace was a key to bringing life back to the Reedy River, the southern end of Main Street, and the West End. (Photograph by Cindy Landrum.)

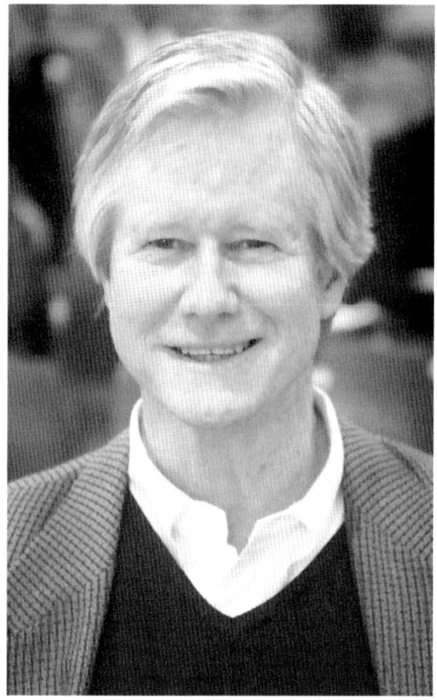

Phillip Rivers Hughes
Phil Hughes orchestrated a land swap that allowed construction of the Upcountry History Museum in Heritage Green. He has also developed apartment complexes and office buildings downtown. (Courtesy of the *Greenville Journal*.)

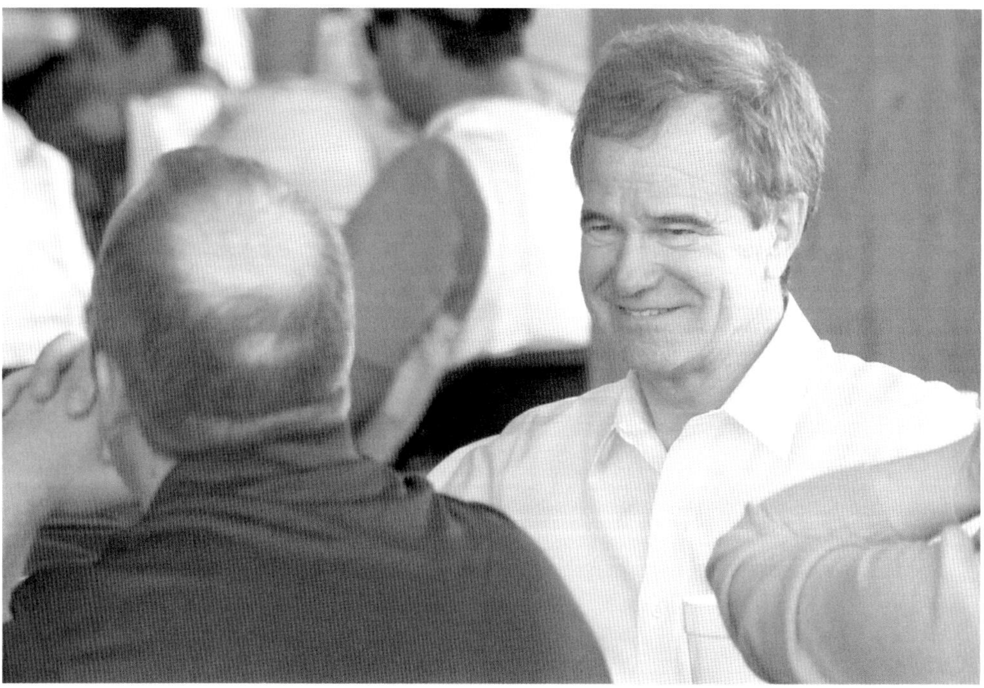

Robert E. Hughes Jr.
Bob Hughes is the developer of ONE, a $100-million, mixed-use development with office space on Main Street. He was a principal partner in Institutional Resources, which orchestrated a controversial $1 billion school construction plan that allowed Greenville County Schools to renovate, expand, or build 70 schools in the late 1990s and early 2000s. (Courtesy of Bob Hughes.)

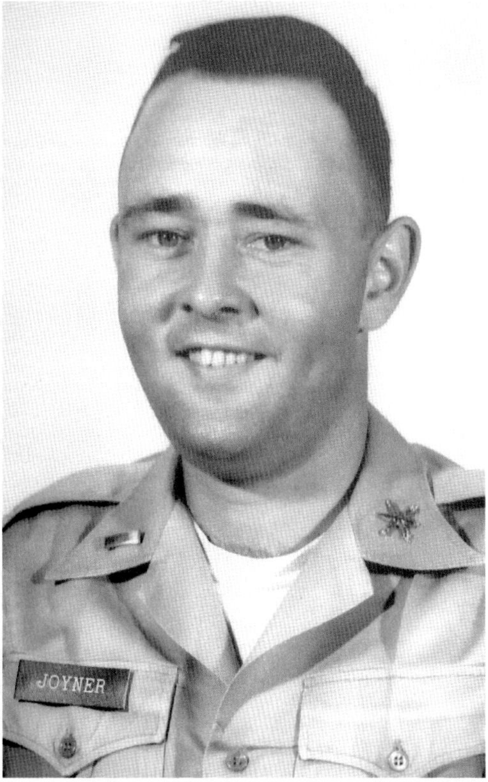

C. Dan Joyner

C. Dan Joyner fell into a real-estate career by accident The man with a congenial personality and firm handshake had just finished a three-year stint in the Army in 1962, and he wanted to come back home to Greenville. A friend suggested real estate, and he joined a small firm. Joyner struggled that first year, calling it the worst of his life. But then, he sold seven houses in five days. The next year, he sold more houses than anybody in Greenville. Joyner opened his firm in 1964 and developed it into one of the top firms in the country. Joyner, who died in 2012, was a committed community servant who helped a number of charities and organizations. He was a fervent supporter of Furman University, his alma mater. He is pictured below on the right with the late Gov. Carroll Campbell. (Both, courtesy of C. Dan Joyner Realtors.)

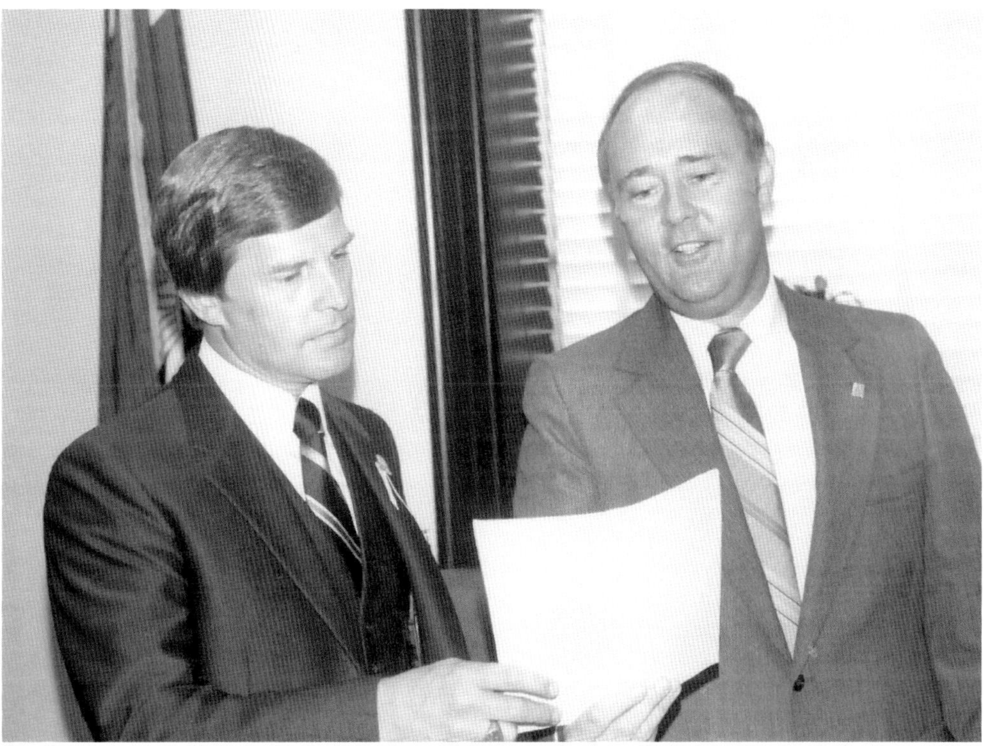

Buck Mickel

Daniel Construction Company grew with the South, and Buck Mickel, whose uncle by marriage was Charles E. Daniel, grew up with it. Mickel joined Daniel Construction and, with the exception of three years of service with the US Army Corps of Engineers in the United States and Germany, stayed with the company until his death in 1998. Mickel negotiated the deal that merged Daniel International Construction with Fluor, eventually creating an international engineering and construction giant. Mickel did a lot of the footwork necessary to open the Greenville-Spartanburg International Airport in 1962, and he marked the occasion by having his family sit in the bleachers behind the podium at GSP's dedication. The crowd cheered for the Blue Angels as they flew above. Mickel's daughter Minor Mickel Shaw now chairs the airport commission. (Courtesy of Fluor Corp.)

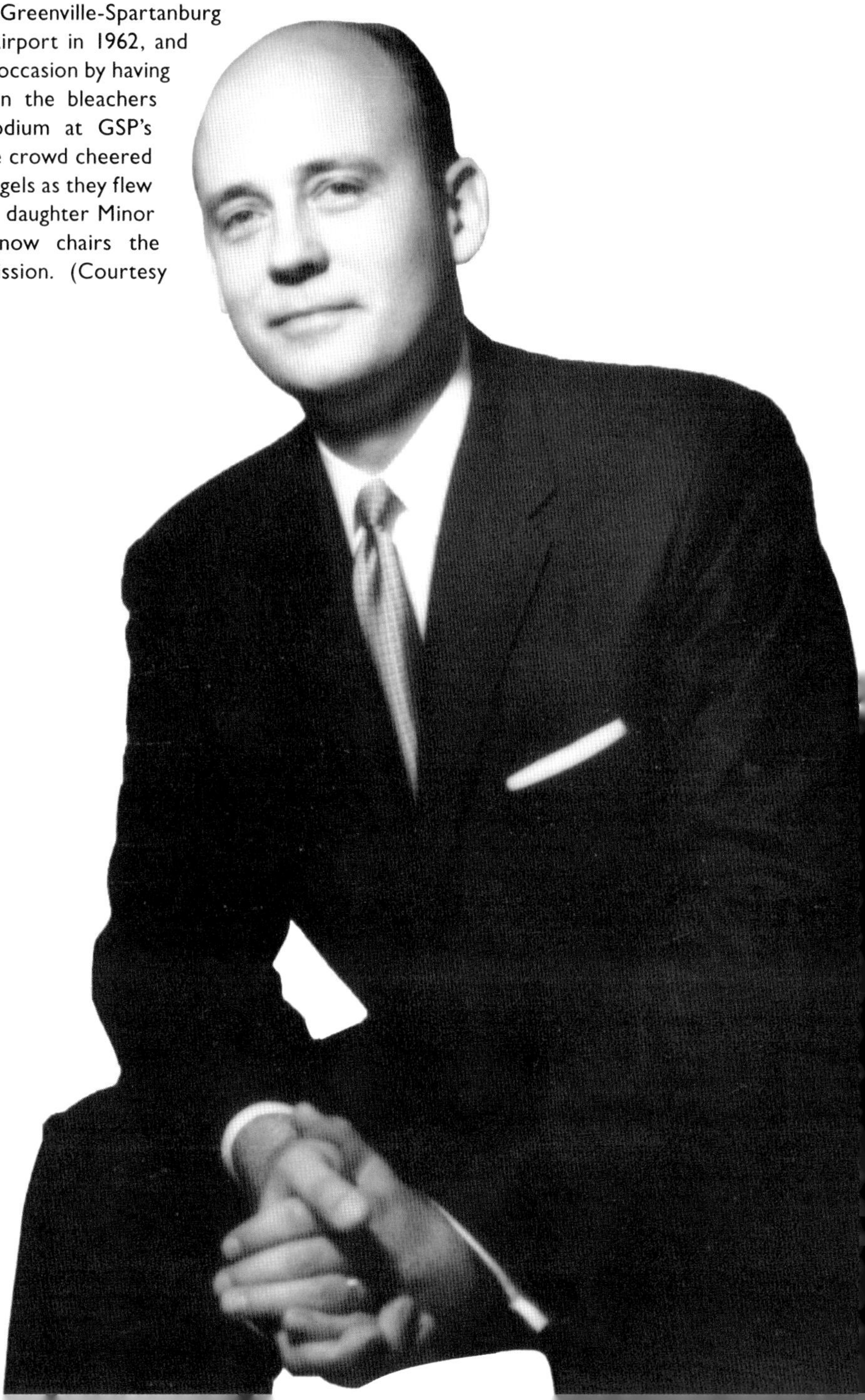

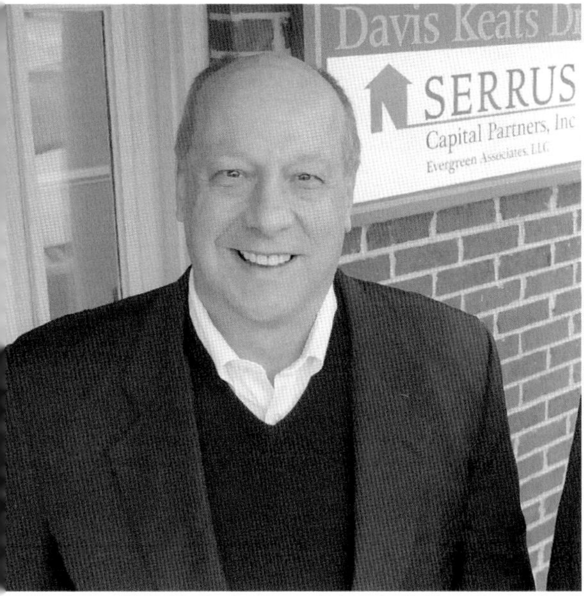

Leighton Cubbage
Leighton Cubbage has always been an entrepreneur. A former Clemson University linebacker, he sold sandwiches in dorms. He paid players from Northern states $5 for game tickets they could not use and resold them for $25, and he delivered pizzas. In 1989, he formed a long-distance telephone company that he and his partner sold in 1995 to LCI International for $164 million. He is now cofounder of Serrus Capital Partners. (Courtesy of the *Upstate Business Journal*.)

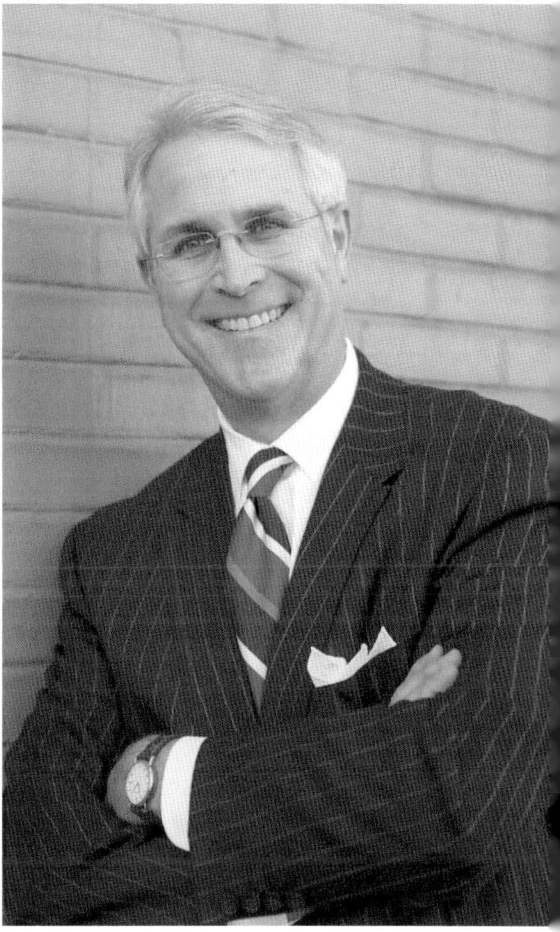

Rush Wilson III
When businesses began abandoning downtown in the 1960s and 1970s for malls, Rush Wilson Limited stayed put. Rush Wilson Jr. started the company in 1950 with a store in North Carolina, and he opened his Greenville store in 1959. Rush Wilson III became president of the company in 1999. With sterling customer service and an ability to adapt, Rush Wilson Limited has become a downtown mainstay. (Courtesy of the *Upstate Business Journal*.)

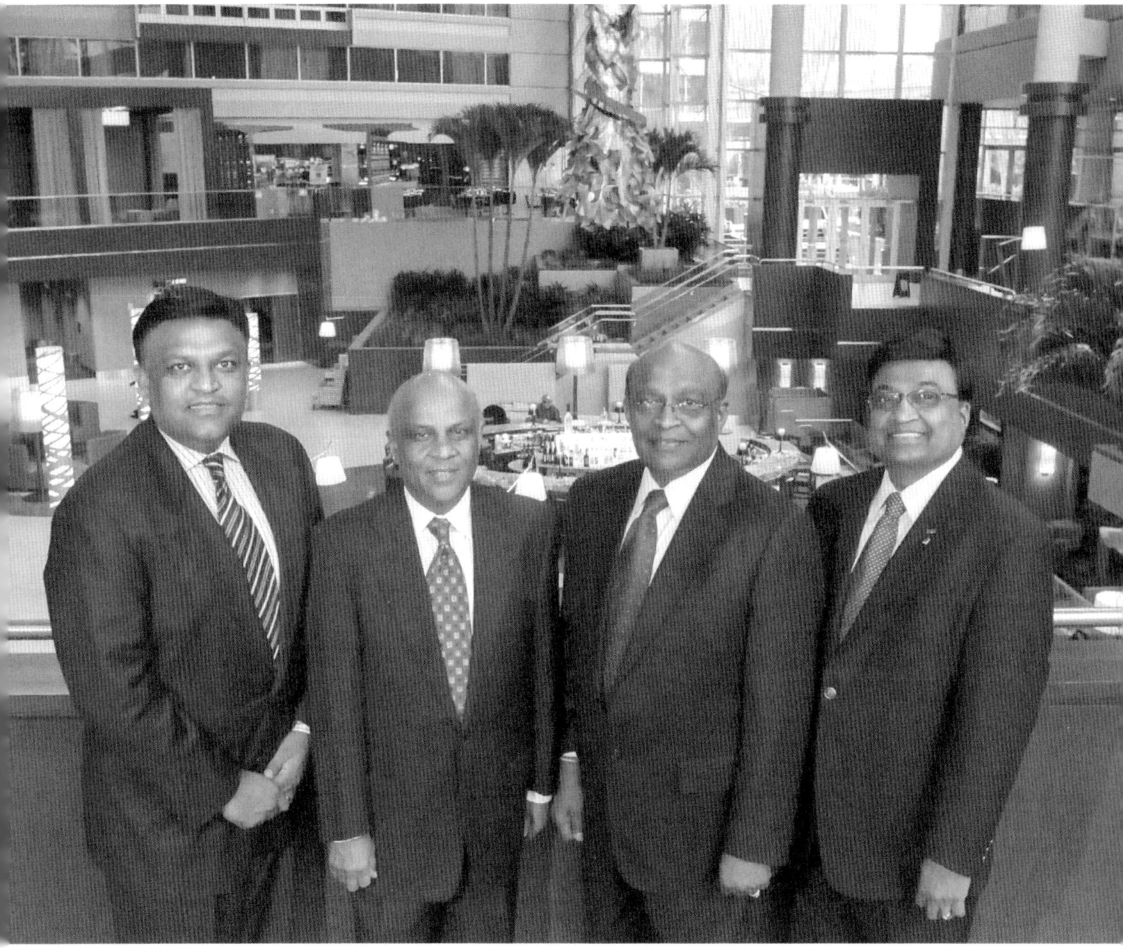

The Ramas

The Rama family has built their legacy in Greenville from the ground up. It started when H.P. Rama left India to pursue an MBA at Xavier University. While a student, he washed dishes and waited tables at a Howard Johnson's hotel restaurant. He bought a 40-room motel in California. Soon, his brothers M.P. and J.P. joined him. They bought the Camelot Inn off I-85 out of bankruptcy in 1976. When the banker asked for a balance sheet, they told him, "Whatever money we make, we will pay you back." JHM Hotels sold the Camelot in 1986. It owns 42 properties, including the Hyatt Regency in Greenville, the hotel credited with sparking downtown revitalization in the 1970s. They bought the Hyatt in 2009 and completed a multimillion-dollar renovation in 2013. The Ramas are, from left to right, D.J. Rama, H.P. Rama, J.P. Rama, and R.O. Rama. (Courtesy of the *Greenville Journal*.)

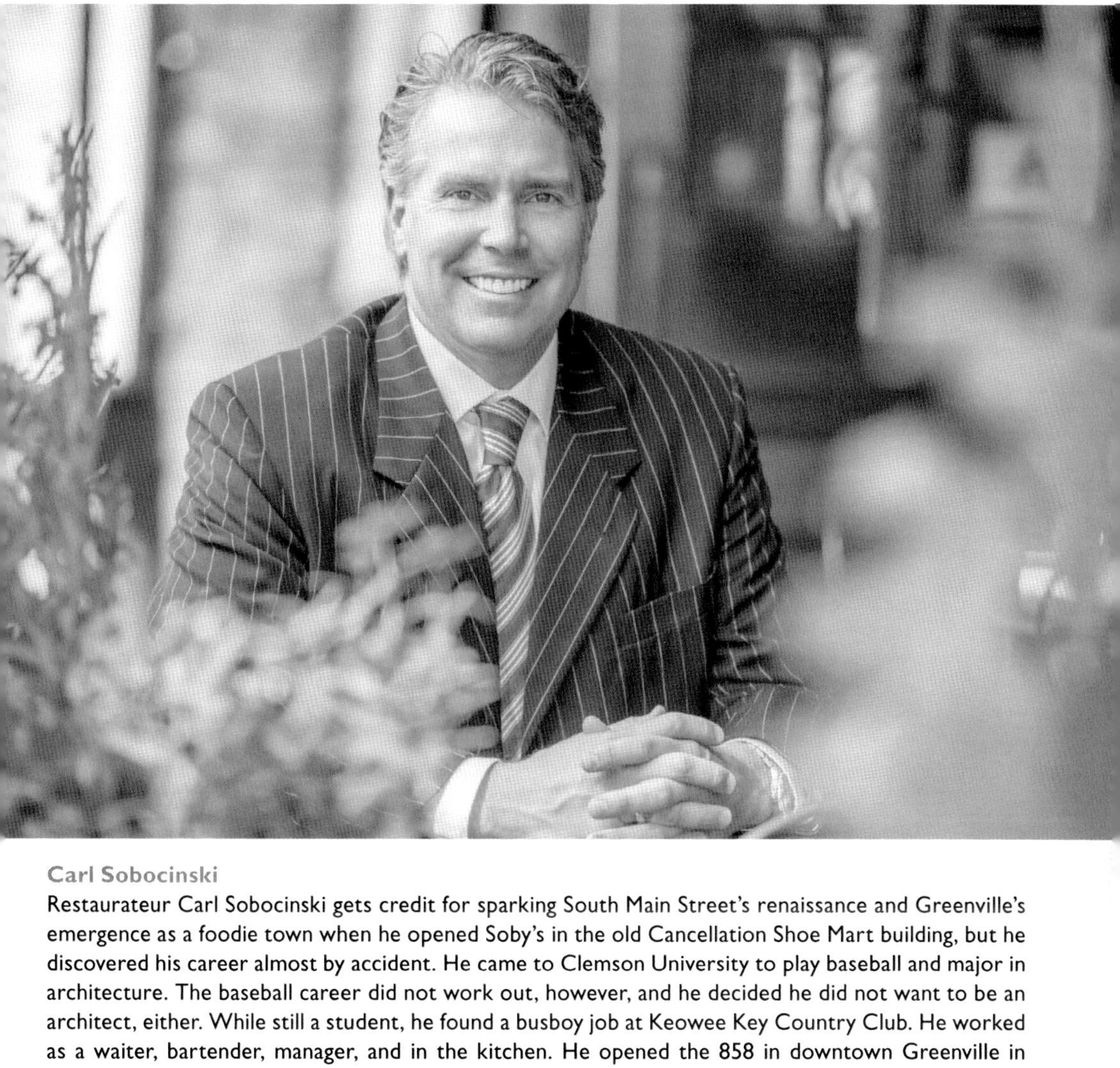

Carl Sobocinski

Restaurateur Carl Sobocinski gets credit for sparking South Main Street's renaissance and Greenville's emergence as a foodie town when he opened Soby's in the old Cancellation Shoe Mart building, but he discovered his career almost by accident. He came to Clemson University to play baseball and major in architecture. The baseball career did not work out, however, and he decided he did not want to be an architect, either. While still a student, he found a busboy job at Keowee Key Country Club. He worked as a waiter, bartender, manager, and in the kitchen. He opened the 858 in downtown Greenville in 1993 and soon left to start Soby's. Now, he owns Table 301, a restaurant group. Sobocinski cofounded Euphoria, Greenville's food, wine, and music festival. (Courtesy of the *Upstate Business Journal* and GetzCreative.)

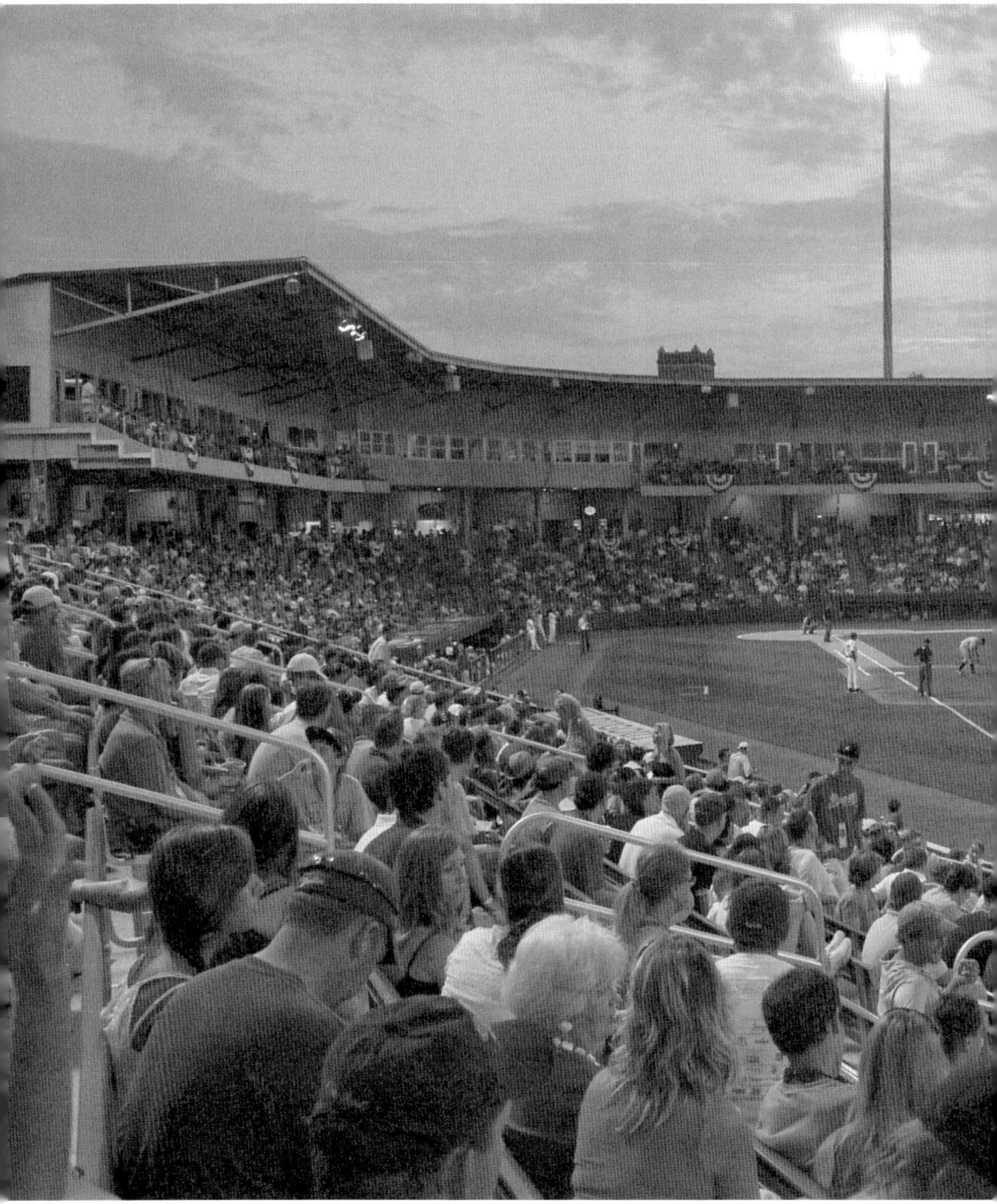

Greenville Drive

Craig Brown's minor-league baseball team, the Capital City Bombers, needed a new stadium, but years of negotiating with Columbia and the University of South Carolina failed to yield results. Greenville was losing the Double AA Greenville Braves and needed a new team. So, Brown and his partners offered to build a new downtown baseball stadium if the city donated the land. Fluor Field, a miniature replica of Fenway Park in Boston, was built in 10 months, in time for the Red Sox-Class A affiliate Greenville Drive

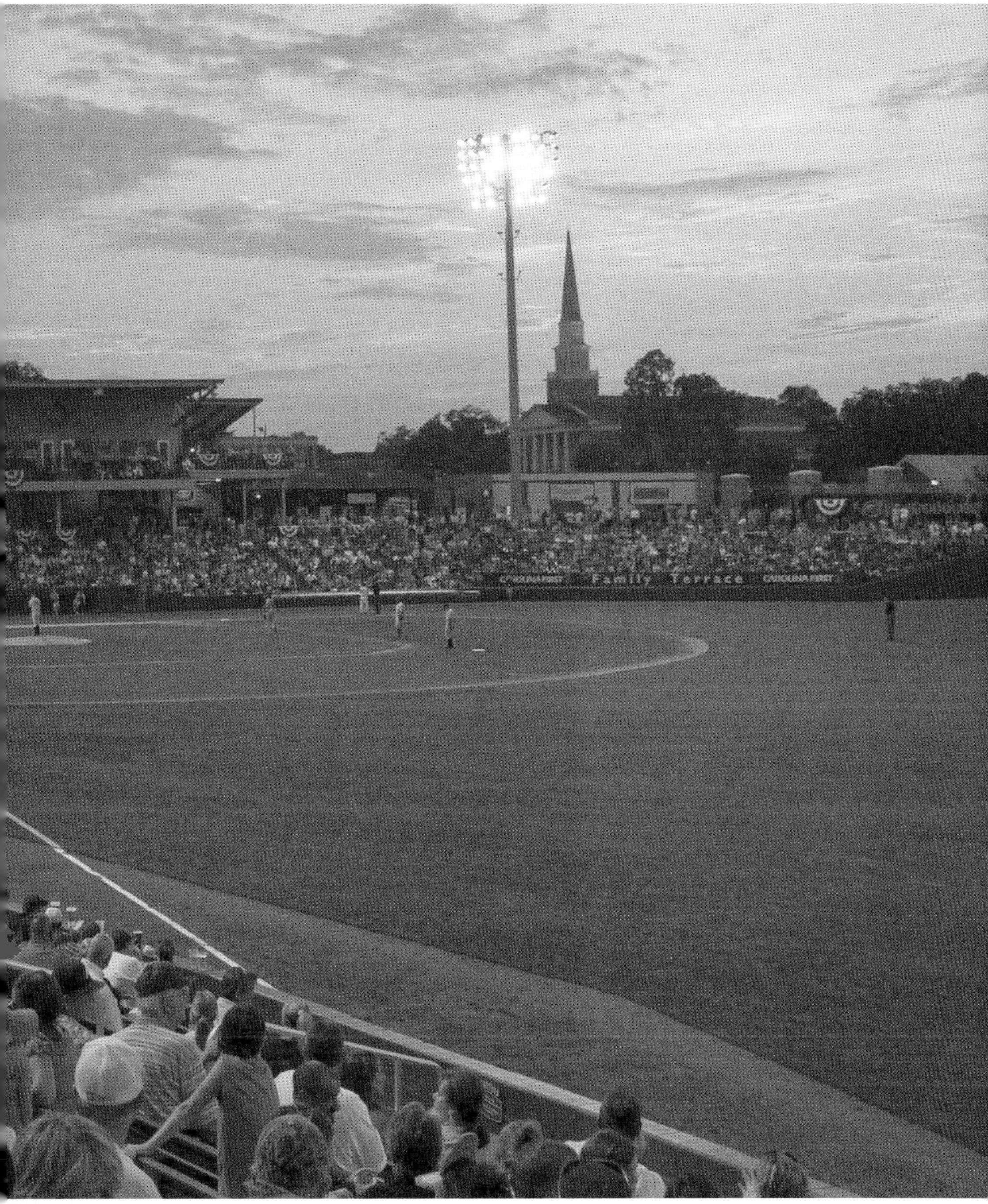

to open the 2006 season. The Drive has repeatedly set single-season attendance records, and Brown has made the team and stadium an integral part of the fabric of the community. Prior to becoming a baseball owner, Brown spent two decades as a New York advertising executive. (Photograph by Cindy Landrum.)

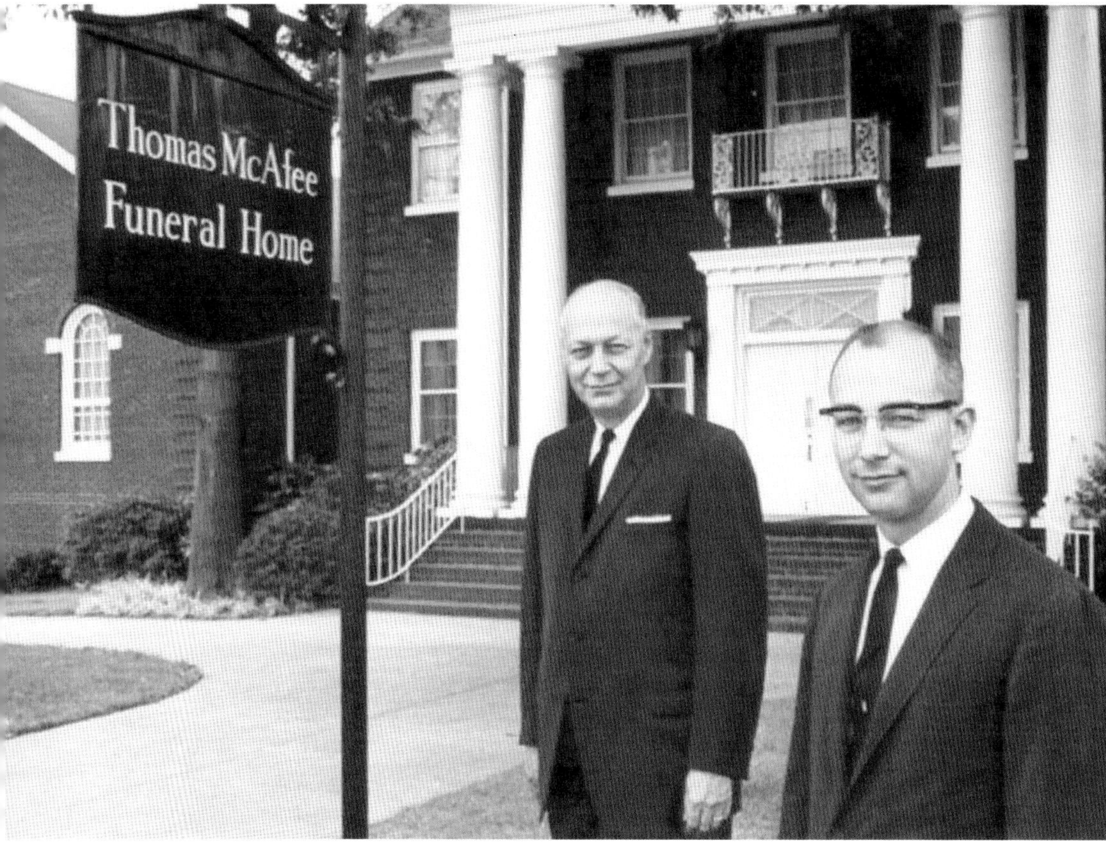

Thomas McAfee

Hearses were still drawn by horses when Thomas McAfee Sr. founded his funeral home in Greenville in 1913. It was not until 1915 that McAfee bought Greenville's first motor ambulance. The fourth generation of McAfees now run the company, located on North Main Street since 1952. Pictured here are Thomas McAfee Jr. (left) and Thomas McAfee III in 1964. (Courtesy of Thomas McAfee Funeral Homes.)

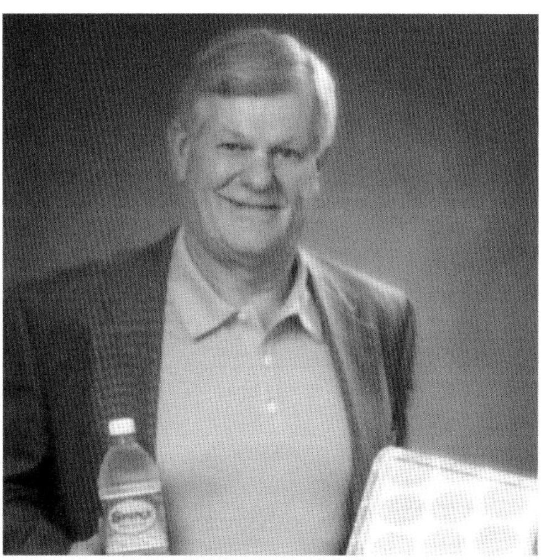

Stewart Spinks

For three weeks after Stewart Spinks quit his job with Shell to start the Spinx Company, he still put his Shell uniform and bow tie on each morning when he left for work. It took him that long to get the nerve to tell his wife that he had quit a secure job to start his own company. Spinx now has more than 70 locations. (Photograph by Fred Rollison Photography; courtesy of Spinx Co.)

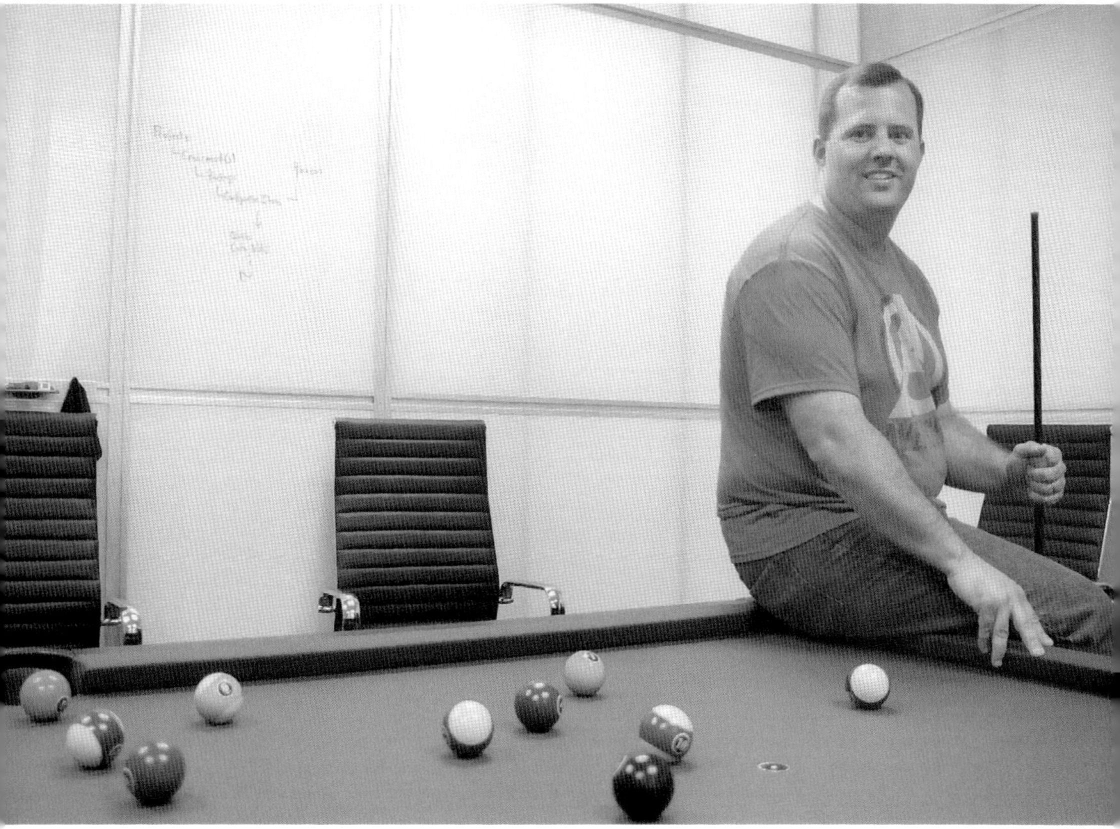

Peter Barth

Peter Barth is not afraid to take chances. He took a chance when he dropped out of Vanderbilt University after two years and moved to New York to work on Wall Street. He walked into a payroll-processing company in Indianapolis, Indiana, with a robust product but a weak front-end program based on old technology and offered the partners a deal. He would rewrite their software at no cost. If it worked, he would come in as a partner. If it did not, he would have worked for six months for free. SharePoint became a powerhouse in the industry, and since 2011, Barth has run the Iron Yard, a high-tech accelerator. (Courtesy of the *Upstate Business Journal.*)

INDEX

INDEX

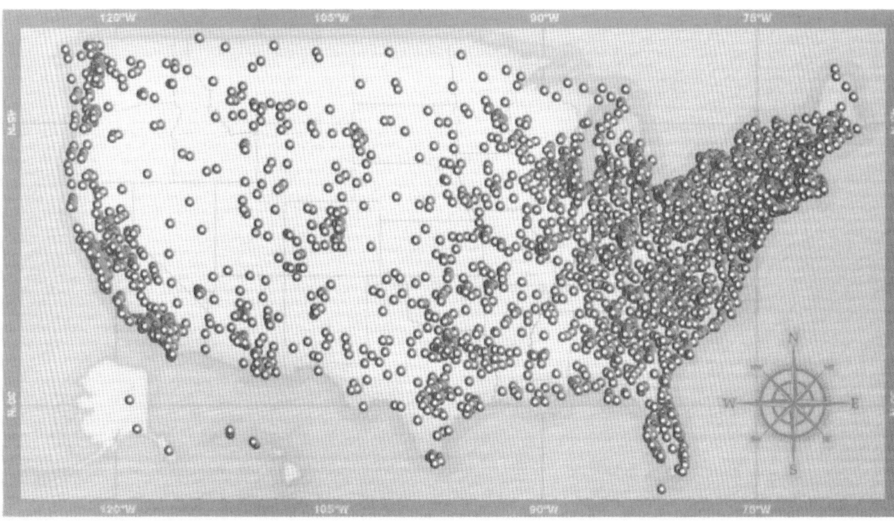